STUDY GUIDE

for

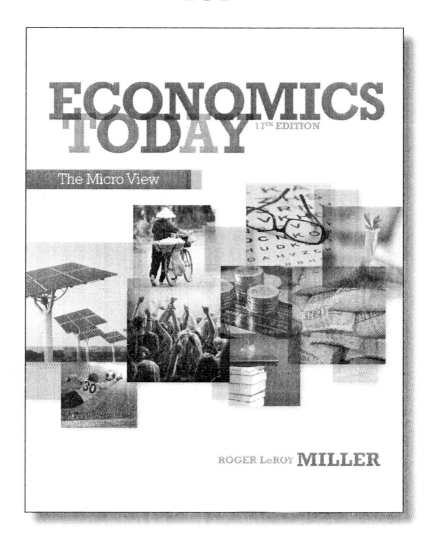

ECONOMICS TODAY 17ᵀᴴ EDITION

The Micro View

ROGER LeROY MILLER

ROGER LeROY MILLER
Research Professor of Economics
University of Texas–Arlington

DAVID D. VAN HOOSE
Baylor University

PEARSON

Boston Columbus Indianapolis New York San Francisco Upper Saddle River
Amsterdam Cape Town Dubai London Madrid Milan Munich Paris Montreal Toronto
Delhi Mexico City São Paulo Sydney Hong Kong Seoul Singapore Taipei Tokyo

Executive Editor: David Alexander
Senior Editorial Project Manager: Carolyn Terbush
Senior Production Project Manager: Kathryn Dinovo
Senior Manufacturing Buyer: Carol Melville

10 9 8 7 6 5 4 3 2 1

www.pearsonhighered.com

ISBN-10:   0-13-295056-1
ISBN-13: 978-0-13-295056-5

Contents

IN THIS VOLUME, CHAPTER 6 IS FOLLOWED BY CHAPTER 19

 **The Nature of Economics**

■ Learning Objectives

After you have read this chapter, you should be able to

1. define economics;

2. distinguish between microeconomics and macroeconomics;

3. be able to list the three fundamental economic questions and discuss two economic systems that offer opposing answers;

4. recognize the rationality assumption;

5. recognize elements of an economic model, or theory;

6. recognize that economics is ultimately concerned with human behavior;

7. define behavioral economics and explain the bounded rationality hypothesis;

8. define resource; and

9. distinguish between positive economics and normative economics, and be able to classify specific statements under each category.

■ Outline

1. Economics is a social science involving the study of how people make choices to satisfy their wants.
    a. Wants are all the things that people would consume if they had unlimited income.
    b. Because wants are unlimited and people cannot satisfy all their wants, individuals are forced to make choices about how to spend their income and how to allocate their time.

2. Economics is broadly divided into microeconomics and macroeconomics.

   a. Microeconomics studies decision making by individuals (or households) and by firms.

   b. Macroeconomics studies the behavior of the economy taken as a whole. It deals with such economy-wide phenomena as unemployment, the price level, and national income.

3. In every nation, there are three fundamental questions that must be addressed, and there are two opposing answers.

   a. The three questions concern the problem of how to allocate society's scarce resources:

      i. What and how much will be produced?

      ii. How will items be produced?

      iii. For whom will items be produced?

   b. How a nation goes about answering these three questions depends on its economic system.

      i. In an economic system of centralized command and control, an authority such as the government decides how to answer the questions.

      ii. In a price system, the answers to the questions are determined by private parties, and prices signal to everyone which resources are relatively scarce and which resources are relatively abundant.

4. Economists assume that individuals are motivated by self-interest and respond predictably to opportunities for gain.

   a. The rationality assumption is that individuals act *as if* they were rational.

   b. Self-interest often means a desire for material well-being, but it can also be defined to incorporate goals relating to love, friendship, prestige, power, and other human characteristics.

   c. By assuming that people act in a rational, self-interested way, economists can generate testable theories concerning human behavior.

5. Economics is a social science.

   a. Economists develop models, or theories, which are simplified representations of the real world.

   b. Models help economists to understand, explain, and predict real-world economic phenomena.

   c. Like other social scientists, economists usually do not perform laboratory experiments. They typically examine what has already occurred in order to test their theories.

   d. Economic theories, like all scientific theories, are simplifications—and hence are "unrealistic."

   e. Economists, as do all scientists, employ assumptions. One important economic assumption is "all other things being equal."

   f. Models are evaluated on their ability to predict and not on the realism of assumptions.

   g. Economic models relate to behavior, not thought processes.

6. Economists maintain that the unit of analysis is the individual. Members of a group are assumed to pursue their own goals rather than the group's objectives.

7. Some economists have proposed an approach known as behavioral economics.
   a. Behavioral economics emphasizes psychological limitations and complications that inhibit rational decision making by individuals.
   b. Proponents of behavioral economics have proposed the bounded rationality hypothesis, which suggests that near, but incomplete, rationality leads people to utilize basic rules of thumb to choose among alternatives.

8. Positive economics is objective and scientific and deals with testable *if this, then that* hypotheses.

9. Normative economics is subjective and deals with value judgments, or with what *ought* to be.

■ Key Terms

Aggregates	Economics	Microeconomics
Behavioral economics	Empirical	Models (or theories)
Bounded rationality	Incentives	Resources
Ceteris paribus assumption	Macroeconomics	Wants

■ Key Concepts

Economic system	Positive economics
Normative economics	Rationality assumption

■ Completion Questions

Fill in the blank, or circle the correct term.

1. Because it is impossible to have all that we want, people are forced to make _____.

2. Economics is a (natural, social) science.

3. Economics is the study of how people make _____ to satisfy their _____.

4. In a price system, _____ signal to everyone which resources are relatively scarce and which resources are relatively abundant.

5. Microeconomics deals with (individual units, the whole economy).

6. A nation's unemployment level is analyzed in (microeconomics, macroeconomics).

7. (Macroeconomics, Microeconomics) studies the causes and effects of inflation.

8. Economists maintain that a member of a group usually attempts to make decisions that are in (her own, the group's) interest.

9. The rationality assumption is that individuals (<u>believe, act as if</u>) they are rational.

10. Economic models are (<u>simplified, realistic</u>) representations of the real world.

11. The *ceteris paribus* assumption permits us to consider (<u>one thing at a time, everything at once</u>).

12. *Ceteris paribus*, payment of bonuses to physicians for pushing preventive health care gives physicians an incentive to (<u>treat only actual illnesses, suggest treatments to deter illnesses</u>).

13. Economists maintain that incentives (<u>are, are not</u>) important to decision making.

14. Economists define self-interest (<u>narrowly, broadly</u>).

15. Economists take the (<u>individual, group</u>) as the unit of analysis.

16. Behavioral economics is an approach that assumes that individuals are (<u>fully, nearly</u>) rational.

17. Economic statements that are testable and are of an "if/then" nature are (<u>positive, normative</u>).

■ True-False Questions

Circle the **T** if the statement is true, the **F** if it is false. Explain to yourself why a statement is false.

T F   1. Economics is the study of how people think about economic phenomena.

T F   2. Economists' definition of self-interest includes only the pursuit of material goods.

T F   3. Macroeconomics deals with aggregates, or totals, of economic variables.

T F   4. The three fundamental economic questions are as follows: (a) Who should decide what to produce, (b) what methods ought to be utilized in production, and (c) who should receive the items that are produced?

T F   5. When economists attempt to predict the number of Web servers that an Internet bank will utilize, they are studying macroeconomics.

T F   6. Economists maintain that people respond in a predictable way to economic incentives.

T F   7. The rationality assumption is that individuals attempt, quite consciously, to make rational economic decisions and will admit to it.

T F   8. It is justifiable to criticize theories on the realism of the assumptions employed.

T F   9. Households cannot be thought of as producers.

T F   10. A statement of fact is an example of a positive statement.

T F   11. Because economics is a science, economists do not make normative statements.

■ Multiple Choice Questions

Circle the letter that corresponds to the best answer.

1. Economics is
   a. a natural science.
   b. nonscientific.
   c. a social science.
   d. usually studied through lab experiments.

2. Wants include desires for
   a. material possessions.
   b. love.
   c. power.
   d. All of the above

3. Which one of the following is NOT one of the three fundamental economic questions?
   a. How will items be produced?
   b. Who deserves produced items?
   c. For whom will items be produced?
   d. What and how much will be produced?

4. Which one of the following areas of study is concerned, primarily, with microeconomics?
   a. the tablet device industry
   b. inflation
   c. the national unemployment rate
   d. national income determination

5. Macroeconomic analysis deals with
   a. the tablet device industry.
   b. how individuals respond to an increase in the price of gasoline.
   c. inflation.
   d. how a change in the price of energy affects a family.

6. Economists maintain that Ms. Chung will usually make decisions that promote the interests of
   a. her colleagues at work.
   b. herself.
   c. her class.
   d. her race.

7. Economic models
    a. use unrealistic assumptions.
    b. are seldom tested in laboratories.
    c. are concerned with how people behave, not with how they think.
    d. All of the above

8. An economic model is justifiably criticized if
    a. its assumptions are not realistic.
    b. it cannot be tested in a controlled, laboratory experiment.
    c. it fails to predict.
    d. All of the above

9. According to the rationality assumption, people
    a. do not intentionally make decisions that would leave them worse off.
    b. do not ever take into account the interests or well-being of others.
    c. can never consider each of the most relevant alternatives.
    d. use rules of thumb to make choices.

10. Economics
    a. is a natural science.
    b. is concerned with how people respond to incentives.
    c. is unconcerned with value judgments.
    d. deals with assumptions and therefore is unrealistic.

11. As is true of a road map showing how a traveler can move about a geographic region, a model of economic behavior typically
    a   omits trivial details and emphasizes factors most relevant to the problem under consideration.
    b. makes no simplifying assumptions, so that every feature of a problem is taken into account.
    c. must be rejected if it leaves out some information, even if it makes correct predictions.
    d. includes each and every element of a problem confronting an individual or group.

12. Which one of the following is a normative economic statement?
    a. If prices rise, people will buy less.
    b. If prices rise, people will buy more.
    c. If prices rise, the poor will be injured. Therefore, prices should not be permitted to rise.
    d. If prices rise, people will buy less. Therefore, we ought to observe that quantity demanded falls.

13. Which one of the following is a positive economic statement?
    a. Full employment policies should be pursued.
    b. If minimum-wage rates rise, then unemployment will rise.
    c. We should take from the rich and give to the poor.
    d. The government should help the homeless.

14. Normative economic statements
    a. are testable hypotheses.
    b. are value-free.
    c. are subjective, value judgments.
    d. can be scientifically established.

15. Which one of the following is a normative economic statement?
    a. When more death-penalty sentences are reduced to life imprisonment, the homicide rate increases.
    b. An increase in the rate of executions is associated with a fall in homicides.
    c. Improved prison conditions increase the disincentive effects of capital punishment.
    d. Capital punishment is a morally wrong way to try to deter homicides.

■ Matching

Choose the item in Column (2) that best matches an item in Column (1).

	(1)		**(2)**
(a)	normative economics	(f)	nonscientific value judgments
(b)	macroeconomics	(g)	objective, scientific hypotheses
(c)	self-interest	(h)	study of individual behavior
(d)	positive economics	(i)	study of economic aggregates
(e)	microeconomics	(j)	rational behavior

■ Answers

Completion Questions

1. choices
2. social
3. choices; wants
4. prices
5. individual units
6. macroeconomics
7. Macroeconomics
8. her own
9. act as if
10. simplified
11. one thing at a time
12. suggest treatments to deter illnesses
13. are
14. broadly
15. individual
16. nearly
17. positive

True-False Questions

1. F   Economics is the study of how people make choices to satisfy their wants.
2. F   Economists have a broader definition of self-interest. Wants include power, friendship, love, and so on.
3. T
4. F   The three fundamental questions are (a) What and how much will be produced, (b) how will items be produced, and (c) for whom will it be produced?
5. F   The example is about microeconomics.
6. T
7. F   That assumption is merely that people act *as if* they are rational.
8. F   All theories employ unrealistic assumptions. What matters is how well they predict.
9. F   Households can be thought of as combining goods and time to produce outputs such as meals.
10. T
11. F   Economists, like other scientists, can and do make normative statements.

Multiple Choice Questions

1. (c)
2. (d)
3. (b)
4. (a)
5. (c)
6. (b)
7. (d)
8. (c)
9. (a)
10. (b)
11. (a)
12. (c)
13. (b)
14. (c)
15. (d)

Matching

(a) and (f)   (d) and (g)

(b) and (i)   (e) and (h)

(c) and (j)

■ Glossary

Aggregates   Total amounts or quantities. Aggregate demand, for example, is total planned expenditures throughout a nation.

Behavioral economics   An approach to the study of consumer behavior that emphasizes psychological limitations and complications that potentially interfere with rational decision making.

Bounded rationality   The hypothesis that people are *nearly*, but not fully, rational, so that they cannot examine every possible choice available to them but instead use simple rules of thumb to sort among the alternatives that happen to occur to them.

***Ceteris paribus* [KAY-ter-us PEAR-uh-bus] assumption**   The assumption that nothing changes except the factor or factors being studied.

Economic system   A society's institutional mechanism for determining the way in which scarce resources are used to satisfy human desires.

Economics   The study of how people allocate their limited resources to satisfy their unlimited wants.

Empirical   Relying on real-world data in evaluating the usefulness of a model.

Incentives   Rewards for engaging in a particular activity.

Macroeconomics   The study of the behavior of the economy as a whole, including such economywide phenomena as changes in unemployment, the general price level, and national income.

Microeconomics   The study of decision making undertaken by individuals (or households) and by firms.

Models, or theories   Simplified representations of the real world used as the basis for predictions or explanations.

Normative economics   Analysis involving value judgments about economic policies; relates to whether outcomes are good or bad. A statement of *what ought to be*.

Positive economics   Analysis that is *strictly* limited to making either purely descriptive statements or scientific predictions; for example, "If A, then B." A statement of *what is*.

Rationality assumption   The assumption that people do not intentionally make decisions that would leave them worse off.

Resources   Things used to produce goods and services to satisfy people's wants.

Wants   What people would buy if their incomes were unlimited.

2 Scarcity and the World of Trade-Offs

■ Learning Objectives

After you have studied this chapter, you should be able to

1. define production, scarcity, resources, land, labor, human and physical capital, entrepreneurship, goods, services, opportunity costs, production possibilities curve, technology, efficiency, inefficient point, law of increasing additional cost, specialization, absolute advantage, comparative advantage, and division of labor;

2. distinguish between a free good and an economic good;

3. determine the opportunity cost of an activity, when given sufficient information;

4. draw production possibilities curves under varying assumptions, and recognize efficient and inefficient points relating to such curves; and

5. understand the difference between a person's or nation's comparative advantage and absolute advantage.

■ Outline

1. Because individuals or communities do not have the resources to satisfy all their wants, scarcity exists.
    a. If society can get all that it wants of good A when the price of good A is zero, good A is not scarce.
    b. If the price of good B is zero, and society cannot get all that it wants of good B, then B is scarce.
    c. Because resources, or factors of production, are scarce, the outputs they produce are scarce.
        i. Land, the natural resource, includes all the gifts of nature.
        ii. Labor, the human resource, includes all productive contributions made by individuals who work.

      iii. Physical capital, the man-made resource, includes the machines, buildings, and tools used to produce other goods and services.

      iv. Human capital includes the education and training of workers.

      v. Entrepreneurship includes the functions of organizing, managing, assembling, and risk-taking necessary for business ventures.

  d. Goods include anything from which people derive satisfaction, or happiness.

      i. Economic goods are scarce.

      ii. Noneconomic goods are not scarce.

      iii. Services are intangible goods.

  e. Economists distinguish between wants and needs. The latter are objectively undefinable.

2. Because of scarcity, choice and opportunity costs arise.

  a. Due to scarcity, people trade off options.

  b. The production possibilities curve (PPC) is a graph of the trade-offs inherent in a decision.

      i. When the amount of one resource or good that must be given up to produce an additional unit of another resource or good remains constant, the PPC is a straight line.

      ii. When the amount of one resource or good that must be given up to produce an additional unit of another resource or good rises, the PPC is bowed outward.

      iii. A point on a PPC is an efficient point. Points inside a PPC are inefficient. Points outside the PPC are unattainable (impossible), by definition.

3. Economic growth can be depicted through PPCs.

  a. There is a trade-off between present consumption and future consumption.

  b. If a nation produces fewer consumer goods and more capital goods now, then it can consume more goods in the future than would otherwise be the case.

4. Specialization occurs because different individuals experience different costs when they engage in the same activities.

  a. People have an economic incentive to specialize in producing an item for which they have a comparative advantage, or a lower opportunity cost of producing that item compared to other products.

  b. Absolute advantage, or the ability to produce more units of an item using a given amount of inputs, does not explain why people specialize and trade. Only comparative advantage matters.

  c. The process of division of labor increases output and permits specialization.

■ Key Terms

Consumption	Human capital	Production
Division of labor	Inefficient point	Production possibilities curve
Economic goods	Labor	Scarcity
Entrepreneurship	Land	Services
Goods	Physical capital	Specialization

■ Key Concepts

Absolute advantage	Efficiency	Opportunity cost
Comparative advantage	Law of increasing additional cost	Technology

■ Completion Questions

Fill in the blank, or circle the correct term.

1. The factors of production include _____, _____,
    _____, _____, and _____.

2. People tend to specialize in those activities for which they have (<u>a comparative, an absolute</u>)
    advantage.

3. When people choose jobs that maximize their income, they are specializing according to their
    _____ advantage.

4. If at a zero price quantity demanded exceeds quantity supplied for a good, that good is
    a(n) _____. If at a zero price quantity supplied exceeds quantity demanded for
    a good, that good is a(n) _____.

5. The _____ of good A is the highest-valued alternative that must be sacrificed
    to attain it.

6. If the opportunity cost of additional units of a good remains constant, the production
    possibilities curve will be (<u>linear, bowed outward</u>). If the opportunity cost of additional units of a
    good rises, the production possibilities curve will be (<u>linear, bowed outward</u>).

7. Because specialized resources are more suited to specific tasks, the opportunity cost of producing
    additional units of a specific good will (<u>rise, fall</u>).

8. If an economy is inefficient, its actual output combination will lie (<u>inside, outside</u>) the
    production possibilities curve.

■ True-False Questions

Circle the **T** if the statement is true, the **F** if it is false. Explain to yourself why a statement is false.

T F   1. Most individuals' needs exceed their wants.

T F   2. Because resources are scarce, the goods that they produce are also scarce.

T F   3. For most activities, no opportunity cost exists.

T F   4. If a production possibilities curve is linear, the opportunity cost of producing additional units of a good rises.

T F   5. At any given moment in time, it is impossible for an economy to be inside its production possibilities curve.

T F   6. The opportunity cost to a motorist of the time that she is stuck in traffic is the next-highest value of the equivalent amount of time.

T F   7. People have little incentive to specialize in jobs for which they have a comparative advantage.

T F   8. Economic growth shifts the production possibilities curve outward.

T F   9. If the price to a specific user is zero, the good must be a noneconomic good.

T F 10. Evidence indicates that developing new technologies, specializing, and engaging in trade helped *Homo sapiens* win out over Neanderthals.

■ Multiple Choice Questions

Circle the letter that corresponds to the best answer.

1. Because of scarcity,
    a. people are forced to make choices.
    b. opportunity costs exist.
    c. people face trade-offs.
    d. All of the above.

2. Which one of the following is **not** considered to be "land?"
    a. bodies of water
    b. fertility of soil
    c. capital
    d. climate

3. Which one of the following words does **not** belong with the others?
   a. opportunity cost
   b. economic "bad"
   c. scarcity
   d. economic good

4. Which statement concerning a production possibilities curve is **not** true?
   a. A trade-off exists along such a curve.
   b. It is usually linear.
   c. Points inside it indicate inefficiency.
   d. A point outside it is currently impossible to attain.

5. When the production possibilities curve is bowed outward, it is because
   a. the additional cost of producing a good rises.
   b. of the law of decreasing additional cost.
   c. all resources are equally suited to the production of any good.
   d. All of the above.

6. When nations and individuals specialize,
   a. overall living standards rise.
   b. trade and exchange increase.
   c. people become more vulnerable to changes in tastes and technology.
   d. All of the above.

7. When a nation expands its capital stock, it is usually true that
   a. it must forgo output of some consumer goods in the present.
   b. the human capital stock must decline.
   c. fewer consumer goods will be available in the future.
   d. no opportunity cost exists for doing so.

8. Ms. Boulware is the best lawyer and the best secretary in town.
   a. She has a comparative advantage in both jobs.
   b. She has an absolute advantage in both jobs.
   c. She has a comparative advantage in being a secretary.
   d. All of the above.

9. From 2:00 to 4:00 on a Thursday afternoon, Mr. Stapleton, a fast-food worker who earns the minimum wage, waits while his daughter is examined at a pediatrician's office. Ms. Rodriguez, a successful marketing consultant who normally charges a fee of $100 per hour and who recently has turned down several potential clients, spends exactly the same amount of time waiting for her own daughter to be examined. The pediatrician charges Mr. Stapleton $100 for the office visit. Ms. Rodriguez also pays the pediatrician $100. We may conclude that during this two-hour period,

    a. both parents incurred identical child-raising costs.
    b. from an economic standpoint, it was irrational for Ms. Rodriguez to wait while the pediatrician examined her child.
    c. Ms. Rodriguez incurred a higher child-raising cost, because she otherwise could have been earning consulting fees during this time.
    d. Mr. Stapleton incurred a higher child-raising cost, because he otherwise could have been looking for a higher-paying job during this time.

■ Matching

Choose the item in Column (2) that best matches an item in Column (1).

(1)	(2)
(a) absolute advantage	(i) production possibilities curve
(b) efficiency	(j) specialization
(c) trade-offs	(k) capital
(d) comparative advantage	(l) ability to produce at a lower unit cost
(e) resource	(m) specializing in one's comparative advantage
(f) economic good	(n) society cannot get all it wants at a zero price
(g) inefficiency	(o) highest-valued forgone alternative
(h) opportunity cost	(p) inside PPC

■ Working with Graphs

1. Given the following information, graph the production possibilities curve in the space provided and then use the graph to answer the questions that follow.

Combination (points)	Laptop Computers (100,000 per year)	Wheat (100,000 tons per year)
A	16	0
B	14	4
C	12	7
D	9	10
E	5	12
F	0	13

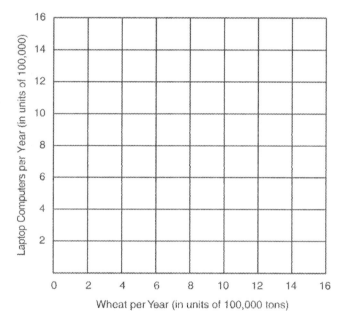

a. If the economy is currently operating at Point C, what is the opportunity cost of moving to Point D? To Point B?

b. Suppose that the economy is currently producing 1,200,000 laptop computers and 200,000 tons of wheat per year. Label this point in your graph with the letter G. At Point G the economy would be suffering from what? At Point G we can see that it is possible to produce more wheat without giving up any laptop computer production, or produce more laptop computers without giving up any wheat production, or produce more of both. Label this region in your graph. This region appears to contradict the definition of a production possibilities curve. What is the explanation for this result?

c. Suppose a new fertilizer compound is developed that will allow the economy to produce an additional 150,000 tons of wheat per year if no laptop computers are produced. Sketch in a likely representation of the effect of this discovery, assuming all else remains constant.

d. What sort of impact (overall) will this discovery have on the opportunity cost of more wheat production at an arbitrary point on the new production possibilities curve, as compared to a point representing the same level of output of wheat on the original curve?

2. Consider the graphs below, then answer the questions that follow.

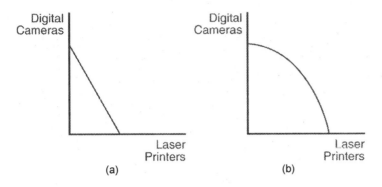

a. Which graph, (a) or (b), shows constant additional costs of producing additional laser printers? Why?

b. Which graph, (a) or (b), shows increasing additional costs of producing additional laser printers? Why?

c. Which graph seems more realistic, (a) or (b)? Why?

3. Graph the probable relationship between

a. income and the amount spent on housing;

b. annual rainfall in New York City and the annual value of ice cream sales in New Orleans;

c. number of vegetarians per 10,000 people and meat sales per 10,000 people.

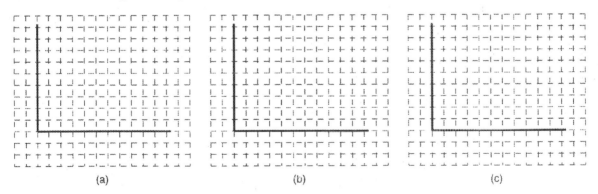

■ Problems

1. If a *nation* wants to increase its future consumption, it must forgo some present consumption because it must allocate some resources to the production of capital goods. Suppose *you* want to increase your future consumption. Given a fixed lifetime income, what can you do?

2. Assume that Ms. Ramirez values her time at $250 per hour because she has the opportunity to do consulting and that Joe College values his time at $18 per hour. Assume that it costs $550 to

fly from their hometown to San Francisco and that the flight takes 6 hours. Assume that it costs $200 to take a bus and that the bus trip takes 24 hours.

    a.   What is the cheaper way to get to San Francisco for Ms. Ramirez? Why?

    b.   Which transportation is cheaper for Joe College? Why?

3.   Suppose you have a friend currently working as a salesperson in a local store that sells digital devices. This friend is thinking about going back to school full-time to finish up work on her computer science degree. She explains to you that she earns $45,000 (after taxes) per year in her current job and that she estimates tuition will cost $4,800 per year. In addition she estimates fees, supplies, books, and miscellaneous expenses associated with attending school will run $2,400 per year. She wants to attend a university that is located directly across the street from the store where she currently works. She claims that she pays $1,050 per month for rent and utilities and that she spends about $600 per month on food, clothing, and related expenses.

Using what you have learned, calculate and explain to your friend the opportunity cost to her of another year back at school.

4.   The Banerjee family consists of Mr. Banerjee, Mrs. Banerjee, and their daughter, Pramila. Assume that Mr. Banerjee can earn $60 per hour (after taxes) any time he chooses, Mrs. Banerjee can earn $10 per hour, and the family values homemaker activities at $12 per hour. Initially, Pramila earns no income.

    a.   Because the family requires income to purchase goods and services, who will be most likely to work in the marketplace?

    b.   Who will probably do the housework?

    c.   If the family must pay $6 per hour for lawn care, who will be assigned that work?

    d.   If Pramila can now earn $8 per hour on a job, who now might care for the lawn?

    e.   If wage rates in the marketplace for Mrs. Banerjee rise to $14 per hour, what is the family likely to do?

■ Answers

Completion Questions

1. land; labor; physical capital; human capital; entrepreneurship
2. a comparative
3. comparative
4. economic good; economic "bad"
5. opportunity cost
6. linear; bowed outward
7. rise
8. inside

True-False Questions

1. F   Wants vastly exceed needs (which cannot be defined anyway) for everyone.
2. T
3. F   An opportunity cost exists for all activities.
4. F   A linear PPC implies a constant cost of production.
5. F   All an economy need be is inefficient to be inside the PPC.
6. T
7. F   People can earn more income in jobs for which they have a comparative advantage.
8. T
9. F   An individual user may pay a zero price for a good, but that does not necessarily mean it is a noneconomic good.
10. T

Multiple Choice Questions

1. (d)   6. (d)
2. (c)   7. (a)
3. (b)   8. (b)
4. (b)   9. (c)
5. (a)

Matching

(a) and (l)   (e) and (k)
(b) and (m)   (f) and (n)
(c) and (i)   (g) and (p)
(d) and (j)   (h) and (o)

Working with Graphs

1. See the following graph.

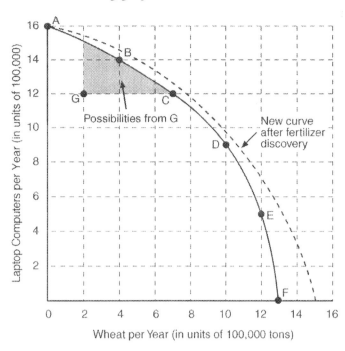

a. The move from Point C to Point D "costs" 300,000 laptop computers—that is, the economy must give up 300,000 laptop computers (1,200,000 – 900,000) to make such a move. The move from Point C to Point B "costs" 300,000 tons of wheat. Notice that in both cases there are gains (Point C to Point D involves 300,000 more tons of wheat, and Point C to Point B means 200,000 more laptop computers are produced), but we measure opportunity costs in terms of movements along a production possibilities curve and what has to be given up to make the choice reflected in the move.

b. See the preceding graph. Remember, the production possibilities curve shows all possible combinations of two goods that an economy can produce by the efficient use of all available resources in a specified period of time. Since Point G is not on the production possibilities curve, the statement contained in this portion of the question does not contradict the definition of the curve. Point G is inside the curve, which implies available resources are not being used efficiently.

c. See the preceding graph.

d. It will lower the opportunity cost of additional wheat production.

2. a. Graph (a) shows constant additional costs because the PPC is linear.

b. Graph (b) shows increasing costs because the PPC is bowed out.

c. Graph (b) is more realistic because it is likely that the production of laser printers and digital cameras requires specialized resources.

3. a. The graph should be upward sloping from left to right.

b. There should be no systematic relationship between these two variables.

c. The graph should be downward sloping from left to right.

Problems

1.   If you want to increase your future consumption—for retirement, say—then you will have to save more out of your current income. The principal and interest that accrue will permit you to purchase more goods in the future than you otherwise would have been able to. Note that by doing so you—as an individual—must forgo some present consumption in order to increase your future consumption. In that sense, what is true for the nation is also true for an individual.

2.   a.   Plane. Flying costs her $550 plus 6 hours times $250 per hour, or $2,050, while taking a bus would cost her $200 plus 24 hours times $250 per hour, or $6,200.
     b.   Bus. Taking the bus costs him a total of $632, while his total cost of flying is $658.

3.   The opportunity cost of another year back at school for your friend is as follows:

Forgone after-tax salary	$45,000
Tuition costs	4,800
Expenses associated with school	2,400
Total opportunity costs	$52,200

4.   a.   Mr. Banerjee
     b.   Mrs. Banerjee or Pramila
     c.   Pramila
     d.   The family (or perhaps Pramila) will hire someone to care for the lawn.
     e.   Mrs. Banerjee may enter the labor force and the family may hire someone to do housework.

■ Glossary

Absolute advantage   The ability to produce more units of a good or service using a given quantity of labor or resource inputs. Equivalently, the ability to produce the same quantity of a good or service using fewer units of labor or resource inputs.

Comparative advantage   The ability to produce a good or service at a lower opportunity cost compared to other producers.

Consumption   The use of goods or services for personal satisfaction.

Division of labor   The segregation of resources into different specific tasks. For instance, one automobile worker puts on bumpers, another doors, and so on.

Economic goods   Goods that are scarce, for which the quantity demanded exceeds the quantity supplied at a zero price.

Efficiency   The case in which a given level of inputs is used to produce the maximum output possible. Alternatively, the situation in which a given output is produced at minimum cost.

Entrepreneurship   The component of human resources that perform the functions of raising capital, organizing, managing, and assembling other factors of production, making basic business policy decisions, and taking risks.

Goods   All things from which individuals derive satisfaction or happiness.

Human capital   The accumulated training and education of workers.

Inefficient point   Any point below the production possibilities curve, at which the use of resources is not generating the maximum possible output.

Labor   Productive contributions of humans who work.

Land   The natural resources that are available from nature. Land as a resource includes location, original fertility and mineral deposits, topography, climate, water, and vegetation.

Law of increasing additional cost   The observation that the opportunity cost of additional units of a good generally increases as people attempt to produce more of that good. This accounts for the bowed-out shape of the production possibilities curve.

Opportunity cost   The highest-valued, next-best alternative that must be sacrificed to attain something or to satisfy a want.

Physical capital   All manufactured resources, including buildings, equipment, machines, and improvements to land that are used for production.

Production   Any activity that results in the conversion of resources into products that can be used in consumption.

Production possibilities curve (PPC)   A curve representing all possible combinations of maximum outputs that could be produced assuming a fixed amount of productive resources of a given quality.

Scarcity   A situation in which the ingredients for producing the things that people desire are insufficient to satisfy all wants at a zero price.

Services   Mental or physical labor or assistance purchased by consumers. Examples are the assistance of physicians, lawyers, dentists, repair personnel, housecleaners, educators, retailers, and wholesalers; items purchased or used by consumers that do not have physical characteristics.

Specialization   The organization of economic activity so that what each person (or region) consumes is not identical to what that person (or region) produces. An individual may specialize, for example, in law or medicine. A nation may specialize in the production of coffee, e-book readers, or digital cameras.

Technology   The total pool of applied knowledge concerning how goods and services can be produced.

3 Demand and Supply

■ Learning Objectives

After you have studied this chapter, you should be able to

1. define demand schedule, quantity demanded, supply schedule, quantity supplied, equilibrium, shortage, and surplus;

2. state both the law of demand and the law of supply;

3. graph demand and supply curves from demand and supply schedules;

4. enumerate five *ceteris paribus* conditions determining demand and five *ceteris paribus* conditions determining supply;

5. predict the effects of a change in the price of one good on the demand for (a) a substitute good, and (b) a complementary good;

6. recognize, from graphs, the difference between a change in demand and a change in quantity demanded, and the difference between a change in supply and a change in quantity supplied;

7. determine from a supply curve and a demand curve what the equilibrium price and the equilibrium quantity will be; and

8. explain how markets eliminate surpluses and shortages.

■ Outline

1. The law of demand states that at higher prices a lower quantity will be demanded than at lower prices, other things being equal.
    a. For simplicity, things other than the price of the good itself are held constant.
    b. Buyers respond to changes in relative, not absolute, prices.

2.   The demand schedule for a good is a set of pair of numbers showing various possible prices and the quantity demanded at each price, for some time period.

   a.   Demand must be conceived of as being measured in constant-quality units.

   b.   A demand curve is a graphical representation of the demand schedule, and it is negatively sloped, reflecting the law of demand.

   c.   A market demand curve for a particular good or service is derived by summing all the individual demand curves for that product.

3.   The determinants of demand include all factors (other than the good's own price) that influence the quantity purchased.

   a.   When deriving a demand curve, other determinants of demand are held constant. When such *ceteris paribus* conditions affecting demand do change, the original demand curve shifts to the left or to the right.

   b.   The major determinants of demand are consumers' income, tastes and preferences, changes in their expectations about future relative prices, the price of substitutes and complements for the good in question, and the number of buyers.

   c.   A change in demand is a shift in the demand curve, whereas a change in quantity demanded is a movement along a given demand curve.

4.   Supply is the relationship between price and the quantity supplied, other things being equal.

   a.   The law of supply generally posits a direct, or positive, relationship between price and quantity supplied.

      i.   As the relative price of a good rises, producers have an incentive to produce more of it.

      ii.   As a firm produces greater quantities in the short run, a firm often requires a higher relative price before it will increase output.

   b.   A supply schedule is a set of numbers showing prices and the quantity supplied at those various prices.

   c.   A supply curve is the graphical representation of the supply schedule. It is positively sloped.

   d.   By summing individual supply curves for a particular good or service, we derive the market supply curve for that good or service.

   e.   The major determinants of supply are the prices of resources (inputs) used to produce the product, technology, taxes and subsidies, price expectations of producers, and the number of firms in an industry.

   f.   Any change in the determinants of supply (listed in part e) causes a change in supply and therefore leads to a shift in the supply curve.

   g.   A change in price, holding the determinants of supply constant, causes a movement along—but not a shift in—the supply curve.

5.   By graphing demand and supply on the same coordinate system, we can find equilibrium at the intersection of the two curves.

   a.   Equilibrium is a situation in which the plans of buyers and of sellers exactly coincide, so that there is neither excess quantity supplied nor excess quantity demanded. At the equilibrium price, quantity supplied equals quantity demanded.

b. At a price below the equilibrium price, quantity demanded exceeds quantity supplied, and *excess quantity demanded*, or a shortage, exists.

c. At a price above the equilibrium price, quantity supplied exceeds quantity demanded, and an *excess quantity supplied*, or a surplus, exists.

d. Seller competition forces price down and eliminates a surplus.

e. Buyer competition forces price up and eliminates a shortage.

■ Key Terms

Ceteris paribus conditions	Market	Money price
Demand curve	Market clearing, or equilibrium, price	Supply curve
Demand schedule	Market demand	Supply schedule

■ Key Concepts

Complements	Law of supply	Subsidy
Equilibrium	Normal goods	Substitutes
Inferior goods	Relative price	Surplus, or excess quantity supplied
Law of demand	Shortage, or excess quantity demanded	

■ Completion Questions

Fill in the blank, or circle the correct term.

1. A(n) _____ relates various possible prices to the quantities demanded at each price, and a(n) _____ relates various prices to the quantities supplied at each price.

2. A change in quantity demanded is a (<u>movement along, shift in</u>) the demand curve. A change in demand is a(n) _____ the demand curve.

3. At the intersection of the supply and demand curves, the quantity supplied equals the quantity demanded, and at that price a(n) _____ exists. At a price above that intersection, quantity supplied exceeds quantity demanded and a(n) _____ exists. At a price below that intersection, quantity demanded exceeds quantity supplied, and a(n) _____ exists.

4. The law of demand states that, other things being equal, more items are purchased at a (<u>lower, higher</u>) price and fewer are purchased at a(n) _____ price.

5. There is (<u>a direct, an inverse</u>) relationship between price and quantity demanded, and demand curves will be (<u>positively, negatively</u>) sloped.

6. When the other determinants of demand change, the entire demand curve shifts. The five major *ceteris paribus* conditions affecting demand are _____,

    _____, _____, _____, and

    _____.

7. If the demand for Internet access services rises, given the supply, then the equilibrium price of Internet access services will (<u>rise, fall</u>) and the equilibrium quantity of Internet access services purchased will _____.

8. The law of supply relates prices to quantities supplied. In general, as price rises, quantity supplied _____. Therefore (a <u>direct, an inverse</u>) relationship exists, and the supply curve is (<u>positively, negatively</u>) sloped.

9. The supply curve is positively sloped because as price rises, producers have an incentive to produce (<u>less, more</u>).

10. When the determinants of supply change, the entire supply curve will shift. Five major determinants of supply are _____, _____,

    _____, _____, and _____.

11. Digital music downloads and iPod music players are (<u>substitutes, complements</u>). If the price of iPod music players rises, then the demand for digital music downloads will _____.

12. When the prices for digital cloud storage services rise, the demand for flash memory drives rises. Digital cloud storage services and flash memory drives are (<u>substitutes, complements</u>).

13. *Analogy*: An excess quantity supplied is to a surplus as a(n) _____ is to a shortage.

14. A rise in demand causes the demand curve to shift to the (<u>left, right</u>). An increase in quantity demanded occurs when there is a movement (<u>up, down</u>) the demand curve.

15. By convention, economists plot (<u>price, quantity</u>) on the vertical axis and (<u>price, quantity</u>) on the horizontal axis.

■ True-False Questions

Circle the **T** if the statement is true, the **F** if it is false. Explain to yourself why a statement is false.

T F   1. A demand schedule relates quantity demanded to quantity supplied, other things being constant.

T F   2. A change in the quantity of cigarettes demanded results from a change in the price of cigarettes.

T F   3. A graphical representation of a demand curve is called a demand schedule.

T F 4. An increase in price leads to a leftward shift in demand and a rightward shift in supply.

T F 5. An increase in the price of MP3 players causes a rise in the supply of MP3 players.

T F 6. Buyers are concerned with absolute, not relative, prices.

T F 7. As producers increase output in the short run, the cost of additional units of output tends to rise.

T F 8. If the price of tennis racquets rises, the demand for tennis balls will tend to rise also.

T F 9. If the price of butter rises, the demand for margarine will rise.

T F 10. If price is below the equilibrium price, a shortage exists.

■ Multiple Choice Questions

Circle the letter that corresponds to the best answer.

1. A demand schedule
   a. relates price to quantity supplied.
   b. when graphed, is a demand curve.
   c. cannot change.
   d. shows a direct relationship between price and quantity demanded.

2. If the price of milk rises, other things being constant,
   a. buyers will drink less milk.
   b. buyers will substitute milk for other beverages.
   c. the demand for milk will fall.
   d. the demand for cola drinks will fall.

3. Which one of the following will **not** occur if the price of widescreen digital televisions falls, other things being constant?
   a. The demand for digital cable services will increase.
   b. People will substitute widescreen digital televisions for standard televisions.
   c. The demand for standard televisions will rise.
   d. The quantity of widescreen digital televisions demanded will increase.

4. If the price of good A rises and the demand for good B rises, then A and B are
   a. substitutes.
   b. complements.
   c. not related goods.
   d. not scarce goods.

5. Consider a city that establishes a law prohibiting the use of lawn sprinklers and limiting showers to four minutes. Which one of the following statements is probably true in this city?
    a. A surplus of water exists.
    b. The price of water is too high.
    c. A shortage of water exists regardless of how high its price got.
    d. The price of water is below the equilibrium price.

6. If the supply of gasoline rises, with a given demand, then
    a. the relative price of gasoline will rise.
    b. the equilibrium price of gasoline will rise.
    c. the equilibrium quantity of gasoline will increase.
    d. the equilibrium price and equilibrium quantity of gasoline will increase.

7. If income falls and the demand for widescreen digital televisions falls, then widescreen digital televisions are a(n)
    a. substitute good.
    b. complement good.
    c. normal good.
    d. inferior good.

    Consider the graph below when answering Questions 8 and 9.

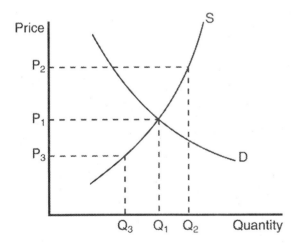

8. Given the graph above,
    a. the equilibrium price is P_1, and the equilibrium quantity is P_2.
    b. the equilibrium quantity is P_1.
    c. the equilibrium price is P_3, and the equilibrium quantity is Q_1.
    d. the equilibrium quantity is Q_1, and the equilibrium price is P_1.

9. Which one of the following is **not** true?
    a. A shortage exists at P_2.
    b. An excess quantity supplied exists at P_2.
    c. An excess quantity demanded exists at P_3.
    d. The equilibrium price is P_1.

10. If the demand for satellite Internet access services increases, with a given supply, then
    a. the supply of satellite Internet access services will rise because price rises.
    b. the equilibrium price of satellite Internet access services will fall, and the equilibrium quantity will rise.
    c. the equilibrium quantity and the equilibrium price of satellite Internet access services will rise.
    d. the quantity supplied of satellite Internet access services will decrease.

11. If a shortage exists at some price, then
    a. sellers can sell all they desire to sell at that price.
    b. sellers have an incentive to raise the price.
    c. buyers cannot get all they want at that price.
    d. All of the above.

12. Which one of the following will lead to a rise in supply?
    a. an increase in the price of the good in question
    b. a technological improvement in the production of the good in question
    c. an increase in the price of labor used to produce the good in question
    d. All of the above.

13. Which one of the following probably will **not** lead to a fall in the demand for hamburgers?
    a. a decrease in income, if hamburgers are a normal good
    b. an expectation that the price of hamburgers will rise in the future
    c. a decrease in the price of hot dogs
    d. a change in tastes away from hamburgers

14. When a demand curve is derived,
    a. quantity is in constant-quality units.
    b. the price of the good is held constant.
    c. money income changes.
    d. consumer tastes change.

15. If a surplus exists at some price, then
    a.   sellers have an incentive to raise the price.
    b.   buyers have an incentive to offer a higher price.
    c.   sellers cannot sell all they wish to at that price.
    d.   seller inventories are falling.

■ Matching

Choose the item in Column (2) that best matches an item in Column (1).

(1)	**(2)**
(a) excess quantity demanded	(k) relation between price and quantity demanded
(b) supply curve	(l) law of supply
(c) demand curve	(m) population increases
(d) bread and butter	(n) raw material prices rise
(e) eyeglasses and contact lenses	(o) community money income falls
(f) demand curve for a normal good shifts to the left	(p) market clearing price
(g) supply shifts to the left	(q) surplus
(h) equilibrium price	(r) complements
(i) equilibrium quantity rises	(s) substitutes
(j) excess quantity supplied	(t) shortage

■ Working with Graphs

1. Use the demand schedule below to plot the demand curve on the following coordinate system. Be sure to label each axis correctly.

Price per Bottle of Shampoo	Quantity Demanded of Bottles of Shampoo per Week (in thousands)
$8	8
$7	10
$6	12
$5	14
$4	16
$3	18

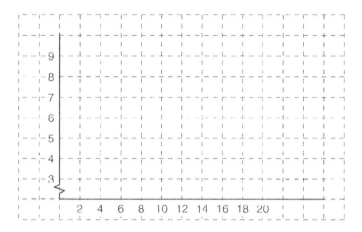

2. Use the supply schedule below to plot the supply curve on the coordinate system in Problem 1.

Price per Bottle of Shampoo	Quantity Supplied of Bottles of Shampoo per Week (in thousands)
$8	18
$7	15
$6	12
$5	9
$4	6
$3	3

3. Using the graphs from Problems 1 and 2, indicate on the graph the equilibrium price and the equilibrium quantity for bottles of shampoo. What is the equilibrium price? The equilibrium quantity?

4. Continuing with the same example, assume that the government mandates that shampoo cannot be sold for more than $5 per bottle. What is the quantity demanded at that price? The quantity supplied? Does a surplus or a shortage exist at that price?

5. Consider the two graphs below, in Panels (a) and (b). Which panel shows an increase in quantity demanded? Which shows a rise in demand?

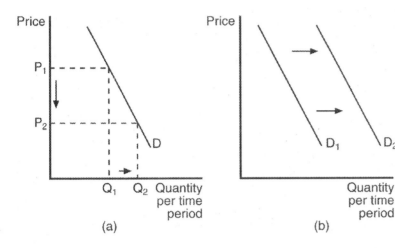

6. Distinguish between a fall in supply and a decrease in quantity supplied, graphically, using the space below. Use two panels.

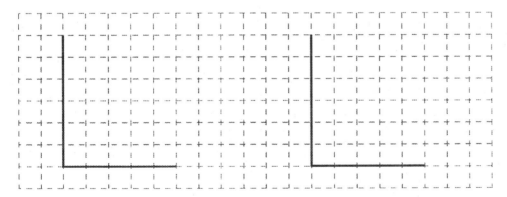

7.   Consider the graphs below in Panel (a). Then show, in Panel (b), the new equilibrium price (label it P_2) and the new equilibrium quantity (label it Q_2) that result due to a change in tastes in favor of the good in question.

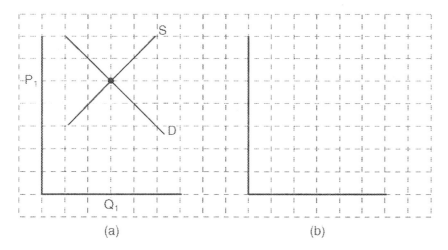

(a)   (b)

■ Problems

1.   In the table below, monthly demand schedules for turkey, a meat commonly prepared in November for Thanksgiving meals in the United States, are indicated. Assume that Column 2 represents quantities demanded in October, Column 3 represents November, and Column 4 represents December.

(1) Price per Pound	(2) Q_d	(3) Q_d	(4) Q_d
5 cents	10,000		16,000
10 cents	8,000		14,000
15 cents	6,000		12,000
20 cents	4,000		10,000
25 cents	2,000		8,000

Fill in Column 3 yourself. What happens to the demand for turkey in November relative to October and December? Why?

2.   List the kinds of changes in the *ceteris paribus* conditions of demand that will lead to a decrease in demand. Be specific.

3.   List the kinds of changes in the *ceteris paribus* conditions of supply that will lead to a rise in supply. Be specific.

4.   Concerning MP3 players, indicate whether each event leads to (i) a rightward shift in demand, (ii) a leftward shift in demand, (iii) an increase in quantity demanded, (iv) a decrease in quantity demanded, (v) a rightward shift in supply, (vi) a leftward shift in supply, (vii) an increase in quantity supplied, or (viii) a decrease in quantity supplied.

(*Note:* Some events may lead to more than one of the above.)

_____   (a) Worldwide spread of a software virus infects large numbers of MP3 files.

_____   (b) Government efforts to protect music copyrights raise the cost of producing MP3 music files.

_____   (c) The price of MP3 players rises.

_____   (d) The price of MP3 players falls.

_____   (e) The federal government requires manufacturers of MP3 players to set and maintain a price of MP3 players below the equilibrium price.

_____   (f) A number of producers of MP3 players leave the industry.

_____   (g) More digital devices, such as iPhones, can be used to play music on MP3 files.

_____   (h) The government subsidizes the production of MP3 players at $10 per MP3 player.

_____   (i) News is released to both consumers and producers of MP3 players that the market price of MP3 players is likely to rise during the coming year.

_____   (j) The price of other digital devices (such as cell phones) that play music on MP3 files rises (assume now that most producers of MP3 players also manufacture these other digital devices).

5.   For each of the statements (a) through (j) in the previous question, decide whether the market clearing (*equilibrium*) price will rise, fall, or be unaffected.

(a) _____   (f) _____

(b) _____   (g) _____

(c) _____   (h) _____

(d) _____   (i) _____

(e) _____   (j) _____

■ Answers

Completion Questions

1. demand curve or schedule; supply curve or schedule
2. movement along; shift in
3. equilibrium; surplus; shortage
4. lower; higher
5. inverse; negatively
6. income; tastes and preferences; prices of related goods; expectations about future relative prices; number of buyers
7. rise; rise
8. increases; direct; positively
9. more
10. prices of inputs; technology; taxes and subsidies; price expectations; number of firms in industry
11. complements; fall
12. substitutes
13. excess quantity demanded
14. right; down
15. price; quantity

True-False Questions

1. F   A demand schedule relates quantity demanded to price.
2. T
3. F   A graphical representation of a demand schedule is a demand curve.
4. F   An increase in price leads to a decrease in quantity demanded and an increase in quantity supplied.
5. F   It increases the quantity of MP3 players supplied, which is a movement along the supply curve, not a shift in the curve.
6. F   Buyers respond to changes in relative prices.
7. T
8. F   The demand for tennis balls will tend to *fall*, because they are complements.
9. T
10. T

Multiple Choice Questions

1. (b)
2. (a)
3. (c)
4. (a)
5. (d)
6. (c)
7. (c)
8. (d)
9. (a)
10. (c)
11. (d)
12. (b)
13. (b)
14. (a)
15. (c)

Matching

(a) and (t)   (f) and (o)

(b) and (l)   (g) and (n)

(c) and (k)   (h) and (p)

(d) and (r)   (i) and (m)

(e) and (s)   (j) and (q)

Working with Graphs

1.   See diagram for Problem 2 below.

2.   See diagram below.

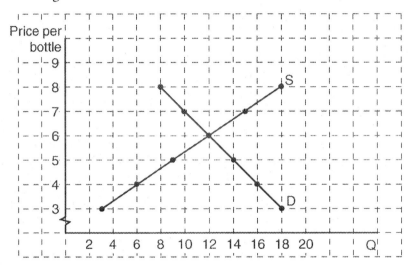

3. $6; 12,000 bottles

4.   14,000 bottles; 9,000 bottles; shortage

5.   Panel (a); Panel (b)

6.

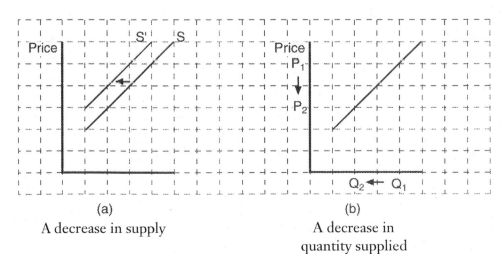

(a)
A decrease in supply

(b)
A decrease in
quantity supplied

7.

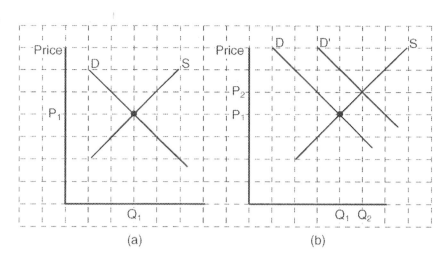

(a)   (b)

Problems

1. Due to Thanksgiving, the quantity of turkey consumed in November at any given price rises significantly relative to October, and (perhaps) slightly relative to December.

2. Income falls for a normal good; change in tastes occurs away from the good; price of a substitute falls or price of a complement rises; expectations exist that the good's future relative price will fall; decrease in the number of buyers occurs.

3. Reduction in the price of inputs; technological advances; decrease in a sales tax on the good or increase in the (per unit) subsidy of the good; expectation that the future relative price will fall; increase in the number of firms in the industry.

4. a. (vi) and (iv)   f. (vi) and (iv)
    b. (vi) and (iv)   g. (ii) and (viii)
    c. (iv) and (vii)   h. (v) and (iii)
    d. (iii) and (viii)   i. (i) and (vi)
    e. (iii) and (viii)   j. (i) and (vi)

5. a. rise   f. rise
    b. rise   g. fall
    c. be unaffected (no change in *equilibrium* price)   h   fall
    d. be unaffected (no change in *equilibrium* price)   i. rise
    e. be unaffected (no change in *equilibrium* price)   j. rise

■ Glossary

***Ceteris paribus* conditions**   Determinants of the relationship between price and quantity that are unchanged along a curve. Changes in these factors cause the curve to shift.

Complements   Two goods are complements when a change in the price of one causes an opposite shift in the demand for the other.

Demand   A schedule showing how much of a good or service people will purchase at any price during a specified time period, other things being constant.

Demand curve   A graphical representation of the demand schedule. It is a negatively sloped line showing the inverse relationship between the price and the quantity demanded (other things being equal).

Equilibrium   The situation when quantity supplied equals quantity demanded at a particular price.

Inferior goods   Goods for which demand falls as income rises.

Law of demand   The observation that there is a negative, or inverse, relationship between the price of any good or service and the quantity demanded, holding other factors constant.

Law of supply   The observation that the higher the price of a good, the more of that good sellers will make available over a specified time period, other things being equal.

Market   All of the arrangements that individuals have for exchanging with one another. Thus we can speak of the labor market, the automobile market, and the credit market.

Market clearing, or equilibrium, price   The price that clears the market, at which quantity demanded equals quantity supplied; the price where the demand curve intersects the supply curve.

Market demand   The demand of all consumers in the marketplace for a particular good or service. The summation at each price of the quantity demanded by each individual.

Money price   That price expressed in terms of today's dollars; also called the *absolute* or *nominal price*.

Normal goods   Goods for which demand rises as income rises. Most goods are normal goods.

Relative price   The money price of one commodity divided by the money price of another commodity; the number of units of one commodity that must be sacrificed to purchase one unit of another commodity.

Shortage   A situation in which quantity demanded is greater than quantity supplied at a price below the market clearing price.

Subsidy   A negative tax; a payment to a producer from the government, usually in the form of a cash grant per unit.

Substitutes   Two goods are substitutes when a change in the price of one causes a shift in demand for the other in the same direction as the price change.

Supply   A schedule showing the relationship between price and quantity supplied for a specified period of time, other things being equal.

Supply curve   The graphical representation of the supply schedule; a line (curve) showing the supply schedule, which generally slopes upward (has a positive slope), other things being equal.

Surplus   A situation in which quantity supplied is greater than quantity demanded at a price above the market clearing price.

4 Extensions of Demand and Supply Analysis

■ Learning Objectives

After you have studied this chapter, you should be able to

1. define price system, voluntary exchange, transaction costs, price controls, price ceiling, price floor, nonprice rationing devices, black market, rent control, minimum wage, and import quota;

2. predict what happens to equilibrium price and equilibrium quantity when supply increases or decreases relative to demand, and when demand increases or decreases relative to supply;

3. predict what happens to the relative price of a good or resource if it becomes more or less scarce;

4. differentiate between the causes of short-run and long-run (prolonged) shortages;

5. recognize various methods of rationing goods and services;

6. recognize, from graphs, how a black market emerges;

7. enumerate several consequences of rent control;

8. recognize several consequences of government quantity restrictions; and

9. recognize the consequences of price floors and the causes of prolonged surpluses.

■ Outline

1. In a price system (free enterprise) voluntary exchange typically determines price. Buyers and sellers transact with a minimum amount of governmental interference.
   a. Under a system of voluntary exchange, the terms of exchange (the terms, usually price, under which trade takes place) are set by the forces of supply and demand.
   b. Markets reduce transaction costs (all the costs associated with exchanging, including such costs associated with gathering information and enforcing contracts).
   c. Under voluntary exchange *both* buyers and sellers are presumed to benefit—otherwise the transactions would not continue.

2.   Changes in demand and/or supply lead to changes in the equilibrium price and the equilibrium quantity.

a.   If demand shifts to the right (left), given supply, then the equilibrium price rises (falls) and the equilibrium quantity rises (falls).

b.   If supply shifts to the right (left), given demand, then the equilibrium price falls (rises) and the equilibrium quantity rises (falls).

c.   When both supply and demand change, it is not always possible to predict the effects on the equilibrium price and the equilibrium quantity.

3.   Prices are not always perfectly flexible.

a.   If prices are inflexible, published prices will not change very much, but hidden price increases through quality reductions might occur.

b.   Markets do not always move to equilibrium (given a change in demand or supply) immediately. Hence, shortages or surpluses can emerge in the short run.

4.   Price reflects relative scarcity and performs a rationing function.

a.   If an input or output becomes less scarce (more scarce), its relative price will fall (rise).

b.   If governments prevent prices from rising to their equilibrium level, via a price control or ceiling, then goods cannot (legally) be allocated to the highest bidders and prolonged shortages result. Other forms of rationing emerge.

c.   During prolonged shortages, such nonprice rationing devices as cheating, long lines, first-come first-served, political power, physical force, and other nonmarket forces arise.

d.   Governments also interfere in markets by putting price floors on price. For example, governments impose minimum wage rates, and they have put price floors on agricultural goods, which have caused surpluses.

5.   Rent controls are governmentally imposed price ceilings on rental apartments, which lead to predictable results. Nonprice rationing for apartments results.

6.   The government has put price floors in several markets.

a.   For many years, price supports created explicit minimum prices for agricultural goods, and in recent years some agricultural price supports have been explicitly created through mechanisms such as marketing loan programs.

b.   When the government sets minimum wages above the equilibrium, some unemployment is created.

c.   Governments sometimes restrict quantity directly through import quotas, which prohibit the importation of more than a specified quantity of a particular good in a one-year period.

■ Key Terms

Black market	Minimum wage	Price floor
Import quota	Price ceiling	Transaction costs

■ Key Concepts

Nonprice rationing devices   Price system
Price controls   Rent control   Voluntary exchange

■ Completion Questions

Fill in the blank, or circle the correct term.

1. Resources are scarce. Therefore, we cannot have all we want at a (<u>zero, positive</u>) price and there will be various ways in which people will _____ for resources.

2. If demand shifts to the left, given supply, then the equilibrium price will (<u>rise, fall</u>) and the equilibrium quantity will _____.

3. If supply shifts to the right, given demand, then the equilibrium price will _____ and the equilibrium quantity will _____.

4. If both demand and supply shift to the right, then the equilibrium price (<u>will rise, will fall, is indeterminate</u>) and the equilibrium quantity (<u>will rise, will fall, is indeterminate</u>).

5. If both demand and supply shift to the left, then the equilibrium price (<u>will rise, will fall, is indeterminate</u>), and the equilibrium quantity (<u>will rise, will fall, is indeterminate</u>).

6. If the demand for good A or resource A rises relative to its supply, A has become relatively (<u>less scarce, more scarce</u>) and its relative price will (<u>rise, fall</u>). If the demand for good B or resource B falls relative to its supply, then B has become relatively _____, and its relative price will _____.

7. If the published price of good A remains constant, but its quality falls, then its relative price has actually (<u>risen, fallen</u>). If the published price of good A remains constant, but people have to wait in line to get it, then the relative price of good A has actually _____, because people have an opportunity cost for their _____.

8. If the demand for a good rises relative to its supply, that good becomes (<u>less scarce, more scarce</u>) and its relative price will (<u>rise, fall</u>). This leads to (<u>a decrease, an increase</u>) in the quantity of the good supplied by producers of the item.

9. Price performs a(n) _____ function. Inputs or outputs go to the _____ bidders, if people are free to exchange voluntarily in markets. If such economic freedoms do not exist, then other (<u>price, nonprice</u>) determinants will allocate goods and services.

10. Price controls that put a price ceiling on goods and services create (<u>surpluses, shortages</u>). Price floors create (<u>surpluses, shortages</u>).

11. If governments place price (<u>floors, ceilings</u>) on goods, then black markets might emerge.

12. Rent control is a form of price (<u>floor, ceiling</u>). Rent control (<u>increases, reduces</u>) the future supply of apartment construction, (<u>increases, reduces</u>) tenant mobility, (<u>improves, causes a deterioration in</u>) the quality of the existing stock of apartments, and hurts

    _____.

13. By prohibiting the sale and use of tobacco products, the government would cause the supply of cigarettes to shift to the (<u>left, right</u>), make cigarettes (<u>more, less</u>) scarce, and cause their relative price to (<u>rise, fall</u>).

14. Import quotas, licensing arrangements, and outright bans on specific goods are forms of government (<u>price, quantity</u>) restrictions.

15. An import quota tends to (<u>lower, raise</u>) the price to consumers.

16. If governments put price floors on agricultural goods, a (<u>shortage, surplus</u>) will result.

■ True-False Questions

Circle the **T** if the statement is true, the **F** if it is false. Explain to yourself why a statement is false.

T F   1. If supply shifts to the left, given demand, then the equilibrium price and the equilibrium quantity will rise.

T F   2. If demand shifts to the left, given supply, then the equilibrium price and the equilibrium quantity will fall.

T F   3. If both supply and demand shift to the right, then the equilibrium price and equilibrium quantity are indeterminate.

T F   4. If the supply of good A increases relative to its demand, then good A is now more scarce, and its relative price will rise.

T F   5. If the published price is constant, but it takes consumers longer to wait in lines, the total price has really risen.

T F   6. If markets are flexible, and no market restrictions exist, then surpluses and shortages will not occur, even in the short run.

T F   7. Minimum-wage laws are a form of price ceiling.

T F   8. Rent controls help the poor who are looking for apartments because rents are lower.

T F   9. Black markets, in effect, cause prices to rise for certain buyers.

T F   10. Agricultural surpluses arise when governments put price ceilings on such goods.

■ Multiple Choice Questions

Circle the letter that corresponds to the best answer.

1. Because resources are scarce,
    a. buyers compete with buyers for outputs.
    b. there must be some method for rationing goods.
    c. people cannot have all they want at a zero price.
    d. All of the above.

2. If markets are free and prices are flexible,
    a. equilibrium price cannot be established.
    b. shortages and surpluses eventually disappear.
    c. shortages and surpluses cannot arise.
    d. equilibrium quantity cannot be established.

3. If demand shifts to the right (given supply), then equilibrium
    a. quantity will rise.
    b. price is indeterminate.
    c. price and equilibrium quantity are indeterminate.
    d. price will fall.

4. If supply shifts to the right (given demand), then equilibrium
    a. quantity will rise.
    b. price will rise.
    c. price and equilibrium quantity will fall.
    d. price and equilibrium quantity rises.

5. If both supply and demand shift to the left, then equilibrium
    a. price is indeterminate, and equilibrium quantity rises.
    b. price is indeterminate, and equilibrium quantity falls.
    c. price falls, and equilibrium quantity falls.
    d. price falls, and equilibrium quantity is indeterminate.

6. If the demand for good A falls relative to its supply, then
    a. good A is now relatively more scarce.
    b. good A is now relatively less scarce.
    c. the relative price of good A will rise.
    d. the total price of good A will rise, even if A is not price flexible.

7. If the demand for good B rises relative to its supply, then
    a. good B is now relatively more scarce.
    b. the relative price of good B will rise.
    c. the total price of good B will rise, even if good B is price inflexible.
    d. All of the above.

8. If the demand for good A rises relative to its supply, and markets are price flexible, then
    a. no shortage of A can exist in the long run.
    b. no shortage of A can exist in the short run.
    c. the published price of A remains constant, but its total price falls.
    d. the published price of A remains constant, but its total price rises.

9. If the demand for good A rises relative to its supply, and markets are price inflexible, then
    a. a shortage can exist in the short run.
    b. a shortage can exist in the long run.
    c. the published price of A might remain constant, but its total price rises.
    d. All of the above.

10. A simultaneous increase in the market clearing price of cheese and decrease in the equilibrium quantity of cheese could result from
    a. a higher price of beef that induces farmers to sell dairy cows for use in beef production, with the milk produced by dairy cows being a key input in cheese production.
    b. a higher price of hormones used to stimulate production of milk in dairy cows, with milk being a key input in the production of cheese.
    c. any factor that reduces the supply of cheese.
    d. All of the above.

11. Which one of the following can influence how a society rations a specific good?
    a. price system that rations to the highest bidder
    b. political power
    c. religion
    d. all of the above

12. Prolonged shortages arise if
    a. demand increases relative to supply.
    b. price floors are set by governments.
    c. prices are not allowed to rise to equilibrium.
    d. buyers are allowed to compete for goods.

13. Black markets may arise if
    a. price ceilings exist.
    b. price floors exist.
    c. governments do not intervene in the market.
    d. equilibrium price is too low.

14. Rent controls
    a. are a form of price floor.
    b. help the homeless who need apartments.
    c. make tenants less mobile.
    d. reduce litigation in society.

15. If an effective minimum wage is imposed, then
    a. more workers will be unable to find jobs.
    b. the quantity of labor demanded will fall.
    c. some workers will move to sectors not covered by minimum wages.
    d. All of the above.

16. Prolonged agricultural surpluses can arise if governments
    a. set price above equilibrium.
    b. institute price floors, or price supports.
    c. purchase the excess supply.
    d. All of the above.

■ Matching

Choose the item in Column (2) that best matches an item in Column (1).

	(1)		(2)
(a)	price floor	(e)	buyer competition
(b)	price ceiling	(f)	rent control
(c)	scarce resources	(g)	minimum-wage law
(d)	nonprice rationing	(h)	black market, long lines

■ Working with Graphs

1.   Consider the graph below, then answer the questions that follow.

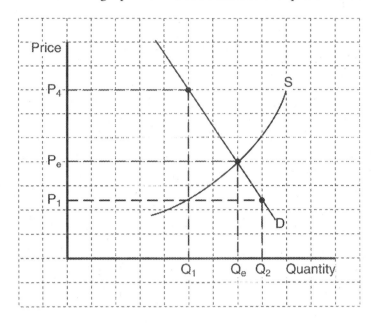

a.   The market clearing price is _____.

b.   If the government imposes a price ceiling at P_1, what will be the quantity supplied? The quantity demanded? What exists at that price?

c.   Given the quantity that will be forthcoming at the permitted price of P_1, what will the actual or black market price be?

d.   Other than via a black market transaction, how can the actual price paid by buyers exceed the permitted price, P_1?

e.   If price had been permitted to rise to equilibrium, what would be the quantity supplied by sellers? Is that amount greater or less than the quantity at P_1? Why?

2. Consider the following supply and demand curves for labor, and then answer the questions.

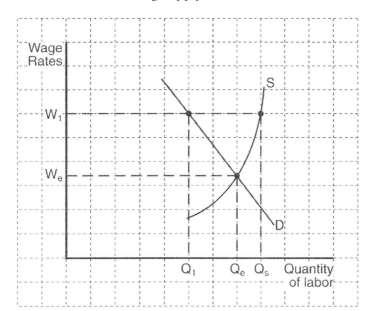

a. What is the equilibrium wage rate? The equilibrium quantity of labor?

b. If the government sets a minimum wage rate at W_1, what is the quantity of labor demanded by employers? The quantity of labor supplied by workers? What exists at the minimum-wage rate?

c. Is there a shortage or surplus of *jobs*? How might such jobs be allocated (that is, how will employers go about deciding who gets the jobs)?

3. During September 1989, the then-"Drug Czar" then-director of the Office of National Drug Control Policy, William T. Bennett, and Nobel Prize winning economist Milton Friedman debated the case for the prohibition of drugs in letters to the editor that appeared in the *Wall Street Journal*. Bennett, who favors prohibition, maintained that if drugs were legalized, then price would fall, and therefore the total amount of drug usage in the United States would rise. Friedman, who favors legalization of drugs (to adults) maintained that, once legalized, the demand for drugs would fall because (1) the appeal to people who want the excitement of doing something "taboo" would disappear, and (2) addicts who have only a $2 a day habit have less of an incentive to get other people hooked on drugs (to support their own habit) than if they had a $200 a day habit. Entering the 2010s, their perspectives continue to summarize arguments favoring prohibition versus legalization of drugs.

a. Is Bennett correct when he says that once legalized, price will fall? Why?

b. If the demand for drugs shifts to the left (Friedman), and the supply of drugs to the right (Bennett), what happens to the market clearing price of drugs?

c. If the demand for drugs shifts to the left (Friedman) and the supply of drugs shifts to the right (Bennett), what happens to the equilibrium quantity of drugs?

d. How does your answer to (c) help you decide whether drug usage will rise or fall if drugs are legalized? What information is necessary to resolve this issue?

■ Problems

1. During the 2000s, New York City relaxed some rent controls by allowing landlords to charge higher rents, albeit at legally permissible levels that typically remained below market-clearing rents. Critics of these actions by the city contended that raising allowable apartment rents has harmed tenants. The critics have proposed that all previously prevailing controls should be reinstituted to protect tenants from economic harm.

    a. How do you imagine that raising allowable rents has affected the shortage of luxury apartments that had prevailed before the relaxation of some of New York City's rent controls?

    b. How were tenants affected by the relaxation of rent controls in New York City? How do you suppose that the relaxation of these controls affect people who previously experienced difficulties in finding apartments?

2. At various times during the 1990s and 2000s, people attending soccer matches around the world died when stadium gates were opened and crowds rushed in to get choice seats in "open seating" sections of the stadiums. What other method of allocating the scarce resource of choice seats would have prevented these tragic events?

■ Answers

Completion Questions

1. zero; compete
2. fall; fall
3. fall; rise
4. is indeterminate; will rise
5. is indeterminate; will fall
6. more scarce; rise; less scarce; fall
7. risen; risen; time
8. more scarce; rise; an increase
9. rationing; highest; nonprice
10. shortages; surpluses
11. ceilings
12. ceiling; reduces; reduces; causes a deterioration in; landlords and low income apartment hunters
13. left; more; rise
14. quantity
15. raise
16. surplus

True-False Questions

1. F   The equilibrium quantity falls.
2. T
3. F   Equilibrium quantity rises.
4. F   Good A is now less scarce, and its relative price will fall.
5. T
6. F   No, surpluses and shortages can exist—in the short run.
7. F   They are a price floor.
8. F   That group is hurt because they will be discriminated against and because the housing stock diminishes.
9. T
10. F   Price ceilings cause shortages.

Multiple Choice Questions

1. (d)	9. (d)
2. (b)	10. (d)
3. (a)	11. (d)
4. (a)	12. (c)
5. (b)	13. (a)
6. (b)	14. (c)
7. (d)	15. (d)
8. (a)	16. (d)

Matching

(a) and (g)   (c) and (e)

(b) and (f)   (d) and (h)

Working with Graphs

1. a. P_e

    b. Q_1; Q_2; shortage

    c. P_4

    d. quality deterioration, long lines that increase opportunity costs

    e. Q_e; greater; a higher price induces sellers to produce more

2. a. W_e; Q_e

    b. Q_1; Q_s; surplus of labor, or unemployment

    c. shortage; family influence, political power, bribes, racial or gender preference

3. a. He is correct because the supply curve will shift to the right as the costs and risks of drug-dealing fall.

    b. The market-clearing price falls (Therefore, Bennett is correct.)

    c. It is impossible to predict the net effect on the equilibrium quantity.

    d. The real issue is an empirical one: Will supply rise by more than demand falls, or vice versa?

Problems

1. a. Under the controls, landlords have to set rents below the market-clearing levels, so the quantity of apartments demanded by prospective renters is greater than the quantity supplied by landlords. The result is a shortage of luxury apartments. The increase in legally permissible rents to levels closer to market-clearing rents has had the effect of reducing the size of this shortage.

    b. People who were already tenants had to pay higher rents than before the relaxation of rent controls. Because landlords supplied more apartments in response to the increase in the legally allowed rental rates, more people who had previously experienced difficulties finding apartments were able to become tenants.

2. Instead of "first-come, first-served seating," ticket sellers for soccer matches could have raised the price of choice seats and used assigned seating.

■ Glossary

Black market   A market in which goods are traded at prices above their legal maximum prices or in which illegal goods are sold.

Import quota   A physical supply restriction on imports of a particular good, such as sugar. Foreign exporters are unable to sell in the United States more than the quantity specified in the import quota.

Minimum wage   A wage floor, legislated by government, setting the lowest hourly rate that firms may legally pay workers.

Nonprice rationing devices   All methods used to ration scarce goods that are price-controlled. Whenever the price system is not allowed to work, nonprice rationing devices will evolve to ration the affected goods and services.

Price ceiling   A legal maximum price that may be charged for a particular good or service.

Price controls   Government-mandated minimum or maximum prices that may be charged for goods and services.

Price floor   A legal minimum price below which a good or service may not be sold. Legal minimum wages are an example.

Price system   An economic system in which relative prices are constantly changing to reflect changes in supply and demand for different commodities. The prices of those commodities are signals to everyone within the system about what is relatively scarce and what is relatively abundant.

Rent control   Price ceilings on rents.

Transaction costs   All of the costs associated with exchange, including the informational costs of finding out the price and quality, service record, and durability of a product, plus the cost of contracting and enforcing that contract.

Voluntary exchange   An act of trading, done on an elective basis, in which both parties to the trade expect to be better off after the exchange.

5 Public Spending and Public Choice

■ Learning Objectives

After you have studied this chapter, you should be able to

1. define antitrust legislation, monopoly, spillover or externality, third parties, effluent fee, market failure, property rights, private goods, public goods, principle of rival consumption, exclusion principle, free-rider problem, government-sponsored good, government-inhibited good, transfer payment, and transfers in kind;

2. enumerate the five economic functions of government;

3. predict whether a specific good will be overproduced, underproduced, or produced in just the right amount if resources are allocated by the price system;

4. identify which graphs take into account an externality and which do not;

5. list the two ways in which a government can correct for negative externalities;

6. identify the three ways in which a government can correct for positive externalities;

7. list four characteristics of public goods that distinguish them from private goods;

8. assess the ways in which Medicare affects the incentives to consume medical services;

9. provide reasons why higher government spending on public education has not necessarily improved student performance; and

10. identify similarities and differences between market and collective decision making.

■ Outline

1. The government performs many economic functions that affect the way in which resources are allocated.

    a. If a benefit or cost associated with an economic activity spills over to third parties, the price system will misallocate resources. A proper role for government is to correct such externalities.

        i. If a negative externality exists, the price system will overallocate resources to that industry. The government can correct this by taxing or regulating such activities.

        ii. If a positive externality exists, the price system will underallocate resources to that industry. The government can correct this by financing additional production, by providing special subsidies, or by regulation.

    b. A legal system that defines and enforces property rights is crucial to the U.S. capitalistic economy.

    c. Because a competitive price system transmits correct signals, an important role for government is to promote competition.

    d. A price system will underallocate resources to the production of public goods.

        i. Characteristics of public goods include the following:

            (1) They are usually indivisible.

            (2) They can be used by more people at no additional cost.

            (3) Additional users of public goods do not deprive others of any of the services of the good.

            (4) It is difficult to charge individual users a fee based on how much they themselves consume of the public good.

        ii. Because public goods must be consumed collectively, individuals have an incentive to take a free ride and not pay for them.

        iii. Because the price system underproduces public goods, a proper role of government may be to ensure their production.

    e. The U.S. government has taken on the economic role of ensuring economy-wide stability: full employment, price stability, and economic growth.

2. The government performs political functions that also affect resource allocation.

    a. Governments subsidize the production of government-sponsored goods and tax or prohibit the production of government-inhibited goods.

    b. By combining a progressive tax structure with transfer payments, the government attempts to redistribute income from higher to lower income groups (although many "loopholes" frustrate such a policy).

3. Governments use tax revenues to fund expenditures on public goods and government-sponsored goods, such as Medicare.

    a. Federal funding of health care services implies that effective prices that consumers pay for health care services are less than the prices that health care providers receive to provide those services, which explains the large quantities of health care services demanded and supplied under Medicare.

      i. Because the government pays a per-unit subsidy for consuming a health care service covered by Medicare, the out-of-pocket expense that a Medicare recipient pays for each unit of service—the effective price to the consumer—is relatively low. Thus, the quantity of health care services demanded by Medicare patients is relatively large.

     ii. Suppliers of health care services are willing to provide the quantity of services demanded by Medicare patients, because the per-unit price they receive is equal to the out-of-pocket expense of Medicare patients plus the government subsidy.

    iii. The Medicare program's total expense for a particular health care service equals the per-unit subsidy times the quantity of the service demanded by Medicare patients. Taxpayers must fund this expense.

  b. In the absence of Medicare subsidies, the equilibrium prices and quantities of health care services both would be lower than they are with the subsidies provided by this federal program.

      i. This means that Medicare has encouraged increased consumption and production of health care services.

     ii. As a result, the total expense of the program—the per-unit government subsidy times the quantity of health care services demanded—is higher than the government estimated using equilibrium quantities as a guide.

  c. To try to contain overall federal spending on Medicare, the government often imposes reimbursement caps, or limits, on specific medical procedures. This can have the unintended effect of worsening patient care and driving the program's costs up even further.

4.   Education is another government-sponsored good that receives considerable public funding, which currently amounts to more than 5 percent of total U.S. national income.

  a. The basic economics of public funding of education is similar to the economics of public subsidies of health care programs such as Medicare. Public schools provide educational services at a price below the market price and provide the amount of services demanded at the below-market price as long as they receive sufficiently large per-unit subsidies from state and local governments.

  b. Measures of student performance have failed to increase even though public spending on education has risen. A possible explanation is that a higher per-pupil subsidy increases the difference between the per-student cost of providing educational services and the lower valuation of the services by parents and students. Thus, schools may have allocated resources to activities that have not necessarily enhanced learning.

5.   The theory of public choice is the study of collective decision making.

  a. Collective decision making involves the actions that voters, politicians, and other interested parties undertake to influence nonmarket choices.

  b. Market and collective decision making are similar in the sense that both involve competition for scarce resources and people motivated by self-interest.

  c. Market and collective decision making are different because the government goods are available for consumption at a price of zero, decisions about what government goods to provide are determined by majority rule, and government can use legally sanctioned force to ensure that its decisions are followed.

■ Key Terms

Antitrust legislation	Majority rule	Subsidy
Collective decision making	Market failure	Third parties
Effluent fee	Monopoly	Transfer payments
Externality	Proportional rule	
Free-rider problem	Public goods	

■ Key Concepts

Government, or political, goods	Medicare subsidies	Public choice
Government-inhibited good	Principle of rival consumption	Theory of public choice
Government-sponsored good	Private goods	Transfers in kind
Incentive structure	Property rights	

■ Completion Questions

Fill in the blank, or circle the correct term.

1. The five economic functions of government in our capitalistic system are
   _____, _____, _____,
   _____, and _____.

2. If there are disputes in an economic arena, the _____ often acts as a
   "referee" to help settle the dispute.

3. Antitrust legislation, in theory, is supposed to (<u>decrease, promote</u>) competition in the private
   sector.

4. If externalities are an important result of an economic activity, then the price system is
   (<u>inefficient, efficient</u>).

5. If Ms. Johnson buys an automobile from Toyota, those people not directly involved in the
   transaction are considered _____.

6. Pollution is an example of a (<u>negative, positive</u>) externality.

7. When there are spillover costs, a price system will (<u>underallocate, overallocate</u>) resources to the
   production of the good in question.

8. If third parties benefit from a transaction, then (<u>negative, positive</u>) externalities exist, and the
   price system will allocate resources (<u>inefficiently, efficiently</u>).

9. Positive and negative externalities are examples of market _____.

10. A government can correct negative externalities by imposing taxes and by _____ the industry or firms in question.

11. A government can correct positive externalities by _____, _____, and _____.

12. If a positive externality exists for good B, a price system will produce too _____ of good B.

13. Public goods have four distinguishing characteristics. They are usually _____. Public goods can be used by more people at _____ additional cost. Additional users (do, do not) deprive others of the services of a public good. It is very (easy, difficult) to charge individuals based on how much they used the public good.

14. A free rider has an incentive (to pay, not to pay) for a public good.

15. Government-inhibited goods are goods for which society wants to (decrease, increase) production.

16. Because the Medicare program pays a per-unit subsidy for health care expenses of people covered by the program, the price that they pay for health care services is (greater than, equal to, less than) the market price, and the quantity of health care services that they desire to consume is (greater than, equal to, less than) the equilibrium quantity.

17. Because the Medicare program pays a per-unit subsidy for health care expenses of people covered by the program, the price that providers receive for health care services is (greater than, equal to, less than) the market price, and the quantity of health care services they are willing to supply is (greater than, equal to, less than) the equilibrium quantity.

18. An increase in the number of people covered by Medicare will tend to cause the demand for covered health care services to _____, thereby causing a(n) _____ in both the equilibrium and actual quantities of the service demanded and supplied.

19. When governments provide subsidies to providers of educational services, the result is that the cost of the last unit of services provided is (lower, higher) than the marginal value of the services to parents and students.

20. Reducing government subsidies paid to public schools causes (a decrease, an increase) in the quantity of educational services provided by these schools and (a decrease, an increase) in the quantity of educational services desired by students and their parents.

21. Many government, or political, goods are provided to consumers at a (zero, positive) price. The opportunity cost to society of providing government goods is (zero, positive).

22. In contrast to goods sold in private markets, government goods are not (scarce, explicitly priced).

23. In the government sector, decisions concerning what goods to produce are determined by (majority, proportional) rule.

■ True-False Questions

Circle the **T** if the statement is true, the **F** if it is false. Explain to yourself why a statement is false.

T F   1. In the U.S. economy, the government plays only a minor role in resource allocation because the country is capitalistic.

T F   2. Governments provide a legal system, but this important function is not considered an economic function.

T F   3. One aim of antitrust legislation is the promotion of competition.

T F   4. If externalities, or spillovers, exist, then a price system misallocates resources so that inefficiency exists.

T F   5. If a negative externality exists, buyers and sellers are not faced with the true opportunity costs of their actions.

T F   6. If a positive externality exists when good A is produced, a price system will underallocate resources into the production of good A.

T F   7. One way to help correct for a negative externality is to tax the good in question because that will cause the price of the good to fall.

T F   8. A price system will tend to overallocate resources to the production of free goods, due to the free-rider problem.

T F   9. Scarcity exists in the market sector but not in the public sector.

T F   10. If third parties are hurt by the production of good B, and they are not compensated, then too many resources have been allocated to industry B.

T F   11. Deciding what is a government-sponsored good and what is a government-inhibited good is easily done and does not require value judgments.

T F   12. The price that Medicare patients pay for covered care that they receive is lower than the market price of that care.

T F   13. Not including any administration costs, the direct expense that taxpayers incur in paying the government's share of the total costs of a particular type of care equals the per-unit subsidy that the government pays times the quantity of care demanded under the subsidy.

T F   14. The price that the supplier of a service covered by Medicare receives is higher than the market price of providing that service.

T F   15. If market demand and supply curves have their normal shapes, then the difference between the market price of a health care service covered by Medicare and the price that Medicare recipients actually pay is equal to the per-unit Medicare subsidy.

T F   16. In recent years, decreases in educational subsidies have generally widened the difference between the cost of the last unit of services provided and the marginal value of the services to parents and students.

T F   17. Government goods are produced solely in the public sector.

T F   18. The best way for the government to prevent the underallocation of resources to production of vaccines against diseases is to require producers to set the price of vaccines below the equilibrium price.

■ Multiple Choice Questions

Circle the letter that corresponds to the best answer.

1. Which one of the following is **not** an economic function of government?
   a. income redistribution
   b. providing a legal system
   c. ensuring economy-wide stability
   d. promoting competition

2. A price system will misallocate resources if
   a. much income inequality exists.
   b. government-inhibited goods are produced.
   c. externalities exist.
   d. All of the above.

3. Which one of the following does **not** belong with the others?
   a. positive externality
   b. negative externality
   c. government-inhibited good
   d. public good

4. The exclusion principle
   a. does not work for public goods.
   b. does not work for private goods.
   c. causes positive externalities.
   d. makes it easy to assess user fees on true public goods.

5. Which one of the following statements concerning externalities is true?
    a. If a positive externality exists for good A, then A will be overproduced by a price system.
    b. If externalities exist, then resources will be allocated efficiently.
    c. Efficiency may be improved if the government taxes goods for which a positive externality exists.
    d. The output of goods for which a positive externality exists is too low, from society's point of view.

6. Which one of the following is **not** a characteristic of public goods?
    a. indivisibility
    b. high extra cost to additional users
    c. exclusion principle does not work easily
    d. difficult to determine how each individual benefits from public goods

7. Market failure exists if
    a. Mr. Smith cannot purchase watermelons in his town.
    b. buyers and sellers must pay the true opportunity costs of their actions.
    c. third parties are injured and are not compensated.
    d. the government must provide government-sponsored goods.

8. Which one of the following will properly correct a negative externality that results from producing good B?
    a. subsidizing the production of good B
    b. letting the price system determine the price and output of good B
    c. forcing buyers and sellers of good B to pay the true opportunity costs of their actions
    d. banning the production of good B

9. Government-sponsored and government-inhibited goods
    a. are examples of public goods.
    b. are examples of externalities.
    c. indicate market failure.
    d. are not easily classified.

10. If Ms. Ayres loves good A, she can convey the intensity of her wants if good A is
    a. a private good.
    b. a public good.
    c. not subject to the exclusion principle.
    d. expensive.

11. The free-rider problem exists
    a. for private goods.
    b. for goods that must be consumed collectively.
    c. only if people can be excluded from consumption.
    d. All of the above.

12. Suppose that the government has been paying a fixed per-unit subsidy for a health care service covered by Medicare. Then officials who administer the program tell patients and doctors and other health care providers that they plan to cut the per-unit subsidy. Other things being equal, the result will be
    a. a rise in the market price and a decline in the equilibrium quantity in the market for the service.
    b. a rise in the price paid by each Medicare recipient, and a reduction in the quantity of the service demanded and supplied.
    c. a rise in the price received by each health care supplier and an increase in the quantity of the service demanded and supplied.
    d. a fall in the price received by each health care supplier and an increase in the quantity of the service demanded and supplied.

13. Suppose that, until this year, a health care service was not covered by Medicare. Recently, however, the government has extended Medicare coverage to this service and has started paying a fixed per-unit subsidy to providers of the service. Other things being equal, the result will be
    a. a fall in the market price and an increase in the equilibrium quantity in the market for the service.
    b. a rise in the price paid by each Medicare recipient and a reduction in the quantity of the service demanded and supplied.
    c. a rise in the price received by each health care supplier and an increase in the quantity of the service demanded and supplied.
    d. a fall in the price received by each health care supplier and an increase in the quantity of the service demanded and supplied.

14. In future years, the number of people covered by Medicare will increase, so the demand for each covered health care service will rise. Suppose that the per-unit subsidy that the government pays for each covered service remains unchanged. Other things being equal, which one of the following will **not** occur as a result?
    a. The market price of the service will increase, and the equilibrium quantity in the market for the service will rise.
    b. There will be a rise in the price paid by each Medicare recipient, and there will be an increase in the quantity of the service demanded.
    c. There will be a rise in the price received by each health care supplier, and there will be an increase in the quantity of the service supplied.
    d. Because the per-unit subsidy paid by the government remains unchanged, the total expense incurred by taxpayers will remain unaffected.

15. Which one of the following is true of both market and collective decision making? Within both contexts,

    a. resources are scarce.
    b. people face identical incentive structures.
    c. production and allocation decisions arise from majority rule.
    d. production and allocation decisions arise from proportional rule.

16. Which one of the following is true of government goods?

    a. They are always produced within the public sector.
    b. They are always produced within the private sector.
    c. They are provided free of charge.
    d. They have no opportunity cost.

■ Matching

Choose the item in Column (2) that best matches an item in Column (1).

(1)		**(2)**	
(a)	antitrust legislation	(h)	pollution
(b)	spillover	(i)	externality
(c)	positive externality	(j)	national defense
(d)	negative externality	(k)	alcohol
(e)	Medicare subsidy	(l)	monopoly
(f)	government good	(m)	flu shots
(g)	government-inhibited good	(n)	difference between the price a consumer pays and the price received by a seller

■ Problems

1. Consider the situation shown in the graph on the next page; in a market for health care services covered by Medicare, the program pays a per-unit subsidy equal to $20 to suppliers. Suppose that the government expands Medicare and increases the per-unit subsidy by $20. What happens to the market price and equilibrium quantity of health care services? What happens to the prices paid by Medicare patients and received by health care providers and to the actual quantity of services consumed and provided under Medicare?

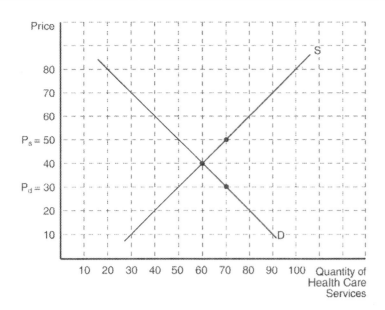

2. In the past, critics have accused the American Medical Association (AMA) of restricting the entry of physicians into markets for health care services. Suppose that these critics are correct and that the AMA successfully reduces the number of physicians offering services at any given price. As a result, the quantity of services provided at each price falls by 20 units. As shown below, the Medicare program pays a per-unit subsidy of $20 to AMA-permitted physicians. Use the diagram below to illustrate the effects of the AMA's action on (1) the equilibrium price and quantity of health care services, (2) the price paid by patients covered by Medicare, and (3) the price received by physicians.

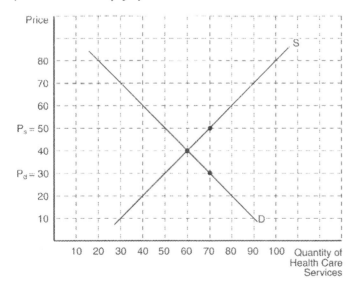

3. One important purely economic function of government is to promote competition, which presumably makes the price system more efficient. During the late 1990s and the 2000s, a wave of mergers among textbook publishers enabled the firms to charge higher textbook prices and earn higher profits. In what ways might various students have reacted to the higher relative price of textbooks? Were such actions rational, from the point of view of the individuals involved? Would such decisions lead to a misallocation of resources from *society's* point of view? (*Hint:* Textbook prices rose because the fall in the number of publishers reduced output and repressed competition.)

4. In the text, five economic and two political functions of the government were analyzed. Place each of the following governmental activities in one (or more) of these seven categories.

    a. Providing aid to welfare recipients   _____
    b. Passing antitrust laws   _____
    c. Subsidizing the arts   _____
    d. Prohibiting the sale and possession of drugs   _____
    e. Providing national defense   _____
    f. Enforcing a progressive tax structure   _____
    g. Enforcing contracts   _____
    h. Providing public education to children   _____
    i. Prosecuting fraud   _____
    j. Providing funds for AIDS research   _____
    k. Creating jobs to reduce unemployment   _____

■ Working with Graphs

1. Consider the graph below, then answer the questions. Assume S represents industry supply and S′ includes pollution costs to society as well as industry private costs.

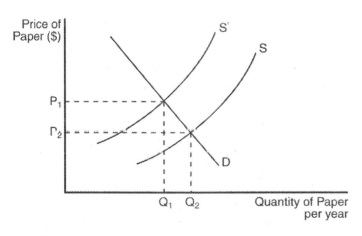

    a. If no governmental intervention takes place, what will be the market equilibrium price? The market equilibrium quantity?
    b. From *society's* point of view, what is the price that reflects the true opportunity costs of paper? From that same point of view, what is the optimal quantity of paper?

c.   Considering your answers in parts a and b, will a price system produce too little or too much paper?

d.   Does a negative externality or a positive externality exist?

2.   Consider the graph below, then answer the questions that follow. Assume that D represents private market demand and that D′ includes benefits that accrue to third parties.

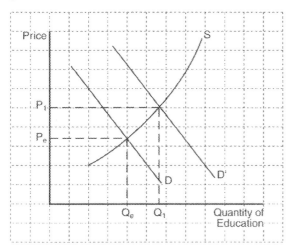

a.   If no government intervention occurs, what will be the market equilibrium price? The market equilibrium quantity?

b.   From *society's* point of view, what is the optimal price and the optimal quantity of education?

c.   In this example, does the price system provide too much or too little education?

d.   Is there a positive externality or a negative externality for this good?

3.   Suppose you know the demand and supply of fertilizer locally, and you have graphed them as shown in the graph to the right. The fertilizer plant that operates in your town is also producing pollution. This pollution is a constant amount per unit of output (proportional to output) at the plant. If the government decides to try to combat the pollution problem by imposing a $20-per-ton tax on fertilizer produced, show graphically what will happen to the fertilizer market. Will the level of pollution in your town be reduced? If so, by how much? If not, can you offer a solution to the pollution problem?

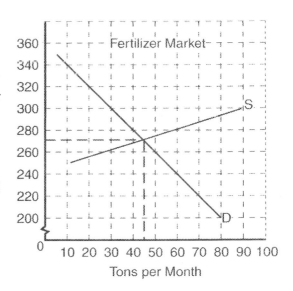

4.   a.   Draw supply and demand curves for good A, for which no externalities exist, and indicate the optimal quantity of output, the price that reflects the opportunity cost to buyers and sellers of that good, and whether the price system has over, or under, or properly allocated resources into Industry A.

     b.   Draw private supply and demand curves for good B, for which negative externalities exist. Draw another curve on that coordinate system that reflects negative externalities. Indicate the optimal output quantity and price from society's point of view, and compare them to the output quantity and price that would result from a price system.

     c.   Draw private supply and demand curves for good C, for which positive externalities exist. Draw another curve that reflects the positive externalities associated with good C. Indicate the optimal price and output quantity of good C from society's point of view, and compare them to the output quantity and price that would result from the price system.

■ Answers

Completion Questions

1. providing a legal system; promoting competition; correcting externalities; providing public goods; ensuring economy-wide stability
2. government
3. promote
4. inefficient
5. third parties
6. negative
7. overallocate
8. positive; inefficiently
9. failure
10. regulating
11. subsidizing production; financing production; regulation
12. little
13. indivisible; zero; do not; difficult
14. not to pay
15. decrease
16. less than; greater than
17. greater than; greater than
18. increase; increase
19. higher
20. a decrease; a decrease
21. zero; positive
22. explicitly priced
23. majority

True-False Questions

1. F Even in capitalist countries the government plays a major role.
2. F It is an economic function because by enforcing contracts government can promote trade and commerce.
3. T
4. T
5. T
6. T
7. F A tax will cause the price of the good to *rise*, which is a movement in the correct direction.
8. F The free-rider problem deals with goods that are *scarce* but for which the exclusion principle does not work well.
9. F Scarcity exists in the public sector, too. After all, the government uses and allocates scarce goods.
10. T
11. F Whether or not a good is a government-sponsored good requires value judgments.
12. T
13. T
14. T
15. F The Medicare subsidy equals the difference between the price that suppliers receive and the price the recipients pay.
16. F A decrease in a per-unit educational subsidy actually narrows this difference.
17. F Governments can also buy privately produced goods for distribution at no charge.

18. F   Requiring vaccine producers to set the price of vaccines lower than the equilibrium price results in a shortage of vaccines. Preventing underallocation of resources to production of a good that creates external benefits, such as vaccines, requires inducing an increase in demand for the good. Hence, government provision of subsidies in the form of vouchers or rebate coupons would more likely generate an increase in demand for vaccines and a resulting increase in the equilibrium quantity of vaccines produced and consumed.

Multiple Choice Questions

1. (a)   9. (d)
2. (c)   10. (a)
3. (c)   11. (b)
4. (a)   12. (b)
5. (d)   13. (c)
6. (b)   14. (d)
7. (c)   15. (a)
8. (c)   16. (c)

Matching

(a) and (l)   (e) and (n)
(b) and (i)   (f) and (j)
(c) and (m)   (g) and (k)
(d) and (h)

Problems

1.   When the subsidy increases, the price paid by Medicare patients declines from $30 per unit to $20 per unit, and the price received by health care providers increases from $50 per unit to $60 per unit. The quantity of services provided under Medicare increases from 70 units to 80 units. The market price remains equal to $40 per unit, and the equilibrium quantity remains equal to 60 units.

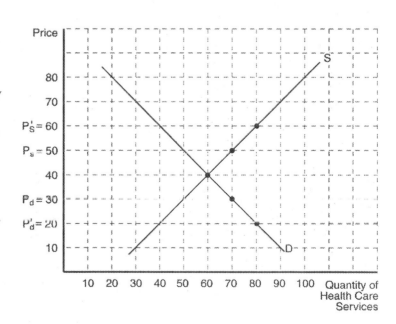

2.   The supply curve shifts leftward, so the market price rises from $40 per unit to $50 per unit, and the equilibrium quantity falls from 60 units to 50 units. The subsidy remains equal to $20 per unit, however, so the price paid by Medicare patients increases from $30 per unit to $40 per unit, and the price received by doctors increases from $50 per unit to $60 per unit.

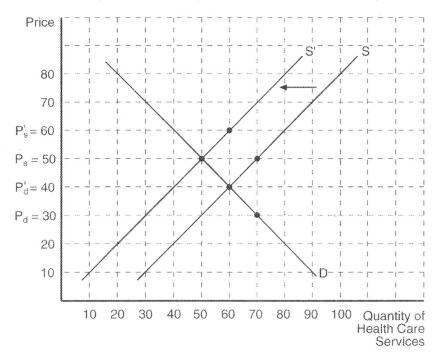

3.   Students shared textbooks, cut back on purchases of optional textbooks and study guides, bought fewer required textbooks, and searched for lower-priced substitutes, such as lower-quality foreign editions of textbooks sold abroad. Such actions were rational because they were responses to a perceived increase in the relative price of textbooks. From society's point of view, it is arguable that such actions could have led to a misallocation because the lack of competition may have caused the price system to transmit an incorrect signal. The signal may have been that textbooks had become more scarce, but the signal was induced by an artificial restriction of supply.

4.   a.   redistribution
     b.   promoting competition
     c.   providing government-sponsored goods
     d.   discouraging government-inhibited goods
     e.   providing public goods
     f.   redistribution
     g.   providing a legal system
     h.   correcting a positive externality
     i.   providing a legal system
     j.   correcting a negative externality
     k.   stabilizing the economy

Working with Graphs

1. a. P_2; Q_2
    b. P_1; Q_1
    c. too much
    d. negative

2. a. P_e; Q_e
    b. P_1; Q_1
    c. too little
    d. positive

3. The supply curve after the tax is imposed shifts to S_1—that is, upward by $20 at each quantity. The equilibrium quantity falls from 45 tons per month to below 40 tons per month as a result. Thus the quantity of fertilizer produced has declined by more than 10 percent. This means that the output of pollution has declined by more than 10 percent, because the output of pollution is a constant per unit of output of fertilizer.

    The result of the analysis should not be extended in a general fashion without regard to other possible effects that a tax of this nature might have. We might also wish to consider other factors before imposing a pollution tax. Among these factors are the effects of the increased price of the fertilizer, the likely reduction in employment as a result of the reduced quantity of fertilizer produced, and the ability of alternative methods of pollution control to achieve the same results.

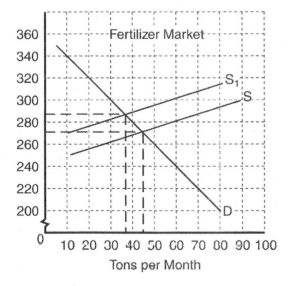

4. a.   The market price and the equilibrium quantity are at the socially optimal values because no externalities exist. Resources are allocated properly into Industry A.

    b.   The *new* curve you draw, which reflects a negative externality, should be a supply curve, S_1, that lies to the left of (above) the original supply curve. The optimal price-quantity combination exists where S_1 intersects the demand curve. The socially optimal price is higher than the market price, and the socially optimal quantity is lower than the market quantity.

    c.   The new curve should be a demand curve, D_1, that lies to the right of (above) the original demand curve. The socially optimal price-output combination is where D_1 intersects the supply curve. Price will be higher and output will be higher than the market price-output combination.

■ Glossary

Antitrust legislation   Laws that restrict the formation of monopolies and regulate certain anticompetitive business practices.

Collective decision making   How voters, politicians, and other interested parties act and how these actions influence nonmarket decisions.

Effluent fee   A charge to a polluter that gives the right to discharge into the air or water a certain amount of pollution; also called a *pollution tax*.

Externality   A consequence of an economic activity that spills over to affect third parties. Pollution is an externality.

Free-rider problem   A problem that arises when individuals presume that others will pay for public goods, so that, individually, they can escape paying for their portion without causing a reduction in production.

Government, or political, goods   Goods (and services) provided by the public sector; they can be either private or public goods.

Government-inhibited good   A good that has been deemed socially undesirable through the political process. Heroin is an example.

Government-sponsored good   A good that has been deemed socially desirable through the political process. Museums are an example.

Incentive structure   The system of rewards and punishments individuals face with respect to their own actions.

Majority rule   A collective decision-making system in which group decisions are made on the basis of more than 50 percent of the vote. In other words, whatever more than half of the electorate votes for, the entire electorate has to accept.

Market failure   A situation in which the market economy leads to too few or too many resources going to a specific economic activity.

Monopoly   A firm that can determine the market price of a good. In the extreme case, a monopoly is the only seller of a good or service.

Principle of rival consumption   The recognition that individuals are rivals in consuming private goods because one person's consumption reduces the amount available for others to consume.

Private goods   Goods that can only be consumed by one individual at a time. Private goods are subject to the principle of rival consumption.

Property rights   The rights of an owner to use and to exchange property.

Proportional rule   A decision-making system in which actions are based on the proportion of the "votes" cast and are in proportion to them. In a market system, if 10 percent of the "dollar votes" are cast for blue cars, 10 percent of automobile output will be blue cars.

Public goods   Goods for which the principle of rival consumption does not apply. They can be jointly consumed by many individuals simultaneously at no additional cost and with no reduction in quality or quantity. Also no one who fails to help pay for the good can be denied the benefit of the good.

Theory of public choice   The study of collective decision making.

Third parties   Parties who are not directly involved in a given activity or transaction.

Transfer payments   Money payments made by governments to individuals for which no services or goods are rendered in return. Examples are Social Security old-age and disability benefits and unemployment insurance benefits.

Transfers in kind   Payments that are in the form of actual goods and services, such as food stamps, subsidized public housing, and medical care, and for which no goods or services are rendered in return.

6 Funding the Public Sector

■ Learning Objectives

After you have studied this chapter, you should be able to

1. define marginal and average tax rates, proportional, progressive, and regressive taxation, capital gain, capital loss, retained earnings, and tax incidence;

2. identify the main ways that governments tax sales of goods and services;

3. distinguish between a marginal and an average tax rate;

4. calculate the tax burden for individuals with different incomes, given different tax structures;

5. recognize the difference between static and dynamic tax analysis; and

6. explain how levying taxes on goods and services affects market prices and equilibrium quantities.

■ Outline

1. The government budget constraint indicates that government spending, transfers, and repayments of borrowed funds are limited to total taxes and user charges that the government collects during a given period.

2. Governments tax in order to obtain revenues to finance expenditures.
   a. The marginal tax rate is the change in the tax payment divided by the change in income.
   b. The average tax rate equals the total tax payment divided by total income.

3. There are three main types of taxation systems.
   a. Under a proportional taxation system, as a person's income rises, the percentage of income paid (rate of taxation) in taxes remains constant.
   b. Under a progressive taxation system, as a person's income rises, the percentage of income paid in taxes rises.
   c. Under a regressive taxation system, as a person's income rises, the percentage of income paid in taxes falls.

4. The federal government imposes income taxes on individuals and corporations, and it collects Social Security taxes and other taxes.

    a. The most important tax in the U.S. economy is the personal income tax. Recently, some have proposed a consumption tax, which taxes people based on what they actually spend.

    b. The difference between the buying and selling price of an asset, such as a share of stock or a plot of land, is called a capital gain if a profit results, and a capital loss if it does not.

5. The corporate income tax is a moderately important source of revenue for the various governments in the U.S. economy.

    a. Corporate stockholders are taxed twice: once on corporate income and again when dividends are received or when the stock is sold.

    b. The incidence of corporate taxes falls on people—consumers, workers, management, and stockholders—not on such inanimate objects as "corporations."

6. An increasing percentage of federal tax receipts is accounted for each year by taxes (other than income) levied on payrolls, such as Social Security taxes and unemployment compensation.

7. Major sources of revenue for states and local governments are sales, excise, and property taxes.

8. When governments attempt to fund their operations by taxing market activities, one issue they must consider is how the tax rates they assess relate to the tax revenues they ultimately receive.

    a. Sales taxes are levied under a system of *ad valorem* taxation, meaning that the tax is applied to the value of final purchases of a good or service, as determined by its market price, which is the sales tax base. The total sales taxes collected by a government equal the sales tax rate multiplied by the sales tax base, so a sales tax is a proportional tax.

    b. Whereas static tax analysis indicates that a government can unambiguously increase its sales tax collections by boosting the sales tax rate, dynamic tax analysis takes into account the fact that higher tax rates give consumers an incentive to cut back on purchases of goods and services. Dynamic tax analysis indicates that at some point a further increase in the tax rate reduces the tax base sufficiently to result in lower tax revenues for the government. Consequently, in principle there is a single tax rate at which the government can collect the maximum possible revenues.

9. When contemplating how to structure a system for taxing market transactions, governments must also consider how the taxes they impose affect market prices and equilibrium quantities.

    a. Excise taxes are taxes on sales of specific commodities, and governments commonly levy certain excise taxes as a constant tax per unit sold, or a unit tax.

    b. Imposing a unit excise tax on a good or service reduces the net price that a producer receives for each unit sold by exactly the amount of the tax. Following assessment of a unit excise tax, a producer will continue to supply any given quantity only if the price received for that quantity is higher by exactly the amount of the tax. Thus levying a unit excise tax on sales of a good or service causes the market supply curve to shift upward by the amount of the tax.

    c. If the demand curve has its usual downward slope, the upward shift in the supply curve caused by imposing a unit excise tax causes the equilibrium quantity produced and consumed to decline. The market price rises by less than the amount of the tax. Producers pay part of the tax in the form of higher per-unit costs, and consumers pay the remainder of the tax when they purchase the item at the higher market price.

Key Terms

Ad valorem taxation	Excise tax	Static tax analysis
Capital gain	Government budget constraint	Tax base
Capital loss	Retained earnings	Unit tax
Dynamic tax analysis	Sales taxes	

Key Concepts

Average tax rate	Progressive taxation	Tax bracket
Marginal tax rate	Proportional taxation	Tax incidence
Payroll tax rate	Regressive taxation	User charges
Payroll tax wage base		

Completion Questions

Fill in the blank, or circle the correct term.

1. Ultimately, all government spending, transfers, and borrowing are primarily financed by (taxes, user charges).

2. The _____ is the limitation that taxes and user charges place on the total amount of government expenditures and transfer payments.

3. If the price of an asset rises after its purchase, the owner receives a(n) _____ gain. If the price falls, the owner suffers a(n) _____ loss.

4. The marginal tax rate applies only to the (first, last) tax bracket.

5. The corporate income tax is paid by one or more of the following groups: _____, _____, and _____.

6. Under an *ad valorem* sales tax system, the government applies a (tax rate, constant tax) to the price of an item to determine the tax owed on the purchase of the item.

7. _____ tax analysis emphasizes the potential for ever-higher tax rates to induce a reduction in the tax base.

8. (A sales, An excise) tax is levied on purchases of a particular good or service.

9. If the demand and supply curves for an item have their typical shapes, then imposing a unit excise tax on the item results in (a decrease, an increase) in the market price of the item and (a decrease, an increase) in the equilibrium quantity purchased and sold.

10. The maximum wage earnings subject to the Social Security payroll tax _____ assessed against the earnings is called the wage _____ of the payroll tax system.

■ True-False Questions

Circle the **T** if the statement is true, the **F** if it is false. Explain to yourself why a statement is false.

T F 1. The federal individual income tax is regressive.

T F 2. The largest source of receipts for the federal government is the individual income tax.

T F 3. In a progressive tax structure, the average tax rate is greater than the marginal tax rate.

T F 4. Positive economics confirms that a progressive taxation system is more equitable than a regressive taxation system.

T F 5. In the United States, the tax system that yields the most revenue to all governments combined is the corporate income tax.

T F 6. When corporations are taxed, consumers and corporate employees are also affected.

T F 7. A sales tax is typically a constant amount charged on the sale of a particular item.

T F 8. Static tax analysis indicates that raising the tax rate by 1 percentage point will always increase tax revenues by an amount equal to 1 percent of the tax base.

T F 9. Every U.S. state government relies on sales taxes to fund at least a portion of its spending and transfer programs.

T F 10. According to dynamic tax analysis, there is likely to be a single tax rate that maximizes government tax collections.

T F 11. Consumers always pay the full amount of a unit excise tax.

■ Multiple Choice Questions

Circle the letter that corresponds to the best answer.

1. A switch from the current progressive income tax to a national sales tax
    a. would not change our tax system very much.
    b. would lead to more taxes on savings.
    c. would cause the current structure of the Internal Revenue Service (IRS) to be greatly reduced.
    d. would cause more IRS agents to be hired.

2. If the government taxes group A and gives to group B, then economic incentives for
    a. group A may be reduced.
    b. group B may be reduced.
    c. both may change so as to reduce output.
    d. All of the above.

3. In a progressive tax structure,
    a. the marginal tax rate exceeds the average tax rate.
    b. equity exists.
    c. the average tax rate rises as income falls.
    d. All of the above.

4. Which one of the following statements is true?
    a. Under a regressive tax structure, the average tax rate remains constant as income rises.
    b. If upper-income people pay more taxes than lower-income people do, equity must exist.
    c. The U.S. federal personal income tax system is progressive.
    d. At very high income levels, the Social Security tax and employee contribution become progressive.

5. The tax incidence of the corporate income tax falls on
    a. corporate stockholders.
    b. corporate employees.
    c. consumers of goods and services produced by corporations.
    d. All of the above.

6. Which one of the following statements about the Social Security tax is **not** true?
    a. It is a progressive tax.
    b. It came into existence in 1935.
    c. It is imposed on employers and employees.
    d. It is a payroll tax.

7. If Mr. Romano faces a 90 percent marginal tax rate,
    a. the next dollar he earns nets him 90 cents.
    b. his total tax payments equal 90 percent of his total income.
    c. he has a strong incentive not to earn extra income.
    d. his average tax rate must be falling.

8. A proportional tax system
    a. is unfair.
    b. cannot be consistent with people's ability to pay such taxes.
    c. means that upper-income people pay smaller percentages of their income in taxes than do lower-income people.
    d. requires upper-income people to pay more tax dollars than lower-income people pay.

9. If the government establishes a sales tax on a broad set of goods and services by levying a tax rate equal to a fraction of the market price of each unit purchased, then it uses a system of
    a. unit taxes.
    b. excise taxes.
    c. *ad valorem* taxes.
    d. constant per-unit taxes.

10. The value of goods, services, or incomes subject to taxation is known as the
    a. tax base.
    b. unit base.
    c. *ad valorem* constraint.
    d. government budget constraint.

11. A key assumption of static tax analysis is that
    a. the tax base declines as the government raises the tax rate.
    b. there is a single tax rate that maximizes government tax revenues.
    c. the government's tax revenues always rise with increases in the tax rate.
    d. the government's tax revenues eventually decline when it levies ever-higher tax rates.

12. Imposing a unit excise tax results in
    a. an upward shift in the market supply curve equal to the amount of the tax.
    b. a downward shift in the market supply curve equal to the amount of the tax.
    c. an upward shift in the market demand curve equal to the resulting price increase.
    d. a downward shift in the market demand curve equal to the resulting price decline.

13. If market demand and supply curves have their normal shapes, then when a government levies a unit excise tax on an item equal to $5 per unit, the market price of the item will
    a. decline by an amount less than $5 per unit.
    b. increase by an amount less than $5 per unit.
    c. decline by an amount more than $5 per unit.
    d. increase by an amount more than $5 per unit.

14. If market demand and supply curves have their normal shapes, then a $1 increase in a unit excise tax on a good causes
    a. the price consumers pay for each unit to rise by $1.
    b. the costs suppliers incur to supply each unit to rise by $1.
    c. the price consumers pay for each unit to rise by more than $1.
    d. the costs suppliers incur to supply each unit to rise by less than $1.

15. Today, the Social Security payroll tax rate is closest to
    a. 2 percent.
    b. 4 percent.
    c. 10 percent.
    d. 14 percent.

■ Matching

Choose an item in Column (2) that best matches an item in Column (1).

(1)

(a) progressive taxation
(b) sales tax
(c) *ad valorem* tax
(d) dynamic tax analysis
(e) static tax analysis

(2)

(f) assumes that ever-higher tax rates eventually reduce the tax base
(g) assumes that ever-higher tax rates leave the tax base unaffected
(h) tax levied as percentage of market price
(i) marginal tax rate rises at higher income levels
(j) tax on market prices of many items

■ Problems

1. Complete the following table for three taxes, and then indicate what type of tax each is.

	Tax 1		Tax 2		Tax 3	
Income	Tax Paid	Average Tax Rate	Tax Paid	Average Tax Rate	Tax Paid	Average Tax Rate
$ 10,000	$ 300	____	$ 100	____	$ 1,000	____
30,000	900	____	600	____	2,700	____
60,000	1,800	____	1,800	____	4,800	____
100,000	3,000	____	4,000	____	7,000	____
150,000	4,500	____	7,500	____	9,000	____
200,000	6,000	____	12,000	____	10,000	____
300,000	9,000	____	21,000	____	12,000	____

2. Suppose the above table had a fourth tax as shown below. Find the average and marginal tax rates, and explain what type of tax it would be.

Income	Tax Paid	Average Tax Rate	Marginal Tax Rate
$ 10,000	$ 300	____	____
30,000	1,200	____	____
60,000	3,000	____	____
100,000	5,000	____	____
150,000	6,000	____	____
200,000	7,000	____	____
300,000	9,000	____	____

■ Answers

Completion Questions

1. taxes
2. government budget constraint
3. capital; capital
4. last
5. stockholders; consumers; employees

6. tax rate
7. Dynamic
8. An excise
9. an increase; a decrease
10. rate; base

True-False Questions

1. F It is progressive.
2. T
3. F For average taxes to rise with income (a progressive tax), the marginal tax rate must exceed the average tax rate.
4. F "Equitable" requires normative statements.
5. F No, the personal income tax does so.
6. T
7. F A sales tax covers a large set of items and typically is levied as a fraction of the price.
8. T
9. F There are no state sales taxes in Delaware, Montana, New Hampshire, Alaska, and Oregon.
10. T
11. F Consumers pay the full tax only if demand is completely unresponsive to price.

Multiple Choice Questions

1. (c)
2. (d)
3. (a)
4. (c)
5. (d)
6. (a)
7. (c)
8. (d)

9. (c)
10. (a)
11. (c)
12. (a)
13. (b)
14. (d)
15. (d)

Matching

(a) and (i)
(b) and (j)
(c) and (h)

(d) and (f)
(e) and (g)

Problems

1. Tax 1: 3 percent; 3 percent; 3 percent; 3 percent; 3 percent; 3 percent; 3 percent; proportional

    Tax 2: 1 percent; 2 percent; 3 percent; 4 percent; 5 percent; 6 percent; 7 percent; progressive

    Tax 3: 10 percent; 9 percent; 8 percent; 7 percent; 6 percent; 5 percent; 4 percent; regressive

2. ATR: 3 percent; 4 percent; 5 percent; 5 percent; 4 percent; 3.5 percent; 3 percent

    MTR: 3 percent; 4.5 percent; 6 percent; 5 percent; 2 percent; 2 percent; 2 percent

    The average tax rate for this tax initially rises and then falls, as does the marginal tax rate. As a result, this tax is progressive up to an income of $60,000, proportional from there to $100,000, and regressive for levels of income above $100,000. Thus this tax is a combination of all three types of taxes as income varies. Can you graph the ATR and MTR for this tax? Can you think of any taxes that might behave in this manner?

■ Glossary

***Ad valorem* taxation**   Assessing taxes by charging a tax rate equal to a fraction of the market price of each unit purchased.

Average tax rate   The total tax payment divided by total income. It is the proportion of total income paid in taxes.

Capital gain   The positive difference between the purchase price and the sale price of an asset. If a share of stock is bought for $5 and then sold for $15, the capital gain is $10.

Capital loss   The negative difference between the purchase price and the sale price of an asset.

Dynamic tax analysis   Economic evaluation of tax rate changes that recognizes that the tax base eventually declines with ever-higher tax rates, so that tax revenues may eventually decline if the tax rate is raised sufficiently.

Excise tax   A tax levied on purchases of a particular good or service.

Government budget constraint   The limit on government spending and transfers imposed by the fact that every dollar the government spends, transfers, or uses to repay borrowed funds must ultimately be provided by the user charges and taxes it collects.

Marginal tax rate   The change in the tax payment divided by the change in income, or the percentage of *additional* dollars that must be paid in taxes. The marginal tax rate is applied to the highest tax bracket of taxable income reached.

Progressive taxation   A tax system in which, as income increases, a higher percentage of the additional income is paid as taxes. The marginal tax rate exceeds the average tax rate as income rises.

Proportional taxation   A tax system in which, regardless of an individual's income, the tax bill comprises exactly the same proportion.

Regressive taxation   A tax system in which as more dollars are earned, the percentage of tax paid on them falls. The marginal tax rate is less than the average tax rate as income rises.

Retained earnings   Earnings that a corporation saves, or retains, for investment in other productive activities; earnings that are not distributed to stockholders.

Sales taxes   Taxes assessed on the prices paid on most goods and services.

Static tax analysis   Economic evaluation of the effects of tax rate changes under the assumption that there is no effect on the tax base, meaning that there is an unambiguous positive relationship between tax rates and tax revenues.

Tax base   The value of goods, services, wealth, or incomes, subject to taxation.

Tax bracket   A specified interval of income to which a specific and unique marginal tax rate is applied.

Tax incidence   The distribution of tax burdens among various groups in society.

Tax rate   The proportion of a tax base that must be paid to a government as taxes.

Unit tax   A constant tax assessed on each unit of a good that consumers purchase.

19 Demand and Supply Elasticity

■ Learning Objectives

After you have studied this chapter, you should be able to

1. define price elasticity of demand, elastic demand, unit elastic demand, inelastic demand, perfectly inelastic demand, perfectly elastic demand, cross price elasticity of demand, income elasticity of demand, price elasticity of supply, perfectly elastic supply, and perfectly inelastic supply;

2. calculate price elasticity of demand in two ways, given the relevant information;

3. predict what will happen to total revenues if there is a change in price, given price elasticity of demand;

4. classify an elasticity coefficient as indicating whether demand is elastic, unit elastic, or inelastic, in the relevant price range;

5. recognize from a graph whether the demand for a good is perfectly elastic or perfectly inelastic in the specified price range;

6. identify the determinants of price elasticity of demand;

7. calculate the cross price elasticity of demand coefficient, and determine from the sign of that coefficient whether or not the goods in question are substitutes or complements;

8. calculate income elasticity of demand from relevant information and distinguish price elasticity of demand from income elasticity of demand; and

9. calculate price elasticity of supply, identify the determinants of price elasticity of supply, and recognize a graph of a perfectly elastic supply curve and a perfectly inelastic supply curve.

■ Outline

1. Elasticity measures quantity responsiveness to price changes.
   a. Price elasticity of demand is defined as the percentage change in quantity demanded divided by the percentage change in price.
      i. Because of the law of demand, the price elasticity of demand is always negative. By convention, however, the sign is ignored.
      ii. Price elasticity of demand relates percentage changes, not absolute changes.
   b. There are two ways to calculate the price elasticity of demand.
      i. Price elasticity of demand may be calculated by dividing the change in quantity demanded over the original quantity demanded by the change in price over the original price. This method yields a different elasticity over the same range of the demand curve, depending on whether price rises or falls.
      ii. In order to get consistent results over the same range of a demand curve, it is possible to calculate price elasticity by using average values for base price and base quantity.

2. If the calculated price elasticity of demand for a good is greater than one, the demand is called elastic. If the price elasticity of demand is equal to one, the demand is called unit elastic. If the price elasticity of demand is less than one, the demand is called inelastic.

3. Elasticity is related to total revenues.
   a. In the range of elastic demand, if price declines, total revenues will rise. If price rises, total revenues will fall.
   b. In the range of unit elastic demand, small changes in price leave total revenues unaltered.
   c. In the range of inelastic demand, if price declines, total revenues will fall. If price rises, total revenues will rise.
   d. Along a linear demand curve (which has a constant slope, by definition), a good has an elastic, a unit elastic, and an inelastic range.
   e. There are two extreme price elasticities of demand.
      i. Perfectly inelastic demand indicates no change in quantity demanded as price changes. Such a demand curve is vertical at the given quantity.
      ii. Perfectly elastic demand indicates that even a slight increase in price will lead to a zero quantity demanded. Such a demand curve is horizontal at the given price.

4. There are three major determinants of the price elasticity of demand.
   a. The closer the substitutes for a particular good, and the more available they are, the greater will be its price elasticity of demand.
   b. The higher the proportion of total expenditures that people allocate to a good, the higher will be that good's price elasticity of demand.
   c. The longer any price change persists, the greater the price elasticity of demand. The distinction between the short-run and long-run consumer adjustment period varies with the good in question.

5.   Cross price elasticity of demand is defined as the percentage change in the demand for one good (holding its price constant) divided by the percentage change in the price of a related good.

   a.   If the sign of the cross price elasticity of demand is positive, the two goods are substitutes.

   b.   If the sign of the cross price elasticity of demand is negative, the two goods are complements.

6.   Income elasticity of demand is defined as the percentage change in the demand for a good (holding its price constant) divided by the percentage change in money income.

7.   Price elasticity of supply is defined as the percentage change in quantity supplied divided by the percentage change in price.

   a.   One extreme is perfectly elastic supply, where a slight decrease in price leads to a zero quantity supplied. Such a supply curve is horizontal at the given price.

   b.   Another extreme is perfectly inelastic supply, where quantity supplied is constant, regardless of what happens to price. Such a supply curve is vertical at the given quantity.

   c.   The longer the time for adjustment, the more price elastic is the supply curve.

   d.   Empirical evidence indicates that short-run elasticities for goods are often considerably smaller than long-run elasticities.

■ Key Terms

Elastic demand   Unit elasticity of demand

Inelastic demand

■ Key Concepts

Cross price elasticity of demand (E_{xy})   Perfectly inelastic demand

Income elasticity of demand (E_i)   Perfectly inelastic supply

Perfectly elastic demand   Price elasticity of demand (E_p)

Perfectly elastic supply   Price elasticity of supply (E_s)

■ Completion Questions

Fill in the blank, or circle the correct term.

1.   Price elasticity of demand is a measure of buyer _____ to price changes.

2.   Price elasticity of demand is defined as the percentage change in _____ divided by the percentage change in _____. The problem with this measure is that we get (<u>the same, a different</u>) numerical value when we move up, as opposed to down, the same range of the demand curve.

3.   In order to correct for the problem in Question 2 above, the _____ value method of calculating the price elasticity of demand can be used.

4. Assume a 1 percent change in price. If quantity demanded changes by less than 1 percent, then we say that in that range the demand for the good is _____. If quantity demanded changes by 1 percent, then in that range demand is _____. If quantity demanded changes by more than 1 percent, then in that range demand is _____.

5. If price falls and total revenues rise, then in that range demand was price _____. If price falls and total revenues remain constant, then in that range demand was price _____. If price falls and total revenues fall, then in that range demand was price _____.

6. If price rises and total revenues fall, then demand was price _____. If total revenues rise, then demand was price _____. If total revenues remain constant, then demand was _____.

7. A demand curve that exhibits zero responsiveness to price changes is _____. Such a demand curve is (<u>horizontal, vertical</u>) at the given quantity. A demand curve in which even the slightest increase in price will lead to a zero quantity demanded is _____. Such a demand curve is (<u>horizontal, vertical</u>) at the given price.

8. The determinants of price elasticity of demand are _____, _____ _____, and _____.

9. Cross price elasticity of demand is defined as the percentage change in the _____ for one good, holding its _____ constant, divided by the percentage change in the _____ of another good.

10. If the cross price elasticity of demand is positive, then the two goods are _____. If the cross price elasticity of demand is negative, the two goods are _____.

11. The income elasticity of demand is defined as the percentage change in _____ for a good, holding its _____ constant, divided by the percentage change in _____.

12. The price elasticity of supply measures the responsiveness of the _____ of a good to a change in its price. A supply curve in which a slight decrease in price leads to a zero quantity supplied is _____. If quantity supplied remains constant no matter what happens to price, the supply curve is _____ .

■ True-False Questions

Circle the **T** if the statement is true, the **F** if it is false. Explain to yourself why a statement is false.

T   F   1. Price elasticity of demand measures the responsiveness of price to changes in quantity demanded.

T   F   2. Because of the law of demand, price elasticity of demand will always (implicitly) be a negative number.

T   F   3. Price elasticity of demand deals with absolute, not relative, values.

T F 4. When price elasticity of demand is calculated by using the average value approach, price elasticity is the same whether price rises or falls over a given demand curve range.

T F 5. If the price elasticity of demand is 3, then over the relevant price range demand is inelastic.

T F 6. When the demand for an item is perfectly elastic, the slightest increase in the price of that item causes the quantity demanded to drop to zero. As a result, the demand curve for the item is horizontal.

T F 7. If price falls and total revenues rise, then over that price range demand is inelastic.

T F 8. If the price elasticity of demand is 0.5 at the current price of an item, an increase in the price of the item will increase revenues.

T F 9. The price elasticity of demand for Microsoft software is less than the price elasticity of demand for software.

T F 10. If the demand for Good A is perfectly elastic, its demand curve is vertical at that price.

T F 11. If the demand for Good A is perfectly inelastic over *all* prices, Good A violates the law of demand.

T F 12. The less time people have to respond to a price change, the higher is the price elasticity.

T F 13. If the cross price elasticity of demand for Goods A and B is negative, A and B are complements.

T F 14. Income elasticity of demand is calculated for a horizontal shift in the demand curve, given price.

T F 15. If supply is perfectly inelastic, the curve will be horizontal at the given quantity.

■ Multiple Choice Questions

Circle the letter that corresponds to the best answer.

1. Price elasticity of demand measures responsiveness of
   a. quantity demanded to changes in price.
   b. quantity demanded to changes in income.
   c. price to changes in quantity demanded.
   d. price to changes in demand.

2. If the price elasticity of demand is 0.33, then
   a. demand is inelastic.
   b. demand is inelastic over that price range.
   c. demand is elastic.
   d. demand is elastic over that price range.

3. Which one of the following is **not** true concerning the price elasticity of demand?
    a. Its sign is always negative, due to the law of demand.
    b. It is a unitless, dimensionless number.
    c. It equals the percentage change in price divided by the percentage change in quantity demanded.
    d. It measures the responsiveness of quantity demanded to changes in price.

4. If price elasticity of demand is calculated using the original price and quantity, then over a given range in the demand curve price elasticity of demand
    a. differs, depending on whether price rises or falls.
    b. is the same, regardless of whether price rises or falls.
    c. is equal to 1.
    d. rises as price falls.

5. If price falls by 1 percent and quantity demanded rises by 2 percent, then the price elasticity of demand
    a. is inelastic over that range.
    b. is 0.5.
    c. is elastic over that range.
    d. cannot be calculated from this information.

6. If price rises and total revenue rises, then the price elasticity of demand over that range is
    a. elastic.
    b. inelastic.
    c. unit elastic.
    d. equal to 1.

7. If price falls and over that price range demand is inelastic, total revenues will
    a. remain constant.
    b. fall.
    c. rise.
    d. fall, then rise.

8. If the demand for Good A is perfectly inelastic at all prices,
    a. quantity demanded does not change as price changes.
    b. the law of demand is violated.
    c. the demand curve is vertical at the given quantity.
    d. All of the above.

9. If the demand for Good A is perfectly elastic,
    a. quantity demanded does not vary with price.
    b. the demand curve is horizontal.
    c. the demand curve is vertical.
    d. the demand curve is positively sloped.

10. Which one of the following is **not** a determinant of the price elasticity of demand?

    a.   existence and closeness of substitutes

    b.   proportion of expenses on the good to the consumer's budget

    c.   price elasticity of supply

    d.   length of time allowed for adjustment to a price change

11. If the cross price elasticity of demand between Goods A and B is positive, the goods are

    a.   substitutes.

    b.   complements.

    c.   unrelated.

    d.   necessities.

12. If the cross price elasticity between Goods A and B is –10, then A and B are

    a.   close substitutes.

    b.   near substitutes.

    c.   strongly complementary.

    d.   mildly complementary.

13. Digitals and downloadable apps are

    a.   substitutes.

    b.   complements.

    c.   not related goods.

    d.   necessities.

14. When the income elasticity of demand for Good A is calculated,

    a.   the price of Good A varies.

    b.   income changes, which lead to horizontal shifts in the demand curve for Good A, are measured.

    c.   a movement along the demand curve for Good A is measured.

    d.   All of the above.

15. *Analogy:* A movement along a demand curve is to price elasticity of demand as a shift in the demand curve is to

    a.   an increase in demand.

    b.   changes in taxes or subsidies.

    c.   income elasticity of demand.

    d.   substitutes and complements.

16. At current prices of a highly addictive drug, the demand for the drug is highly price

    a.   elastic.

    b.   inelastic.

    c.   cross elastic.

    d.   unit elastic.

17. Which of the following goods is probably the most highly income elastic?
    a. salt
    b. food
    c. alcoholic beverages
    d. private education

18. A perfectly inelastic supply curve
    a. shows great quantity supplied responsiveness to price changes.
    b. is horizontal at the given price.
    c. indicates zero quantity supplied responsiveness to price changes.
    d. is a normal situation.

19. If the supply of Good B is perfectly elastic and price falls, quantity supplied will
    a. remain unchanged.
    b. rise.
    c. fall.
    d. fall to zero.

20. If price rises, the quantity supplied will be greater the
    a. longer the time that elapses.
    b. more income elastic is the good.
    c. higher the price elasticity of demand for the good.
    d. All of the above.

■ Matching

Choose the item in Column (2) that best matches an item in Column (1).

(1)		(2)	
(a)	perfectly inelastic demand	(h)	elasticity coefficient less than 1
(b)	perfectly elastic demand	(i)	horizontal supply curve
(c)	perfectly inelastic supply	(j)	complementary or substitute goods
(d)	perfectly elastic supply	(k)	quality of substitutes
(e)	determinant of price elasticity	(l)	horizontal demand curve
(f)	cross-price elasticity of demand	(m)	vertical demand curve
(g)	inelastic	(n)	vertical supply curve

■ Problems

1. Suppose you are given the following data on the market demand and supply for online movies at Web sites. (Use the average elasticity measure.)

Price	Quantity Demanded (per day)	Quantity Supplied (per day)
$4.00	50	10
4.50	45	15
5.00	40	25
5.50	35	35
6.00	30	45

   a. What is the equilibrium price of online movies?
   b. What is the price elasticity of demand over the price range $4.50 to $5? Over the range $5.50 to $6?
   c. What is the price elasticity of supply over the same two ranges of price?
   d. Now suppose that consumers' incomes have increased. As a result, at each price, two more movies per day are demanded. Calculate the price elasticity of demand over the same ranges as in part (b).
   e. After comparing your answers from parts (b) and (d), what can you conclude about the price elasticity of demand as the demand curve shifts to the right?

2. Suppose we have the following information for a low-income family:

	Income per Month	Quantity of Hamburger Demanded per Month	Quantity of Steak Demanded per Month
Period 1	$750	8 lbs.	2 lbs.
Period 2	$950	5 lbs.	4 lbs.

   a. What is the income elasticity of demand for hamburger?
   b. What is the income elasticity of demand for steak?
   c. From our study of demand in an earlier chapter, we know _____ is a normal good, whereas _____ is an inferior good.

3. Suppose the price of printing paper for digital cameras has recently risen by 10 percent due to an increase in the cost of materials used in the finish for the paper. As a result, less photo printing paper is being sold in the office supply store where you work. You do some checking and find that digital camera sales are down by 4 percent. What is the cross-price elasticity of photo printing paper and digital cameras? Are these two goods complements or substitutes?

■ Answers

Completion Questions

1. responsiveness
2. quantity demanded; price; a different
3. average
4. inelastic; unit elastic; elastic
5. elastic; unit elastic; inelastic
6. elastic; inelastic; unit elastic
7. perfectly inelastic; vertical; perfectly elastic; horizontal
8. closeness of available substitutes; proportion of the good in consumer budgets; length of time to respond
9. demand; price; price
10. substitutes; complements
11. demand; price; money income
12. quantity supplied; perfectly elastic; perfectly inelastic

True-False Questions

1. F It measures quantity demanded responsiveness to price changes.
2. T
3. F It deals with relative values.
4. T
5. F It is price elastic because the coefficient exceeds 1.
6. T
7. F It must have been elastic.
8. T
9. F It is greater, because there are more substitutes for Microsoft's software than for software in general.
10. F It is horizontal at that price.
11. T
12. F Elasticity increases over time because substitutes become more readily available over time.
13. T
14. T
15. F It will be vertical at the given quantity.

Multiple Choice Questions

1. (a)	11. (a)
2. (b)	12. (c)
3. (c)	13. (b)
4. (a)	14. (b)
5. (c)	15. (c)
6. (b)	16. (b)
7. (b)	17. (d)
8. (d)	18. (c)
9. (b)	19. (d)
10. (c)	20. (a)

Matching

(a) and (m)	(e) and (k)
(b) and (l)	(f) and (j)
(c) and (n)	(g) and (h)
(d) and (i)	

Problems

1. a. $5.50
   b. 1.12; 1.77
   c. 4.75; 2.88
   d. 1.07; 1.67
   e. As the demand curve shifts to the right, for any price range, demand becomes less elastic—or, alternatively stated, more inelastic.

2. a. −1.96
   b. 2.83
   c. steak; hamburger

3. −0.4; complements

■ Glossary

Cross price elasticity of demand (E_{xy})   The percentage change in the amount of an item demanded (holding its price constant) divided by the percentage change in the price of a related good.

Elastic demand   A demand relationship in which a given percentage change in price will result in a larger percentage change in quantity demanded.

Income elasticity of demand (E_i)   The percentage change in the amount of a good demanded, holding its price constant, divided by the percentage change in income; the responsiveness of the amount of a good demanded to a change in income, holding the good's relative price constant.

Inelastic demand   A demand relationship in which a given percentage change in price will result in a less-than-proportionate percentage change in the quantity demanded.

Perfectly elastic demand   A demand that has the characteristic that even the slightest increase in price will lead to a zero quantity demanded.

Perfectly elastic supply   A supply characterized by a reduction in quantity supplied to zero when there is the slightest decrease in price.

Perfectly inelastic demand   A demand that exhibits zero responsiveness to price changes. No matter what the price is, the quantity demanded remains the same.

Perfectly inelastic supply   A supply for which quantity supplied remains constant, no matter what happens to price.

Price elasticity of demand (E_p)   The responsiveness of the quantity demanded of a commodity to changes in its price; defined as the percentage change in quantity demanded divided by the percentage change in price.

Price elasticity of supply (E_s)   The responsiveness of the quantity supplied of a commodity to a change in its price; the percentage change in quantity supplied divided by the percentage change in price.

Unit elasticity of demand   A demand relationship in which the quantity demanded changes exactly in proportion to the change in price.

20 Consumer Choice

■ Learning Objectives

After you have studied this chapter, you should be able to

1. define utility, util, marginal utility, marginal analysis, diminishing marginal utility, consumer optimum, substitution effect, principle of substitution, purchasing power, and real income effect;

2. distinguish between total utility and marginal utility, and answer questions that require an understanding of how they are related;

3. define marginal utility, and answer questions that require an understanding of this concept;

4. apply the concept of diminishing marginal utility to the law of demand;

5. predict what happens to the marginal utility per dollar's worth of a good when (a) its price changes, other things being constant and (b) more or less is consumed, other things being constant;

6. predict what a consumer will do if the marginal utility per dollar's worth of Good A is greater (less) than the marginal utility per dollar's worth of Good B;

7. predict how a change in price generates a real income effect and a substitution effect; and

8. answer questions that require an understanding of how economists can explain the diamond-water paradox.

■ Outline

1. Utility analysis is the study of consumer decision making based on utility maximization.
    a. A util is an artificial unit by which utility is measured.
    b. Total utility is the sum of all the utils derived from consumption; marginal utility is the change in total utility due to a one-unit change in the quantity of a good consumed.
    c. Economists maintain that economic decisions are made by comparing the marginal benefit of an activity with its marginal cost.
    d. As long as marginal utility is positive, total utility will rise.
    e. If marginal utility becomes negative—the good becomes a nuisance—total utility will fall.

2. The principle of diminishing marginal utility states that as more of any good or service is consumed, eventually its extra benefit declines.

3. Consumers are assumed to optimize their consumption choices. The consumer attempts to maximize total utility subject to such constraints as income and relative prices.

4. When relative price changes, the consumer optimum is affected, and the consumer reacts consistently and predictably.
    a. A consumer is optimizing when she allocates all of her money income in such a way that the marginal utility per dollar's worth of each good and service purchased is equal.
    b. If the relative price of a good falls, consumers will substitute it for the now relatively more expensive substitutes, which is the substitution effect.
    c. If the price of a good falls, given money income and given the prices of all other goods, a consumer's real income rises and she normally will purchase more of that good whose price has fallen, which is the real income effect.
    d. The substitution effect and the income effect help to explain the law of demand.

5. The "law" of diminishing marginal utility can account for the law of demand. Because the marginal benefit falls to consumers as they consume more per unit of time, price must fall to induce them to purchase more.

6. The diamond-water paradox is that diamonds are unessential to life and have a high relative price, while water is essential to life yet has a low relative price.
    a. The total utility of water to humans far exceeds the total utility of diamonds to humans, but the marginal utility of water is relatively low while the marginal utility of diamonds is high.
    b. The price of a good, therefore, reflects its value on the margin—not its total or average value.

■ Key Terms

Marginal utility   Utility
Util

■ Key Concepts

Consumer optimum	Real income effect
Diminishing marginal utility	Substitution effect
Principle of substitution	Utility analysis
Purchasing power	

■ Completion Questions

Fill in the blank, or circle the correct term.

1. The want-satisfying power that a good or service possesses is referred to as _____.

2. The _____ is an artificial unit by which utility is measured.

3. The change in total utility due to a one-unit change in quantity consumed is called _____.

4. _____ analysis is the study of what happens when small changes take place relative to the status quo.

5. If marginal utility is positive, total utility must (<u>fall, rise</u>). If marginal utility is negative, total utility must _____. If marginal utility falls (but is positive) then total utility must (<u>fall, rise</u>) at a decreasing rate.

6. Economists maintain that as more of a good or service is consumed, per unit of time, its marginal benefit (<u>falls, rises</u>). Therefore, before buyers will purchase more and more of a good, its price must (<u>fall, rise</u>).

7. The consumer optimum exists when consumers _____ their total utility, subject to such constraints as _____ and relative price. In order to optimize, a consumer should allocate his income so that the marginal utility per dollar's worth of each good or service he purchases is _____.

8. Assume a consumer is in consumer optimum and then the price of Good A rises, other things being constant. It is now true that the marginal utility per dollar's worth of Good A is (<u>less, greater</u>) than the marginal utility per dollar's worth of other goods. The consumer will now feel (<u>richer, poorer</u>) and probably spend (<u>more, less</u>) on Good A. Furthermore, the consumer will tend to substitute (<u>A for other goods, other goods for A</u>).

9. Although the (<u>marginal, total</u>) utility of water is greater than that of diamonds, the (<u>marginal, total</u>) utility of diamonds is higher. The price of a good reflects its (<u>marginal, total</u>) utility.

10. The explicit price of time spent surfing the Internet is (<u>zero, infinite</u>), but the law of diminishing marginal utility implies that a person who places a relatively high value on her time will tend to spend (<u>more, less</u>) time "Net-surfing."

■ True-False Questions

Circle the **T** if the statement is true, the **F** if it is false. Explain to yourself why a statement is false.

T   F   1. Economists today maintain that utility can be measured cardinally.

T   F   2. It is possible for a person's marginal utility to be negative if consuming more of an item causes the individual's total utility to decline.

T   F   3. Positive economics permits economists to say that Person 1 gets more utility from ice cream than does Person 2.

T   F   4. If total utility rises at a decreasing rate, then marginal utility must be falling.

T   F   5. If marginal utility is positive, then consuming the last unit of output reduced total utility.

T   F   6. Economists typically assume that as a person consumes more of any good, that good's total utility must fall.

T   F   7. If the MU of Good X/price of Good X exceeds the MU of Good Y/price of Good Y, the consumer can increase her total utility by substituting Good X for Good Y.

T   F   8. The law of diminishing marginal utility implies the law of demand, assuming consumers wish to optimize.

T   F   9. When the prices of digital apps fall, other things constant, everyone's real income will rise.

T   F   10. When the price of butter falls, other things constant, people will tend to substitute butter for margarine.

T   F   11. Because price reflects total utility rather than marginal utility, diamonds are more expensive than water.

■ Multiple Choice Questions

Circle the letter that corresponds to the best answer.

1. If marginal utility is positive, but falling, then total utility
   a. falls.
   b. falls at a decreasing rate.
   c. rises.
   d. rises at a decreasing rate.

2. Which one of the following words is most **unlike** the others?
    a. Marginal
    b. Average
    c. Incremental
    d. Extra

3. When an individual's total utility increases with consumption of one more unit of an item, it must be true that the person's marginal utility
    a. from consuming this unit is negative.
    b. from consuming this unit is positive.
    c. is increasing at the current level of consumption.
    d. is decreasing at the current level of consumption.

4. As more of Good A is consumed per week, over broad ranges
    a. the marginal utility of Good A falls.
    b. the total utility of Good A rises.
    c. the total utility of Good A rises at a decreasing rate.
    d. All of the above.

5. If marginal utility is negative, then
    a   total utility falls.
    b. total utility rises at a decreasing rate.
    c. total utility must be negative.
    d. None of the above.

6. Which one of the following helps to explain the law of demand?
    a. The law of diminishing marginal utility
    b. The substitution effect
    c. The income effect
    d. All of the above.

7. Consumer optimizing requires that the consumer
    a. maximize income.
    b. maximize total utility, subject to an income constraint.
    c. maximize income, subject to a marginal utility constraint.
    d. maximize marginal utility, subject to an income constraint.

8. If the marginal utility per dollar's worth of Good A exceeds that of Good B for Mr. Capra, then he
    a. is optimizing.
    b. will substitute Good A for Good B.
    c. will substitute Good B for Good A.
    d. is minimizing, not maximizing.

9. If the price of Good A rises, other things being constant, then
    a. the marginal utility of Good A falls.
    b. the marginal utility of Good A rises.
    c. the marginal utility per dollar's worth of Good A falls.
    d. the relative price of Good A falls.

10. If the price of steak rises, other things constant,
    a. everyone's real income will rise.
    b. everyone's money income will rise.
    c. the real income of steak buyers will rise.
    d. the real income of steak buyers will fall.

11. If the price of steak rises, other things constant,
    a. a real income effect will induce people to purchase less steak.
    b. people will substitute hamburger for steak.
    c. the quantity of steak demanded will fall.
    d. All of the above.

12. Diamonds have a higher price than water because
    a. people are shallow and shortsighted.
    b. price reflects total, not marginal, utility.
    c. price reflects marginal, not total, utility.
    d. the total utility of diamonds is greater, but the marginal utility of water is greater.

■ Working with Graphs

1.   Use the information given below to complete the table.

Hamburgers Consumed per Month	Total Utility (in utils)	Marginal Utility (in utils)
0	0	
1	5	_____
2	14	_____
3	22	_____
4	28	_____
5	33	_____
6	36	_____
7	35	_____
8	32	_____

a.   Graph the total and marginal utility curves on the graph provided below. (Plot the marginal utilities at the midpoint between quantities.)

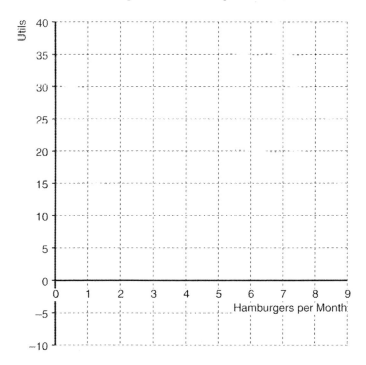

b.   At what quantity does diminishing marginal utility set in?

2.   Consider the graphs below, then answer the questions that follow.

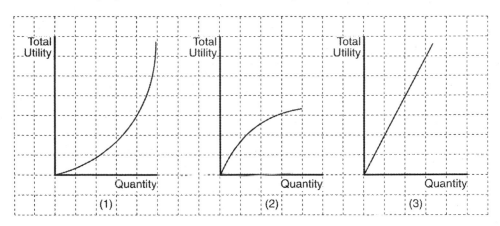

a.   Which panel indicates constant marginal utility?
b.   Which panel indicates increasing marginal utility?
c.   Which panel indicates decreasing marginal utility?

■ Problems

1.   Consider the following information.

Quantity	Candy Bars		Apples	
Consumed per Week	Total Utility	Marginal Utility	Total Utility	Marginal Utility
0	0		0	
1	10	_____	15	_____
2	18	_____	24	_____
3	25	_____	30	_____
4	29	_____	32	_____
5	31	_____	31	_____
6	30	_____	29	_____

a.   Complete the columns containing the marginal utilities of each good.
b.   With unlimited income, a consumer described by the above information would consume _____ candy bars and _____ apples.
c.   If candy bars cost 25 cents each and apples are two for a quarter (12.5 cents each) and the consumer has $1.50 to spend on candy and apples, what quantity of candy bars and apples will allow the above individual to reach consumer optimum?
d.   Now suppose the consumer suffers a loss of income and has 20 cents to spend. In addition, the price of candy bars is now 10 cents and the price of apples is 2 cents. What quantities of each will allow the individual to reach consumer optimum?

2. Mr. Garcia does not believe that economists are correct when they say that diminishing marginal utility is the rule for most goods. He claims that *increasing* marginal utility is the rule: As he consumes more and more of any good, his marginal utility rises.

    Assume that Mr. Garcia spends his income one dollar at a time, and that he can purchase one dollar's worth of any good. Assume further that he wishes to maximize his total utility.

    On what good does Mr. Garcia spend his first dollar? The second? The third? What predictions can you make about his behavior? Do most people behave that way? Does anyone?

3. Conduct the same analysis that you did in Question 2 above for Mrs. Garcia, who claims that, for her, *constant* marginal utility is the rule.

    a.   How do your answers differ from those in Question 2?

    b.   Can you think of *anything* for which diminishing marginal utility does not occur eventually, *per unit of time*?

■ Answers

Completion Questions

1. utility
2. util
3. marginal utility
4. Marginal
5. rise; fall; rise

6. falls; fall
7. maximize; income; equal
8. less; poorer; less; other goods for A
9. total; marginal; marginal
10. zero; less

True-False Questions

1. F   They need only to assume that it can be measured ordinally.
2. T
3. F   Interpersonal utility comparisons require normative judgments.
4. T
5. F   Marginal utility is positive only if total utility increased with the last unit consumed.
6. F   They assume that its *marginal utility* falls.
7. T
8. T
9. F   Only buyers of digital apps will experience an increase in real income.
10. T
11. F   Price reflects marginal utility.

Multiple Choice Questions

1. (d)
2. (b)
3. (b)
4. (d)
5. (a)
6. (d)

7. (b)
8. (b)
9. (c)
10. (d)
11. (d)
12. (c)

Working with Graphs

1.   a.   5; 9; 8; 6; 5; 3; –1; –3

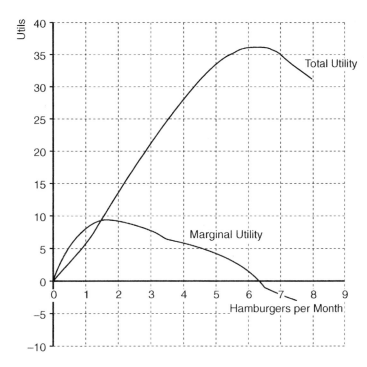

     b.   with the third hamburger consumed each month

2.   a.   3
     b.   1
     c.   2

Problems

1.   a.   marginal utility of candy bars: 10, 8, 7, 4, 2, –1; marginal utility of apples: 15, 9, 6, 2, –1, –2
     b.   5, 4
     c.   4 candy bars and 4 apples
     d.   1 candy bar and 4 apples. Note that the consumer has 2 cents left over, cannot purchase another candy bar, and will not purchase another apple, since the additional apple has a negative marginal utility (total utility declines).

2.   Mr. Garcia will spend every dollar of his income on the same good—that which gives him the highest marginal utility per dollar's worth of his first dollar spent. Only drug addicts, perhaps, behave that way.

3.   a.   The answers are the same as in Problem 2 above.
     b.   Given the qualifications in the question, it is difficult to think of any good for which that is not the case.

■ Glossary

Consumer optimum   A choice of a set of goods and services that maximizes the level of satisfaction for each consumer, subject to limited income.

Diminishing marginal utility   The principle that as more of any good or service is consumed, its extra benefit declines. Otherwise stated, increases in total utility from the consumption of a good or service become smaller and smaller as more is consumed during a given time period.

Marginal utility   The change in total utility due to a one-unit change in the quantity of a good or service consumed.

Principle of substitution   The principle that consumers shift away from goods and services that become priced relatively higher in favor of goods and services that are now priced relatively lower.

Purchasing power   The value of money for buying goods and services. If your money income stays the same but the price of one good that you are buying goes up, your effective purchasing power falls, and vice versa.

Real-income effect   The change in people's purchasing power that occurs when, other things being constant, the price of one good they purchase changes. When that price goes up, real income, or purchasing power, falls, and when that price goes down, real income increases.

Substitution effect   The tendency of people to substitute cheaper commodities for more expensive commodities.

Util   A representative unit by which utility is measured.

Utility   The want-satisfying power of a good or service.

Utility analysis   The analysis of consumer decision making based on utility maximization.

21 Rents, Profits, and the Financial Environment of Business

■ Learning Objectives

After you have studied this chapter, you should be able to

1. define economic rent, firm, proprietorship, partnership, corporation, unlimited liability, limited liability, explicit costs, implicit costs, accounting profit, economic profit, normal rate of return, opportunity cost of capital, interest, nominal rate of interest, real rate of interest, present value, rate of discount, discounting financial capital, dividends, share of stock, bond, reinvestment, random walk theory, and inside information;

2. understand the allocative function of economic rents;

3. distinguish among proprietorships, partnerships, and corporations;

4. identify the advantages and disadvantages of proprietorships, partnerships, and corporations;

5. distinguish between accounting profits and economic profits and between explicit costs and implicit costs;

6. explain the importance of earning a normal rate of return and taking into account the opportunity cost of capital;

7. explain the distinction between the nominal interest rate and the real interest rate and calculate the (approximate) nominal interest rate, given the real interest rate and the anticipated rate of inflation;

8. list three factors that account for variations in interest rates;

9. calculate the present value of an amount of money to be received at a future date; and

10. describe the differences between stocks and bonds and the basic features of securities markets.

■ Outline

1. *Economic rent* is a payment for the use of any resource that is in fixed supply.
   a. Land is often believed to be in fixed supply.

---

   b. Even if land is absolutely in fixed supply, rent payments help society to decide how land is to be used.

   c. Economic rents also accrue to factors of production other than land.

   d. Rents help society decide how to allocate a factor fixed in supply.

2. A firm is an organization that brings together different factors of production, such as labor, land, capital, and entrepreneurial skill, to produce a product or service that it is hoped can be sold for a profit.

3. A proprietorship is owned by a single individual who makes the business decisions, receives all the profits, and is legally responsible for all the debts of the firm.

   a. *Advantages:* A proprietorship is easy to form and dissolve. All decision-making powers reside with the sole proprietor. A proprietorship is taxed only once.

   b. *Disadvantages:* The proprietorship faces unlimited liability for debts of the firm and has limited ability to raise funds. The business normally ceases to exist with the death of the proprietor.

4. A partnership is owned by two or more individuals who share profits or losses.

   a. *Advantages:* Partnerships are easy to form, experience relatively low costs of monitoring job performance, permit more specialization than sole proprietorships, and are only taxed once.

   b. *Disadvantages:* Partnerships face unlimited liability and more difficulty in decision making (relative to proprietorship). Dissolution of the partnership is usually necessary when a partner dies or leaves the partnership.

5. A corporation is a legal entity that may conduct business in its own name, just as an individual does. The owners of the corporation are its shareholders.

   a. *Advantages:* Shareholders enjoy limited liability. A corporation continues to exist even if some owners cease to remain owners. A corporation has the ability to raise large sums of money for investments.

   b. *Disadvantages:* Owners are subject to double taxation because corporations pay taxes on profits and shareholders pay taxes on dividends received. Ownership and control are separated in a corporation.

      i. Professional managers, who may have little or no ownership in the firm, may pursue their own, not shareholder-owner, interests.

     ii. Shareholders may experience high costs to monitor the behavior of professional managers.

6. It is widely assumed by economists that the goal of the firm is to maximize economic profits.

   a. Accounting profits equal total revenues minus explicit costs.

   b. The opportunity cost of capital, or the normal rate of return to invested capital, is the rate of return that must be paid to an investor to induce him or her to invest in a business.

   c. There is also an opportunity cost to labor. Single-owner proprietors, after all, could earn wages elsewhere.

      i. There is an opportunity cost to all inputs.

     ii. Economic profits equal total revenues minus the opportunity cost of all inputs. Stated differently, economic profits equal total revenues minus the sum of explicit and implicit costs.

7. The term *interest* is used to mean two things: (1) the price paid by debtors to creditors for the use of loanable funds, and (2) the market return earned by (nonfinancial) capital as a factor of production.

    a. Interest is the payment for obtaining credit.

    b. Interest rates vary with the length of loan, risk, and handling charges.

    c. The *nominal interest* rate is (approximately) equal to the sum of the real interest rate and the expected rate of inflation.

    d. The interest rate, ultimately, allocates physical capital to various firms for investment projects.

8. Interest rates link the present with the future.

    a. A money value in the future can be expressed in today's value by a process referred to as *discounting* to present worth.

    b. Discounting is the method by which the present value of a future sum, or a stream of future sums, is obtained.

    c. The *rate of discount* is the interest rate used in the discounting to present worth equation.

9. Stocks, bonds, and reinvestment of retained earnings are the most important sources of corporate financing.

    a. From the investor's point of view, stocks offer the highest risk (and, therefore, the highest potential rate of return), and the greatest control over the firm's decisions.

    b. Bonds are relatively safer (and yield a correspondingly lower rate of return) and provide little control over decision making.

10. Some people believe that the stock market is an efficient market, in the sense that it follows a random walk.

    a. The random walk theory predicts that the best forecast of tomorrow's stock price is today's price, because today's price incorporates all the information important to stock price determination.

    b. Only inside information will permit people to beat the stock market.

■ Key Terms

Accounting profit	Financial capital	Partnership
Bond	Implicit costs	Proprietorship
Corporation	Interest	Rate of discount
Dividends	Nominal rate of interest	Real rate of interest
Economic profits	Normal rate of return	Share of stock
Explicit costs		

■ Key Concepts

Discounting	Limited liability	Random walk theory
Economic rent	Opportunity cost of capital	Reinvestment
Inside information	Present value	Unlimited liability

■ Completion Questions

Fill in the blank or circle the correct term.

1. A payment for the use of any resource that is _____ in supply is an economic rent.

2. The three major forms of U.S. business organizations are _____, _____, and _____.

3. While the highest percentage of U.S. firms are (<u>proprietorships, partnerships, corporations</u>), the highest percentage of total business revenue is attributed to _____.

4. A _____ is a legal entity that may conduct business in its own name, just as an individual does. Its owners are called (<u>shareholders, bondholders</u>), and such owners enjoy (<u>unlimited, limited, partially limited</u>) liability.

5. (<u>Explicit, Implicit</u>) costs are usually considered by accountants, but _____ costs typically are not.

6. Economists consider implicit costs because such costs (<u>do, do not</u>) include the opportunity costs of the resources used.

7. Accounting profits equal _____ minus _____. Economic profits equal _____ minus _____. Economic profits are less than accounting profits because economic profits subtract _____ costs from total revenues.

8. Economists usually assume that the firm's goal is _____.

9. Interest is the cost of obtaining _____. Interest is used to mean two different things: (1) _____, and (2) _____.

10. Interest rates vary due to _____, _____, and _____.

11. The nominal interest rate (approximately) equals the real interest rate plus the _____. Ultimately, the interest rate allocates _____ to various firms for investment projects.

12. The process of finding the value today of a sum of money in the future is called _____. The interest rate used in that process is called the _____ rate.

13. According to the efficient markets theory, the stock market is a _____ walk. The best prediction of tomorrow's price is _____.

■ True-False Questions

Circle the **T** if the statement is true, the **F** if it is false. Explain to yourself why a statement is false.

T   F   1.   Economic rent accrues only to the factor land.

T   F   2.   Economic rent is the price paid to a factor that is perfectly elastic in supply.

T   F   3.   If economic rent was totally taxed away, society would have to decide who gets to use the resource in question.

T   F   4.   For a factor fixed in supply, economic rent has no economic function.

T   F   5.   Economic rent occurs because specific resources have perfect substitutes.

T   F   6.   If a rock star prices tickets at a price way below equilibrium, that is an efficient way to help poor people.

T   F   7.   Corporations are the most common form of business organization in the United States.

T   F   8.   Proprietorships account for the highest percentage of total business revenues in the United States.

T   F   9.   Proprietors and partners face unlimited liability for the debts of their firms.

T   F   10.   The main advantage of corporations is that they offer limited liability to shareholders.

T   F   11.   Accountants typically do not consider implicit costs.

T   F   12.   Explicit costs include the opportunity cost of a resource.

T   F   13.   Accounting profits equal total revenues minus explicit costs.

T   F   14.   Accounting profits always exceed economic profits.

T   F   15.   Economists usually assume that the firm's goal is to maximize profits.

T   F   16.   Other things being constant, the greater the risk of nonrepayment, the higher the interest rate.

T   F   17.   The nominal interest rate (approximately) equals the real rate of interest plus the expected interest rate.

T   F   18.   Ultimately, the interest rate allocates physical capital to specific firms and households.

T   F   19.   Discounting is the process of converting future money values to present worth.

T   F   20.   Stocks offer a higher risk and return, relative to bonds, but bonds offer investors greater control over the firm's decisions.

T   F   21.   Reinvestment of retained earnings is the most important source of corporate finance.

T   F   22.   According to the efficient market theory, the best prediction of tomorrow's stock price is today's price.

T F 23. According to the efficient market theory, the only way to earn abnormal profits (in the long run) is to have inside information.

■ Multiple Choice Questions

Circle the letter that corresponds to the best answer.

1. For a factor that earns economic rent,
    a. its quantity varies only in the long run.
    b. its supply is perfectly elastic.
    c. its supply curve is perfectly inelastic.
    d. no taxation is possible because no surplus exists.

2. In David Ricardo's economic model,
    a. land was fixed in supply.
    b. wages and salaries were set by government.
    c. land rent falls as industrialization occurs.
    d. All of the above.

3. Economic rents
    a. have no allocative function.
    b. have no economic function.
    c. do not bring forth a greater quantity of the resource.
    d. exist only for land.

4. Economic rents
    a. accrue only to land.
    b. accrue only to labor.
    c. accrue only to entrepreneurs.
    d. can accrue to any factor, in principle.

5. Which one of the following is **not** true, concerning a proprietorship?
    a. Most U.S. firms are proprietorships.
    b. They are easy to form and to dissolve.
    c. They offer limited liability.
    d. The owner is taxed only once on business income.

6. Which one of the following is a disadvantage of a proprietorship?
    a. Unlimited liability for the firm's debts.
    b. Limited ability to raise funds.
    c. The firm ends with the death of the proprietor.
    d. All of the above.

7. Which one of the following is **not** true, concerning partnerships?

    a.   There are fewer partnerships than proprietorships in the United States.

    b.   They permit more effective specialization than proprietorships.

    c.   Business income is taxed only once.

    d.   Partners have limited liability for the firm's debts.

8. Which one of the following is an advantage of partnerships?

    a.   Partners have unlimited liability.

    b.   They enjoy reduced cost in monitoring job performance.

    c.   They must be dissolved if one partner dies.

    d.   All of the above.

9. A corporation

    a.   is a legal entity that conducts business in its own name.

    b.   permits unlimited liability to shareholders.

    c.   must be dissolved if a majority stockholder dies.

    d.   has severely limited abilities to attract financial resources.

10. Explicit costs are

    a.   considered by accountants.

    b.   greater than implicit costs.

    c.   considered irrelevant by economists.

    d.   considered by accountants, but not by economists.

11. Implicit costs

    a.   are considered important to accountants, but not to economists.

    b.   are usually less than explicit costs.

    c.   include the opportunity costs of resources.

    d.   are considered irrelevant by businesses.

12. Accounting profits

    a.   equal total revenues minus explicit costs.

    b.   exceed economic profits.

    c.   do not take implicit costs into account.

    d.   All of the above.

13. The opportunity cost of capital is

    a.   an explicit cost of doing business.

    b.   not an important cost of doing business.

    c.   the normal rate of return on capital invested in a business.

    d.   purely a technological concept.

14. Which one of the following is **not** explicit?
    a. wages
    b. opportunity cost of capital
    c. taxes
    d. rent

15. *Analogy:* Rent is to explicit costs as _____ are to implicit costs.
    a. labor services of a proprietor
    b. taxes
    c. wages
    d. accounting profits

16. Which one of the following goals of the firm is most widely assumed by economists?
    a. Staff maximization
    b. sales maximization
    c. growth maximization
    d. profit maximization

17. Other things being constant, the interest rate varies with the
    a. length of a loan.
    b. risk of nonrepayment.
    c. handling charges.
    d. All of the above.

18. The nominal interest rate approximately equals the real interest rate
    a. minus the expected interest rate.
    b. plus the expected interest rate.
    c. plus the expected rate of inflation.
    d. minus the expected inflation rate.

19. Interest rates
    a. have no economic function.
    b. allocate financial capital to less efficient firms.
    c. allocate physical capital to firms in a random manner.
    d. allocate physical capital to specific firms for investment projects.

20. Discounting
    a. converts future dollar values into present values.
    b. connects the future with the present.
    c. uses the interest rate.
    d. All of the above.

21. If the interest rate is 5 percent, the present value of $100 that is to be received one year from now is about
    a. $90.
    b. $950.
    c. $95.
    d. $105.

22. When Ms. Stephenson won the $1,000,000 lottery in Florida, she found out that the money would be paid to her at the rate of $50,000 per year for the next 20 years. Which of the following can be determined with certainty?
    a. Ms. Stephenson will refuse the money, after she finds out what the lottery is really worth.
    b. The lottery winnings are worth considerably less than $1 million.
    c. Ms. Stephenson would *prefer* to receive her lottery winnings over 20 years, instead of all at once.
    d. Ms. Stephenson would have preferred to receive $25,000 per year for 40 years.

23. Shareholders
    a. are the owners of corporations.
    b. are less at risk than are bondholders.
    c. are subject to unlimited risk.
    d. have less control over firm decisions than do bondholders.

24. According to the efficient market theory, in an efficient market
    a. only lucky people can earn abnormal profits in the long run.
    b. tomorrow's price is easily determined.
    c. only inside information permits abnormal profits.
    d. a pattern of price changes will emerge.

■ Matching

Choose the item in Column (2) that best matches an item in Column (1).

(1)	**(2)**
(a) economic rent	(h) corporate debt
(b) share of stock	(i) payment to resource fixed in supply
(c) bond	(j) limited liability
(d) present value calculation	(k) total revenues less implicit and explicit costs
(e) economic profits	(l) corporate ownership
(f) corporation	(m) discount rate
(g) real rate of interest	(n) inflation expectation

■ Working with Graphs

Use the following diagram to answer the questions that follow.

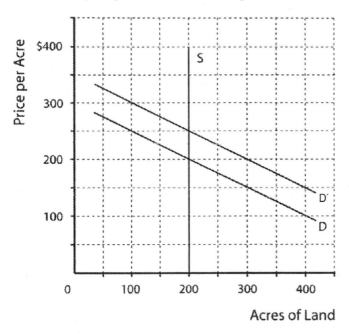

1. If the demand for land is represented by D, what is the total rent received by the owner of the 200 acres of land?

2. If the demand for land increases to D′, what is the rent received by the landowner?

■ Problems

1. Suppose you win a lottery that offers the following payoff. At the end of each year for the next three years you are to receive $1,000. At the end of each of the following three years you will receive $500, for a total of $4,500 over the six-year period. If the current going rate of interest is 8 percent, what is the present value of your winnings? If someone offered you $3,700 today for your lottery ticket, should you take it?

2. Francisco Martinez just learned that a long-lost aunt has set up a trust for him, whereby he will receive $1 million exactly 10 years from now. Assume that the relevant interest rate is 10 percent.
   a. Can Francisco sell his inheritance, right now, for $1 million? Why or why not?
   b. What is the present value of the inheritance that Francisco has received?

3. Suppose that you had used a discount rate of 20 percent in Question 2 above. How would you answer (a) and (b) now? (c) How are present value and the interest rate related?

■ Answers

Completion Questions

1. fixed
2. proprietorships; partnerships; corporations
3. proprietorships; corporations
4. corporation; shareholders; limited
5. Explicit; implicit
6. do
7. total revenues; explicit costs; total revenues; implicit plus explicit costs; implicit
8. profit maximization
9. credit; price paid by debtors to creditors, return to capital
10. length of loan, risk of nonrepayment, handling charges
11. expected inflation rate; physical capital
12. discounting; discount
13. random; today's price

True-False Questions

1. F   It accrues to any factor fixed in supply.
2. F   It is the price paid to a perfectly *in*elastic resource supply.
3. T
4. F   It allocates the fixed factor to its highest valued use.
5. F   Rent is earned by resources that cannot be replicated exactly.
6. F   Giving them money income directly would be more efficient.
7. F   Proprietorships account for about 70 percent of total business organizations.
8. F   Corporations do.
9. T
10. T
11. T
12. F   Implicit costs do.
13. T
14. T
15. T
16. T
17. F   Plus the expected *inflation* (not *expected interest*) rate.
18. T
19. T
20. F   Stocks also give investors greater control than bonds.
21. T
22. T
23. T

Multiple Choice Questions

1. (c)	13. (c)
2. (a)	14. (b)
3. (c)	15. (a)
4. (d)	16. (d)
5. (c)	17. (d)
6. (d)	18. (c)
7. (d)	19. (d)
8. (b)	20. (d)
9. (a)	21. (c)
10. (a)	22. (b)
11. (c)	23. (a)
12. (d)	24. (c)

Matching

(a) and (i)	(e) and (k)
(b) and (l)	(f) and (j)
(c) and (h)	(g) and (n)
(d) and (m)	

Working with Graphs

1. $40,000

2. $50,000

Problems

1.   From Table 21-3 on page 473 of your text we can see:

Year	Present Value	(Found by)
1	$926.00	(0.926 × 1000)
2	857.00	(0.857 × 1000)
3	794.00	(0.794 × 1000)
4	367.50	(0.735 × 500)
5	340.50	(0.681 × 500)
6	315.00	(0.630 × 500)
Total	$3,600.00	

Yes, you would be $100 better off, as is seen by the present value calculation.

2.   a.   No, no one would give him $1 million right now because such a sum could be invested and earn interest for 10 years, and at the end of that period it would be worth $1 million plus the accumulated interest.

   b. $\dfrac{\$1,000,000}{(1.1)^{10}} = \dfrac{\$1,000,000}{2.5937425} = \$385,543$; or from Table 21-3, use the discount factor

   of 0.385 for an answer of $385,000.

3.   a.   See Problem 2(a).

   b. $161,506 (or rounded to $162,000 if the discount factor of 0.162 from Table 21-3 is used)

   c.   They are inversely related.

■ Glossary

Accounting profit   Total revenues minus total explicit costs.

Bond   A legal claim against a firm, usually entitling the owner of the bond to receive a fixed annual coupon payment, plus a lump sum payment at the bond's maturity date. Bonds are issued in return for funds lent to the firm.

Corporation   A legal entity that may conduct business in its own name just as an individual does. The owners of a corporation, called shareholders, own shares of the firm's profits and enjoy the protection of limited liability.

Discounting   The method by which the present value of a future sum or a future stream of sums is obtained.

Dividends   Portion of a corporation's profits paid to its owners (shareholders).

Economic profits   Total revenues minus total opportunity costs of all inputs used, or the total of all implicit and explicit costs.

Economic rent   A payment for the use of any resource over and above its opportunity cost.

Explicit costs   Costs that business managers must take account of because they must be paid. Examples are wages, taxes, and rent.

Financial capital   Funds used to purchase physical capital goods, such as buildings and equipment, and patents and trademarks.

Firm   A business organization that employs resources to produce goods or services for profit. A firm normally owns and operates at least one "plant" or facility in order to produce.

Implicit costs   Expenses that managers do not have to pay out of pocket and hence normally do not explicitly calculate, such as the opportunity cost of factors of production that are owned. Examples are owner-provided capital and owner-provided labor.

Inside information   Information that is not available to the general public about what is happening in a corporation.

Interest   The payment for current rather than future command over resources; the cost of obtaining credit.

Limited liability   A legal concept in which the responsibility, or liability, of the owners of a corporation is limited to the value of the shares in the firm that they own.

Nominal rate of interest   The market rate of interest expressed in today's dollars.

Normal rate of return   The amount that must be paid to an investor to induce investment in a business. Also known as the *opportunity cost of capital*.

Opportunity cost of capital   The normal rate of return, or the available return on the next-best alternative investment. Economists consider this a cost of production, and it is included in our cost examples.

Partnership   A business owned by two or more joint owners, or partners, who share the responsibilities and profits of the firm and are individually liable for all the debts of the partnership.

Present value   The value of a future amount expressed in today's dollars; the most that someone would pay today to receive a certain sum at some point in the future.

Proprietorship   A business owned by one individual who makes the business decisions, receives all the profits, and is legally responsible for the debts of the firm.

Random walk theory   The theory that there are no predictable trends in securities prices that can be used to "get rich quick."

Rate of discount   The rate of interest used to discount future sums back to present value.

Real rate of interest   The nominal rate of interest minus the anticipated rate of inflation.

Reinvestment   Profits (or depreciation reserves) used to purchase new capital equipment.

Securities   Stocks and bonds.

Share of stock   A legal claim to a share of a corporation's future profits. If it is *common stock,* it incorporates certain voting rights regarding major policy decisions of the corporation. If it is *preferred stock,* its owners are accorded preferential treatment in the payment of dividends but do not have any voting rights.

Unlimited liability   A legal concept whereby the personal assets of the owner of a firm may be seized to pay off the firm's debts.

22 The Firm: Cost and Output Determination

■ Learning Objectives

After you have studied this chapter, you should be able to

1. define short run, long run, production, production function, law of diminishing marginal product, average physical product, marginal physical product, total costs, fixed costs, variable costs, average fixed costs, average variable costs, average total costs, marginal costs, planning horizon, long-run average cost curve, planning curve, economies of scale, constant returns to scale, diseconomies of scale, and minimum efficient scale;

2. distinguish between the firm's short run and its long run;

3. apply the law of diminishing marginal product to account for the shape of the firm's short-run marginal cost curve, average total cost curve, and average variable cost curve;

4. classify firm costs as fixed or variable costs;

5. calculate average total costs, average fixed costs, average variable costs, and marginal costs, given sufficient information;

6. apply the concepts of economies of scale, diseconomies of scale, and constant returns to scale to predict the shape of a firm's long-run average cost curve;

7. list reasons for economies of scale and for diseconomies of scale; and

8. understand the concept of minimum efficient scale (MES).

■ Outline

1. The short run is defined as that time period in which a firm cannot alter its current size of plant. The long run is that time period in which all factors of production can be varied.

2. Total costs are identical to total fixed costs plus total variable costs.
   a. Total fixed costs do not vary with output.
   b. Total variable costs are the sum of all those costs that vary with output.
   c. There are several short-run average cost curves.
      i. Average total costs equal total costs divided by output.
      ii. Average variable costs equal total variable costs divided by output.
      iii. Average fixed costs equal total fixed costs divided by output.
   d. Marginal cost equals the change in total costs divided by the change in output.
   e. When marginal cost is above average cost, average cost rises. When marginal cost is below average cost, average cost falls. When marginal cost equals average cost, average cost remains constant.
   f. The marginal cost curve intersects the average total cost curve and the average variable cost curve at their respective minimum points.

3. The production function is a relationship between inputs and outputs. The production function is a technological, not an economic, relationship.
   a. The law of diminishing marginal product comes into play when the firm increases output in the short run.
   b. The marginal physical product is the change in total product that occurs when a variable input is increased and all other inputs are held constant.
   c. The law of diminishing marginal product implies that the marginal physical product of labor eventually falls.

4. Diminishing marginal product causes the marginal cost curve, the average total cost curve, and the average variable cost curve to rise.

5. In the long run, all inputs are variable, and long-run cost curves must take this into account.
   a. The long-run average cost curve is the locus of points representing the minimum unit cost of producing any given rate of output, given current technology and resource prices.
   b. Another name for the long-run average cost curve is the planning horizon.

6. The long-run average cost curve is U-shaped.
   a. Initially a firm experiences economies of scale due to specialization, a dimensional factor, or improved productive equipment.
   b. Eventually a firm might experience diseconomies of scale because a disproportionate increase in management and staff may be needed, and because the costs of information and communication also grow more than proportionally with output.

7. The minimum efficient scale is the lowest rate of output per unit time period at which average costs reach a minimum for a particular firm.

■ Key Terms

Average fixed costs	Economies of scale	Planning curve
Average physical product	Fixed costs	Plant size
Average total costs	Long-run average cost curve	Production
Average variable costs	Marginal costs	Total costs
Constant returns to scale	Marginal physical product	Variable costs

■ Key Concepts

Diseconomies of scale	Planning horizon
Law of diminishing marginal product	Production function
	Short run
Long run	
Minimum efficient scale	

■ Completion Questions

Fill in the blank, or circle the correct term.

1. Our definition of the short run is the time during which _____ is fixed, but _____ is variable.

2. In the long run (<u>no, all</u>) factors are variable.

3. Fixed costs (<u>do, do not</u>) vary with output. Variable costs (<u>do, do not</u>) vary with output.

4. (<u>Rent, Wages</u>) and (<u>mortgage interest payments, raw materials costs</u>) are examples of fixed costs. (<u>Rent, Wages</u>) and (<u>mortgage interest payments, raw materials costs</u>) are examples of variable costs.

5. Short-run average cost curves eventually are upward sloping due to _____.

6. If marginal cost exceeds average total cost, then average total cost will (<u>fall, rise, remain constant</u>).

7. At the minimum of the average total cost curve, marginal cost is (<u>less than, greater than, equal to</u>) average total cost.

8. If marginal cost is less than average total cost, then average total cost will (<u>fall, rise, remain constant</u>).

9. Because of the law of diminishing marginal product, in the (<u>short, long</u>) run the marginal product of labor will eventually (<u>fall, rise, remain constant</u>).

10. The long-run cost curve typically is U-shaped because initially, as a firm expands its scale of operations, it realizes _____ of scale. Then the firm may realize _____ returns to scale. Eventually, the firm realizes _____ of scale.

11. Reasons for economies of scale include _____, _____, and _____.

12. A firm might experience diseconomies of scale due to _____ and _____.

■ True-False Questions

Circle the **T** if the statement is true, the **F** if it is false. Explain to yourself why a statement is false.

T F   1. Short-run cost curves that include variable costs eventually reflect the influence of the law of diminishing marginal product.

T F   2. Fixed costs vary with output.

T F   3. Eventually, as output expands, the short-run marginal cost curve must rise.

T F   4. When average total cost exceeds marginal cost, marginal cost must be rising.

T F   5. When average variable cost is less than marginal cost, marginal cost must be falling.

T F   6. At the minimum average total cost output level, marginal cost equals average total cost.

T F   7. In the short run, the supply of labor to the firm is usually fixed.

T F   8. Because of the law of diminishing marginal product, the marginal product of labor will rise.

T F   9. Long-run cost curves are U-shaped due to the law of diminishing marginal product.

T F   10. The minimum efficient scale is the lowest scale of output at which long-run average total cost is as low as possible.

■ Multiple Choice Questions

Circle the letter that corresponds to the best answer.

1. In the short run, for our purposes,
   a. all factors are variable.
   b. labor is variable.
   c. capital is variable.
   d. both capital and labor are variable.

2. The long run
    a. permits the variation of all factors of production.
    b. is different for different firms.
    c. permits a firm to avoid the consequences of the law of diminishing marginal product.
    d. All of the above.

3. Fixed costs
    a. vary with output.
    b. do not vary with output.
    c. reflect the effect of diminishing marginal product.
    d. include labor and raw materials costs.

4. In the short run, which cost is **not** fixed?
    a. rent
    b. wages
    c. opportunity cost of capital
    d. interest payments on borrowed money

5. If marginal cost is above average total cost, then average total cost
    a. will rise.
    b. will fall.
    c. will remain constant.
    d. cannot be calculated.

6. At that output where average total cost is at a minimum,
    a. marginal cost equals average total cost.
    b. marginal cost equals average variable cost.
    c. average total cost is rising.
    d. total cost is constant.

7. Which short-run curve is not U-shaped?
    a. average total cost
    b. marginal cost
    c. average variable cost
    d. average fixed cost

8. The production function
    a. is a technological relationship.
    b. is not an economic relationship.
    c. relates output to inputs.
    d. All of the above.

9. Because of the law of diminishing marginal product,
   a. long-run average cost eventually rises.
   b. marginal cost falls.
   c. the marginal product of labor eventually falls.
   d. the average total cost curve falls.

10. Which is **not** due to the law of diminishing marginal product?
    a. rising short-run marginal cost
    b. rising long-run average total cost
    c. rising short-run average variable cost
    d. rising short-run average total cost

11. *Analogy:* Diminishing marginal product is to rising short-run average total costs as _____ is to rising long-run average total costs.
    a. economies of scale
    b. diseconomies of scale
    c. law of diminishing marginal product
    d. constant returns to scale

12. Which of the following helps to account for a U-shaped short-run average total cost curve?
    a. economies of scale
    b. diseconomies of scale
    c. law of diminishing marginal product
    d. constant returns to scale

13. A firm might experience diseconomies of scale due to
    a. disproportionate rises in specialization.
    b. dimensional factors.
    c. information and communication costs that rise disproportionately.
    d. the ability to use larger-volume machinery that is efficient only at large outputs.

14. If the minimum efficient scale is relatively low, then
    a. there will likely be a relatively large number of firms in the industry.
    b. there will likely be a relatively small number of firms in the industry.
    c. economies of scale are very great.
    d. long-run average costs decline over broad ranges of output.

■ Matching

Choose the item in Column (2) that best matches an item in Column (1).

(1)	**(2)**
(a) long run	(i) falling long-run average cost
(b) short run	(j) rising long-run average cost
(c) fixed cost	(k) fixed plant size
(d) variable cost	(l) diminishing marginal product
(e) marginal cost	(m) overhead
(f) economies of scale	(n) wages of laborers
(g) diseconomies of scale	(o) additional cost of producing next unit
(h) law of diminishing marginal product	(p) all factors variable

■ Working with Graphs

1. Assume that the High Rise Bakery produces a single product: loaves of bread. Further assume that the bread is produced using a fixed plant size, with 10 ovens and varying quantities of labor. John Doe, the owner and manager of the High Rise Bakery, notices that as he hires additional workers, the total output of bread goes up for a while. Then he finds that after hiring several additional workers, the workers begin to get in one another's way, and extra output begins to decline. John knows the principles of economics and something about diminishing marginal physical product. Given the information in the table on the next page, calculate the marginal physical product of John's bakers. Graph total and marginal products on the next page and tell John how many bakers he can employ before diminishing marginal product sets in. (Plot the marginal product at the midpoint between the number of bakers employed.)

Bakers	Output (loaves per day)	Marginal Product
0	0	
1	8	_____
2	19	_____
3	32	_____
4	45	_____
5	60	_____
6	71	_____
7	75	_____
8	77	_____
9	77	_____
10	75	_____
11	65	_____

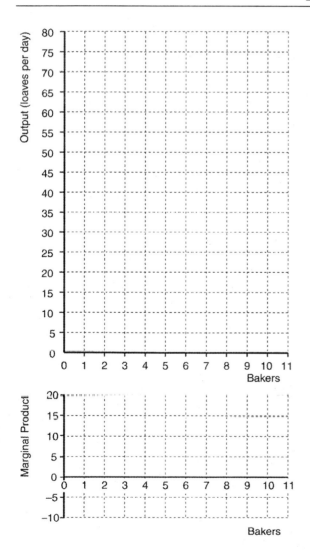

2.   Complete the following table of cost figures and then graph the information on the graphs provided below. Assume total fixed costs are $3.

Output	Total Variable Costs	Total Costs	Average Variable Cost	Average Total Cost	Marginal Cost
0	0.00	3.00	____	____	____
1	3.00	____	____	____	____
2	____	____	____	4.00	____
3	____	9.20	____	____	____
4	____	____	____	____	2.30
5	____	____	2.38	____	____
6	____	____	____	____	5.00
7	23.90	____	____	____	____
8	____	36.90	____	____	____

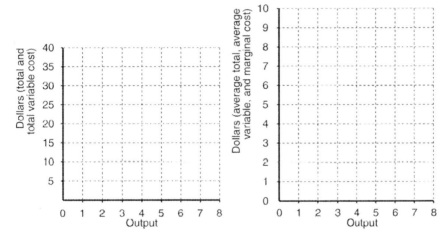

3.   Use the graph below to answer the questions that follow.

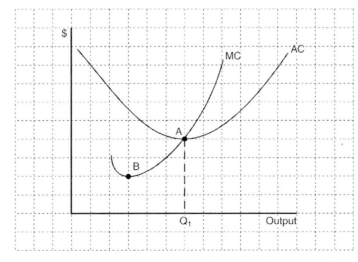

a.   At what point does marginal product begin to diminish?

b.   At any output less than Q_1, why is *AC* falling?

    c.   At any output greater than Q_1, why is *AC* rising?

    d.   What is *AC* doing at the exact output Q_1?

4.   Use the graph below to answer the questions that follow. Assume that *A* and *B* are minimum points.

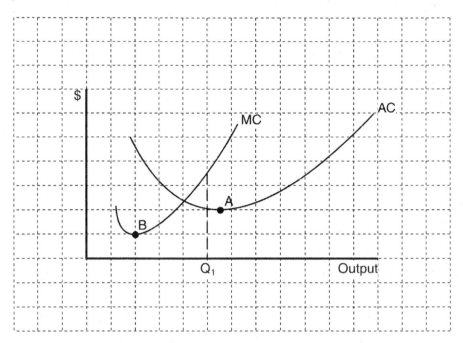

    a.   Something is wrong with the graph above. What is it?

    b.   According to the graph above, what is happening at output Q_1, with respect to *MC* and *AC*? Is this possible?

■ Problems

1.   Fill in the information in each blank below so that the equation is correct. (*Note:* Q is quantity of output.)

    a. $TC = TFC + \underline{\hspace{2cm}}$

    b. $AFC = \underline{\hspace{2cm}} - AVC$

    c. $ATC = (TVC/Q) + \underline{\hspace{2cm}}$

    d. $TFC = Q \times \underline{\hspace{2cm}}$

    e. $AVC = (TC/Q) - \underline{\hspace{2cm}} /Q$

    f. $TVC = (Q \times ATC) - Q \times \underline{\hspace{2cm}}$

■ Answers

Completion Questions

1. capital; labor
2. all
3. do not; do
4. rent; mortgage interest payments; wages; raw material costs
5. diminishing marginal product
6. rise
7. equal to
8. fall
9. short; fall
10. economies; constant; diseconomies
11. specialization; dimensional factors; improved productive equipment
12. disproportionate requirements for managers and staff; disproportionate costs of information and communication

True-False Questions

1. T
2. F   By definition they do not.
3. T
4. F   Not necessarily.
5. F   When *AVC* is less than *MC*, the *MC* curve has already crossed through the minimum point of *AVC*, so *MC* must be rising.
6. T
7. F   Capital is fixed in the short run.
8. F   It falls due to the law of diminishing marginal product.
9. F   Diminishing marginal product occurs in the short run.
10. T

Multiple Choice Questions

1. (b)
2. (d)
3. (b)
4. (b)
5. (a)
6. (a)
7. (d)
8. (d)
9. (c)
10. (b)
11. (b)
12. (c)
13. (c)
14. (a)

Matching

(a) and (p)
(b) and (k)
(c) and (m)
(d) and (n)
(e) and (o)
(f) and (i)
(g) and (j)
(h) and (l)

Working with Graphs

1. Marginal product: 8; 11; 13; 13; 15; 11; 4; 2; 0; –2; –10

   Diminishing marginal product sets in when John hires the sixth baker.

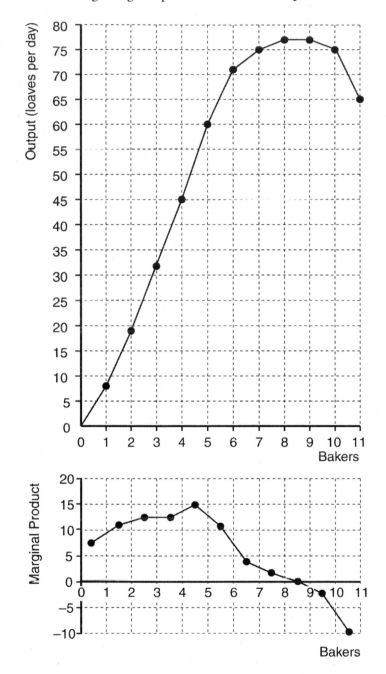

2.

Output	Total Variable Costs	Total Costs	Average Variable Cost	Average Total Cost	Marginal Cost
0	0.00	3.00	——	——	——
1	3.00	6.00	3.00	6.00	3.00
2	5.00	8.00	2.50	4.00	2.00
3	6.20	9.20	2.07	3.07	1.20
4	8.50	11.50	2.13	2.88	2.30
5	11.90	14.90	2.38	2.98	3.40
6	16.90	19.90	2.82	3.32	5.00
7	23.90	26.90	3.41	3.84	7.00
8	33.90	36.90	4.24	4.61	10.00

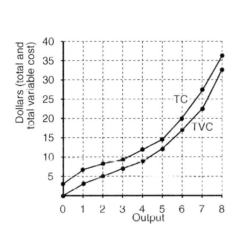 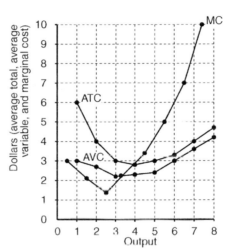

3.   a.   *B*

   b.   *MC* is below *AC*, due to specialization.

   c.   *MC* is above *AC*.

   d.   *AC* is constant, because *MC* = *AC*.

4.   a.   *MC* cuts the *AC* curve to the left of *AC*'s minimum point.

   b.   *MC* > *AC*, yet *AC* is falling. No.

Problems

1.   a.   *TVC*

   b.   *ATC*

   c.   *AFC*

   d.   *AFC*

   e.   *TFC*

   f.   *AFC*

■ Glossary

Average fixed costs   Total fixed costs divided by the number of units produced.

Average physical product   Total product divided by the variable input.

Average total costs   Total costs divided by the number of units produced; sometimes called *average per-unit total costs*.

Average variable costs   Total variable costs divided by the number of units produced.

Constant returns to scale   No change in long-run average costs when output increases.

Diseconomies of scale   Increases in long-run average costs that occur as output increases.

Economies of scale   Decreases in long-run average costs resulting from increases in output.

Fixed costs   Costs that do not vary with output. Fixed costs include such expenses as rent on a building. These costs are fixed for a certain period of time (in the long run, though, they are variable).

Law of diminishing marginal product   The observation that after some point, successive equal-sized increases in a variable factor of production, such as labor, added to fixed factors of production will result in smaller increases in output.

Long run   That time period during which all factors of production can be varied.

Long-run average cost curve   The locus of points representing the minimum unit cost of producing any given rate of output, given current technology and resource prices.

Marginal costs   The change in total costs due to a one-unit change in production rate.

Marginal physical product   The physical output that is due to the addition of one more unit of a variable factor of production. The change in total product occurring when a variable input is increased and all other inputs are held constant. Also called *marginal product*.

Minimum efficient scale (MES)   The lowest rate of output per unit time at which long-run average costs for a particular firm are at a minimum.

Planning curve   The long-run average cost curve.

Planning horizon   The long run, during which all inputs are variable.

Plant size   The physical size of factories that a firm owns and operates to produce its output. Plant size can be defined by square footage, maximum physical capacity, and other physical measures.

Production   Any activity that results in the conversion of resources into products that can be used in consumption.

Production function   The relationship between inputs and maximum physical output. A production function is a technological, not an economic, relationship.

Short run   The time period during which at least one input, such as plant size, cannot be changed.

Total costs   The sum of total fixed costs and total variable costs.

Variable costs   Costs that vary with the rate of production. They include wages paid to workers and purchases of materials.

23 Perfect Competition

■ Learning Objectives

After you have studied this chapter, you should be able to

1. define price taker, total revenues, marginal revenue, short-run shutdown price, short-run break-even price, industry supply curve, long-run industry supply curve, constant-cost industry, increasing-cost industry, decreasing-cost industry, and marginal cost pricing;

2. list four characteristics of the perfect competition market structure;

3. recognize the shape of a perfectly competitive firm's demand curve and recognize reasons for its shape;

4. determine a perfect competitor's optimal output rate, given sufficient information;

5. calculate the value of a perfect competitor's short-run profits, given sufficient information;

6. recognize and determine the perfectly competitive firm's short-run shutdown price and its short-run break-even price;

7. recognize a perfectly competitive firm's short-run supply curve and recognize how an *industry* short-run supply curve is derived;

8. distinguish among constant-cost, increasing-cost, and decreasing-cost industries;

9. recognize the long-run equilibrium position for a firm in a perfectly competitive industry;

10. indicate why a perfectly competitive market structure is socially efficient; and

11. recognize how the asymmetry of information problem affects the perfect competition model.

■ Outline

1. There are four major characteristics of the perfect competition market structure: a large number of buyers and sellers, homogeneous product, unimpeded industry exit and entry, and equally good information for both buyers and sellers.

---

2. Because in the perfect competition model many firms produce a homogeneous product, a single firm's demand curve is perfectly elastic at the "going" market price.

3. In order to predict how much the perfect competitor will produce, we assume that it wants to maximize total profits.

   a. Total revenues equal quantity sold times price per unit.

   b. In the short run, total costs are the sum of total fixed costs and total variable costs.

   c. Total revenues minus total costs equal total profits.

   d. Marginal revenue equals the change in total revenue divided by the change in output.

   e. Total profits are maximized at that rate of output where marginal revenue equals marginal cost.

4. Because a normal rate of return to investment is included in the average total cost curve, the "profits" we calculate are economic profits.

5. The firm's short-run shutdown price occurs at its minimum average variable cost value: At a higher price, the firm should produce and contribute to payment of fixed costs. The firm should not produce at a lower price.

6. The firm's short-run break-even price is found at the minimum point on its average total cost curve: At a higher price the firm will earn abnormal profits, at a lower price it suffers economic losses, and at the minimum point, economic profits equal zero.

7. The firm's short-run supply curve is its marginal cost curve above the short-run shutdown point.

8. The short-run industry supply curve is derived by summing horizontally all the firm supply curves. The industry supply curve shifts when nonprice determinants of supply change.

9. In a perfectly competitive market, the "going" price is set where the market demand curve intersects the industry supply curve.

10. In the long run, because abnormal industry profits induce entry and because negative industry profits induce exit, firms in a perfectly competitive industry will earn zero economic profits.

    a. Long-run supply curves relate price and quantity supplied after firms have time to enter or exit from an industry.

    b. A constant-cost industry is one whose long-run supply curve is horizontal because input prices are unaffected by output.

    c. An increasing-cost industry is one whose long-run supply curve is positively sloped because the price of specialized (or essential) inputs rises as industry output increases.

    d. A decreasing-cost industry is one whose long-run supply curve is negatively sloped because specialized input prices fall as industry output expands.

11. In a perfectly competitive industry, a firm operates where price equals marginal revenue equals marginal cost equals short-run minimum average cost equals long-run minimum average cost—in the long run.

   a. Perfectly competitive industries are efficient from society's point of view because for such industries price equals marginal cost in long-run equilibrium.

   b. They are also efficient because in long-run equilibrium the output rate is produced at minimum average cost.

   c. The perfectly competitive model is not a realistic description of any real-world industry. Nevertheless, the model of perfect competition helps economists explain and predict economic events.

■ Key Terms

Industry supply curve

Long-run industry supply curve

Marginal revenue

Market failure

Perfectly competitive firm

Short-run break-even price

Short-run shutdown price

Total revenues

■ Key Concepts

Constant-cost industry

Decreasing-cost industry

Increasing-cost industry

Marginal cost pricing

Perfect competition

Price taker

Profit maximizing rate of production

Signals

Total costs

■ Completion Questions

Fill in the blank, or circle the correct term.

1. The four major characteristics of a perfect competition market structure are _____, _____, _____, and _____.

2. The demand curve facing a perfect competitor is _____ elastic.

3. We assume that the goal of the firm is to _____. If so, the perfect competitor should produce up to the point where MR equals _____. Total profits are defined as _____ minus _____.

4. Marginal revenue equals _____ divided by _____.

5. Because we include the opportunity cost of capital as a cost of production, the profits we define are (accounting, economic) profits.

6. If the firm's selling price cannot cover its short-run variable costs, then it should _____. If the selling price equals minimum average total cost, the firm is just _____, and its economic profits are (<u>negative, positive, zero</u>).

7. If the firm is earning zero economic profits, it (<u>will, will not</u>) continue to operate.

8. The perfectly competitive firm's short-run supply curve is the portion of its _____ curve lying above minimum *AVC*. The industry short-run supply curve is derived by _____ all the firm supply curves.

9. In the long run, a firm in a perfectly competitive industry will earn exactly zero economic profits. This is true because if economic profits are positive, some firms will _____ the industry, and price will fall. If economic profits are negative, some firms will _____ the industry, and price will rise.

10. If an industry expands and input prices do not change, such an industry is a(n) _____ -cost industry and the long-run supply curve is horizontal. If input prices rise, the industry is a(n) _____ -cost industry and the long-run industry supply curve is _____ sloping. If input prices fall, the industry is a(n) _____ -cost industry and the industry's long-run supply curve is _____ sloping.

11. In the long run, a perfectly competitive firm will earn (<u>negative, positive, zero</u>) economic profits. Its price will be (<u>greater than, less than, equal to</u>) marginal cost, and output (<u>will, will not</u>) be produced at minimum average total cost. From society's point of view, all of this is (<u>efficient, inefficient</u>).

■ True-False Questions

Circle the **T** if the statement is true, the **F** if it is false. Explain to yourself why a statement is false.

T F   1. A firm in a perfectly competitive industry is a price taker.

T F   2. Because firms in a perfectly competitive industry are all price takers, price cannot change in that industry.

T F   3. The demand curve facing a perfect competitor is perfectly elastic.

T F   4. The perfectly competitive firm attempts to maximize marginal profits.

T F   5. The total profit maximization output occurs at the point where the firm's marginal cost equals its marginal revenue.

T F   6. Marginal revenue minus average cost equals total profits.

T F   7. If price is below minimum average variable costs in the short run, the firm will shut down, assuming output is where *MR – MC*.

T F   8. If price is below minimum average total cost, economic profits will be negative, assuming that output is where $MR = MC$.

T F   9. The firm's short-run supply curve is its average variable cost curve.

T F   10. The industry supply curve is derived by summing horizontally all the firm supply curves.

T F   11. Because of the law of diminishing returns, the firm's short-run supply curve will be upward sloping.

T F   12. Because of free exit and entry, long-run accounting profits for a perfect competitor must be zero.

T F   13. A constant-cost industry has an upward-sloping long-run industry supply curve.

T F   14. If demand falls in a decreasing-cost industry, in the long run both output and price will fall.

T F   15. In the long-run equilibrium situation, the perfectly competitive firm will earn zero economic profits and produce at minimum average cost.

T F   16. Because of excessive competition, the perfectly competitive industry is believed to be inefficient from society's point of view.

■ Multiple Choice Questions

Circle the letter that corresponds to the best answer.

1. Which one of the following is **not** a characteristic of the perfect competition market structure?
    a. equally good information for both buyers and sellers
    b. homogeneous product
    c. large number of buyers and sellers
    d. restricted entry and exit

2. The demand curve facing the perfect competitor is
    a. perfectly elastic.
    b. vertical at the going price.
    c. perfectly inelastic.
    d. negatively sloped.

3. In the perfect competition model,
    a. each seller is a price taker.
    b. all firms together can affect price.
    c. all firms produce a homogeneous product.
    d. All of the above.

4. We assume the firm wants to maximize _____ profits.
   a. marginal
   b. average
   c. total
   d. fixed

5. The firm maximizes total profits at that output at which
   a. $MC = MR$.
   b. $MC > MR$.
   c. $P = AC$.
   d. $AR = AC$.

6. In which one of these cases are economic profits necessarily negative?
   a. Total revenues exceed total costs.
   b. Marginal revenue exceeds average cost.
   c. Price is below minimum average total cost.
   d. Marginal revenue is equal to price.

7. The perfect competitor
   a. can sell all it wants to sell at the going price.
   b. can sell nothing at a price higher than the going price.
   c. faces a perfectly elastic demand curve.
   d. All of the above.

8. The perfectly competitive firm's short-run total profits equal
   a. price minus average cost times quantity sold.
   b. price minus average cost.
   c. price minus marginal cost.
   d. price minus average variable cost.

9. If selling price equals the firm's minimum average variable cost, then
   a. that is the firm's shutdown point.
   b. economic profits are negative.
   c. the firm is indifferent between producing and shutting down.
   d. All of the above.

10. At the short-run break-even price,
    a. accounting profits equal economic profits.
    b. economic profits are negative.
    c. economic profits are zero.
    d. economic profits are positive.

11. The firm's short-run supply curve is its
    a. marginal cost curve above the shutdown point.
    b. average cost curve above its minimum point.
    c. average variable cost curve above the shutdown point.
    d. marginal revenue curve.

12. The industry supply curve is derived by summing horizontally all the firms'
    a. marginal cost curves above their shutdown points.
    b. average total cost curves.
    c. total revenue curves.
    d. marginal revenue curves.

13. Which one of the following will **not** shift the industry supply curve?
    a. change in price
    b. change in the cost of raw materials
    c. change in number of firms in the industry
    d. change in wage rates

14. If economic profits are negative in an industry, then
    a. firms will enter that industry.
    b. some firms will exit from that industry.
    c. price is above minimum average total costs.
    d. accounting profits must also be negative.

15. In long-run equilibrium, a perfectly competitive firm
    a. earns zero economic profits.
    b. produces at minimum average cost.
    c. produces where price equals marginal cost.
    d. All of the above.

16. If demand falls in an increasing-cost industry, then in the long run
    a. price will fall.
    b. price will return to its previous level.
    c. output will rise.
    d. output will return to its previous level.

17. In a decreasing-cost industry, the long-run industry supply curve is
    a. downward sloping.
    b. upward sloping.
    c. horizontal.
    d. perpendicular.

18. The marginal cost of producing good A
    a. includes fixed costs.
    b. represents the opportunity cost to society of producing one more unit of good A.
    c. is found by reading the average variable cost curve.
    d. includes only labor costs.

■ Matching

Choose the item in Column (2) that best matches an item in Column (1).

(1)	**(2)**
(a) long-run equilibrium	(h) horizontal long-run industry supply curve (given input prices)
(b) constant returns to scale	
(c) price taker	(i) perfectly competitive firm
(d) decreasing-cost industry	(j) zero economic profits
(e) short-run shutdown price	(k) marginal cost curve above shutdown point
(f) short-run supply curve	(l) falling long-run industry supply curve
(g) profit maximizing output	(m) $P = $ minimum AVC
	(n) $MR = MC$

■ Working with Graphs

1. Use the graph below to answer the following questions. Assume that the firm is a profit maximizer operating in a perfectly competitive market.
    a. How many units of output will the firm produce and sell?
    b. What is *TR* at this level of output?
    c. What is the *ATC* at this level of output?
    d. What is the *TFC* at this level of output?
    e. What is the *AVC* at this level of output?
    f. What is *TC* at this level of output?
    g. What is the total profit or loss at this level of output?

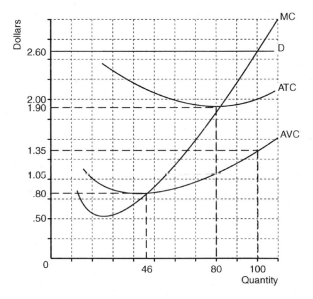

2.   Use the graph below to answer the questions that follow.

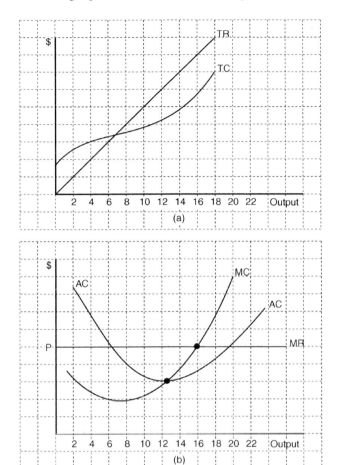

a.   The total revenue curve is linear. Therefore, the slope of the total revenue curve is a
     _____. This slope equals what economic concept?
b.   The slope of a tangent to a point on the *TC* curve is defined as what?
c.   The firm tries to (<u>minimize, maximize</u>) _____ the positive difference between *TR* and
     TC. At what output level does that occur?
d.   In Panel (b), what is the firm's profit-maximizing output? Why?
e.   How are your answers to parts (c) and (d) related?

■ Problems

1. Suppose you are hired as an economic consultant for Profmax Consulting Company. Your job is to advise the company's clients on the appropriate action to take in the short run in order to maximize the profits (or minimize the losses) of each firm. The firms you are to analyze produce indistinguishable products, and each operates independently in a different perfectly competitive market. You may assume that each is currently operating at an output level where marginal cost is increasing. Fill in the missing information, and make your suggestions about the appropriate action for each firm by placing one of the following symbols in the last row of the table of information that follows.

> C = currently operating at the correct level of output
>
> I = increase the level of output
>
> D = decrease the level of output
>
> SD = shut down the plant

Firm	A	B	C	D	E	F	G
Price	$0.50	___	$3.50	___	$3.00	$5.00	___
Output	___	300	750	700	___	___	1,000
TR	$500	$300	___	$2,800	$1,800	$4,000	$5,000
TC	___	$525	$2,625	$2,975	___	___	___
TFC	___	___	___	___	$180	$1,200	___
TVC	$300	___	___	$2,450	___	___	$3,000
ATC	$0.40	___	Minimum	___	___	$5.50	$5.50
AVC	___	$1.20	$3.00	___	$2.00	Minimum	___
MC	$0.40	$1.00	___	$4.00	$3.50	___	$5.75
Suggestion	___	___	___	___	___	___	___

■ Answers

Completion Questions

1. large number of buyers and sellers; homogeneous product; equally good information for both buyers and sellers; unimpeded entry or exit
2. perfectly
3. maximize total profits; *MC*; total revenues; total costs
4. change in total revenue; change in output
5. economic
6. shut down; breaking even; zero
7. will
8. *MC*; summing horizontally
9. enter; exit
10. constant; increasing; upward; decreasing; downward
11. zero; equal to; will; efficient

True-False Questions

1. T
2. F   Price is a constant to an *individual* firm but not to the group of firms.
3. T
4. F   Firms attempt to maximize *total* profits.
5. T
6. F   It equals average profits.
7. T
8. T
9. F   The firm's marginal cost curve above minimum *AVC* is its short-run supply curve.
10. T
11. T
12. F   Long-run *economic* profits must be zero.
13. F   It is horizontal.
14. F   Price will rise.
15. T
16. F   It is efficient because $P = MC$ and economic profits = 0 in the long run.

Multiple Choice Questions

1. (d)	10. (c)
2. (a)	11. (a)
3. (d)	12. (a)
4. (c)	13. (a)
5. (a)	14. (b)
6. (c)	15. (d)
7. (d)	16. (a)
8. (a)	17. (a)
9. (d)	18. (b)

Matching

(a) and (j)	(e) and (m)
(b) and (h)	(f) and (k)
(c) and (i)	(g) and (n)
(d) and (l)	

Working with Graphs

1. a. 100
   b. $260
   c. $2
   d. $65
   e. $1.35
   f. $200
   g. $60 profit

2. a. constant; MR (or P)
   b. MC
   c. maximize; 16 units of output
   d. 16 units of output; because $MC = MR$ at that output level
   e. $MC = MR$ at 16 units of output

Problems

1.

Firm	A	B	C	D	E	F	G
Price	$0.50	$1.00	$3.50	$4.00	$3.00	$5.00	$5.00
Output	1,000	300	750	700	600	800	1,000
TR	$500	$300	$2,625	$2,800	$1,800	$4,000	$5,000
TC	$400	$525	$2,625	$2,975	$1,380	$4,400	$5,500
TFC	$100	$165	$375	$525	$180	$1,200	$2,500
TVC	$300	$360	$2,250	$2,450	$1,200	$3,200	$3,000
ATC	$0.40	$1.75	Minimum	$4.25	$2.30	$5.50	$5.50
AVC	$0.30	$1.20	$3.00	$3.50	$2.00	Minimum	$3.00
MC	$0.40	$1.00	$3.50	$4.00	$3.50	$4.00	$5.75
Suggestion	I	SD	C	C	D	I	D

■ Glossary

Constant-cost industry   An industry whose total output can be increased without an increase in long-run per-unit costs. Its long-run supply curve is horizontal.

Decreasing-cost industry   An industry in which an increase in output leads to a reduction in long-run per-unit costs, such that the long-run industry supply curve slopes downward.

Increasing-cost industry   An industry in which an increase in industry output is accompanied by an increase in long-run per-unit costs, such that the long-run industry supply curve slopes upward.

Industry supply curve   The locus of points showing the minimum prices at which given quantities will be forthcoming; also called the *market supply curve*.

Long-run industry supply curve   A market supply curve showing the relationship between prices and quantities after firms have been allowed the time to enter into or exit from an industry, depending on whether there have been positive or negative economic profits.

Marginal cost pricing   A system of pricing in which the price charged is equal to the opportunity cost to society of producing one more unit of the good or service in question. The opportunity cost is the marginal cost to society.

Marginal revenue   The change in total revenues resulting from a one-unit change in output (and sale) of the product in question.

Market failure   A situation in which an unrestrained market operation leads to either too few or too many resources going to a specific economic activity.

Perfect competition   A market structure in which the decisions of *individual* buyers and sellers have no effect on market price.

Perfectly competitive firm   A firm that is such a small part of the total *industry* that it cannot affect the price of the product it sells.

Price taker   A perfectly competitive firm that must take the price of its product as given because the firm cannot influence its price.

Profit-maximizing rate of production   The rate of production that maximizes total profits, or the difference between total revenues and total costs. Also, it is the rate of production at which marginal revenue equals marginal cost.

Short-run break-even price   The price at which a firm's total revenues equal its total costs. At the break-even price, the firm is just making a normal rate of return on its capital investment. (It is covering its explicit and implicit costs.)

Short-run shutdown price   The price that covers average variable costs. It occurs just below the intersection of the marginal cost curve and the average variable cost curve.

Signals   Compact ways of indicating to economic decision makers information needed to make decisions. An effective signal not only conveys information but also provides the incentive to react appropriately. Economic profits and economic losses are such signals.

Total revenues   The price per unit times the total quantity sold.

24 Monopoly

■ Learning Objectives

After you have studied this chapter, you should be able to

1. define monopolist, natural monopoly, price discrimination, price differentiation, price searcher, and tariffs;

2. list the characteristics of a monopoly and distinguish them from the characteristics of the perfectly competitive firm;

3. distinguish between the monopolist's demand curve and the perfect competitor's demand curve;

4. determine the profit-maximizing output for the monopolist, given sufficient information, and determine the price that a monopolist would charge, given the profit-maximizing output;

5. list possible barriers to entry into an industry;

6. calculate a monopolist's total profits, given sufficient information;

7. recognize some misconceptions concerning monopoly;

8. distinguish between price discrimination and price differentiation, and list the conditions necessary for price discrimination; and

9. list and recognize two costs to society of monopolies.

■ Outline

1. A monopolist is a single supplier that constitutes an entire industry. The monopolist produces a good for which there are no close substitutes.

2. Barriers to entry are impediments that prevent new firms from entering an industry. There are numerous potential barriers to entry.
   a. Some monopolists gain power through the exclusive ownership of a raw material that is essential to produce a good.
   b. Licenses, franchises, and certificates of convenience also constitute potential barriers to entry.

c. Patents issued to inventors constitute, for a time, effective barriers to entry.

d. If economies of scale are great relative to market demand, new entrants into an industry will be discouraged. Persistent economies of scale could lead to a natural monopoly.

e. Governmental safety and quality regulations may raise fixed costs to firms in an industry significantly enough so as to deter new entrants.

f. If tariffs on imports are sufficiently high, then producers can gain some measure of monopoly power.

3. The monopolist faces the industry demand curve because the monopolist is the entire industry. Examples of monopolies include local electric power companies and the post office.

4. It is instructive to compare the monopolist with the perfect competitor.

a. The perfect competitor's demand curve is perfectly elastic at the "going" price.

b. The monopolist's demand curve is negatively sloped. Price falls, and therefore, marginal revenue is less than price because the monopolist must lower its price on all the units it sells and not just on the marginal unit.

5. Where marginal revenue equals zero, total revenue is maximized; at the point on the demand curve corresponding to zero marginal revenue, the price elasticity of demand equals 1. At higher prices (lower outputs) demand is elastic, and at lower prices (higher outputs) demand is inelastic.

6. By assuming that the monopolist wants to maximize total profits and that the short-run cost curves are similar in shape to those of the perfect competitor, we can determine the monopolist's optimal output-price combination.

a. The monopolist's total revenue curve is nonlinear (unlike the perfect competitor's). Profit-maximizing output is reached at a rate at which the positive difference between total costs and total revenues is maximized.

b. Stated differently, optimal output exists where $MR = MC$.

c. If $MR > MC$, the firm can increase total profits by increasing output. If $MC > MR$, then the firm can increase total profits by reducing output.

d. Once the profit-maximizing output is determined, the monopolist's price is already determined. The price is determined on the demand curve at that quantity.

7. Graphically, total profits are calculated by subtracting average costs from price and multiplying that value by the quantity produced.

8. If its average cost curve lies entirely above its demand curve, the monopolist will experience economic losses.

9. If the monopolist can prevent the resale of its homogeneous output and if it can separate its customers into different markets with different price elasticities, then it can price discriminate—and earn higher profits.

10. Monopolies are inefficient because they charge a price that is too high ($P > MC$) and because they produce an output that is too low.

■ Key Terms

Monopolist   Price discrimination

Price differentiation   Tariffs

■ Key Concepts

Natural monopoly   Price searcher

■ Completion Questions

Fill in the blank, or circle the correct term.

1. A monopolist is a(n) _____ supplier that constitutes the entire industry. The monopolist's demand curve is _____ sloped.

2. Before a monopolist can earn long-run monopoly profits, there must be _____ to entry.

3. Examples of barriers to entry include _____, _____, _____, _____, _____, and _____.

4. Because the perfect competitor's demand curve is perfectly elastic, its selling price is constant. Therefore, the perfect competitor's per-unit revenue (<u>falls, rises, remains constant</u>) and its marginal revenue (<u>falls, rises, remains constant</u>).

5. Because the monopolist's demand curve is negatively sloped, its selling price falls with output. Therefore, the monopolist's per-unit revenue (<u>falls, rises, remains constant</u>), and its marginal revenue (<u>falls, rises, remains constant</u>).

6. If a monopolist must charge the same price to everyone, when it produces more, its marginal revenue will be (<u>less than, greater than, equal to</u>) its price.

7. When marginal revenue equals zero, total revenue is (<u>minimized, maximized</u>). At that point on the demand curve, the price elasticity of demand equals the number _____. At a higher price, total revenues would fall, and therefore, demand would be (<u>elastic, inelastic</u>). At a lower price, total revenues would fall, and therefore, demand would be _____.

8. One misconception about monopoly is that the monopolist can sell any quantity that it chooses to at any _____. Instead, the monopolist can sell any specific quantity at only one price. Another misconception is that a monopolist must earn economic profits. The monopolist will not if the _____ curve is above the monopolist's demand curve.

9. The monopolist maximizes total profits at that output for which _____ equals _____. Given its profit-maximizing output, the monopolist (<u>need not, must</u>) charge a price consistent with that quantity.

10. If a monopolist need not charge the same price to everyone, then it can _____, and its profits will rise. A monopolist can charge different prices to different groups if it can prevent the _____ of its product.

11. A monopolist charges a price that is too _____, and it produces an output that is too _____. Therefore, monopoly is (<u>less, more</u>) socially efficient than perfect competition.

■ True-False Questions

Circle the **T** if the statement is true, the **F** if it is false. Explain to yourself why a statement is false.

T F   1. The more broadly we define an industry, the less likely it is to be a monopoly.

T F   2. Because of barriers to entry, a monopolist must earn long-run profits.

T F   3. The monopolist's marginal revenue curve lies below its demand curve.

T F   4. A monopolist must charge the same price to all buyers.

T F   5. The monopolist's total revenue curve is linear.

T F   6. At that output for which total revenue is maximized, price elasticity of demand equals 1.

T F   7. The profit-maximizing monopolist will never produce on the inelastic portion of its demand curve.

T F   8. Total profits are maximized where total revenue equals total costs.

T F   9. If *MR* > *MC*, the firm can increase profits if it produces less.

T F   10. A monopolist can select only one profit-maximizing price, given the output it chooses to produce, assuming no price discrimination.

T F   11. If possible, a monopolist will charge a higher price to a price inelastic group than to a price elastic group.

T F   12. A monopolist tends to produce too little and to sell at a price that is too high.

T F   13. A monopolist is a price taker.

T F   14. Because there are no close substitutes for a monopolist's output, its demand curve is inelastic throughout.

■ Multiple Choice Questions

Circle the letter that corresponds to the best answer.

1. Which one of the following is **not** a characteristic of the monopoly market structure?
    a. one seller
    b. homogeneous product
    c. restricted entry
    d. price taker

2. Which one of the following is a potential barrier to entry?
    a. government license requirement
    b. sole ownership of a key resource
    c. great economies of scale, relative to demand
    d. All of the above.

3. Which one of the following is **not** true about monopolies?
    a. linear total revenue curve
    b. may earn long-run economic profits
    c. negatively sloped demand curve
    d. marginal revenue below price

4. The firm maximizes total profits at that output at which
    a. total revenue equals total cost.
    b. marginal revenue equals marginal cost.
    c. the elasticity of demand equals 1.
    d. All of the above.

5. Once a monopolist produces a profit-maximizing output,
    a. the price is determined for it, given its demand curve.
    b. it can select any price it wants.
    c. its competitors select price.
    d. price cannot be determined.

6. If $MR < MC$, then the firm
    a. is maximizing total profits.
    b. can increase total profits by producing more.
    c. can increase total profits by producing less.
    d. is maximizing total revenues.

7. Monopoly profit
   a. equals (price – average cost) times quantity sold.
   b. equals price times quantity sold.
   c. exists only in the short run.
   d. exists because no entry barriers exist.

8. A monopolist will price discriminate if
   a. price differentiation exists.
   b. it can separate markets by different price elasticities of demand and prevent resales.
   c. it chooses to maximize marginal revenue.
   d. all buyers have the same price elasticity of demand.

9. Which one of the following is an example of price differentiation?
   a. Students pay a higher rental price for apartments than do nonstudents because they cause more damage.
   b. Women pay higher prices for haircuts because it takes longer to cut their hair.
   c. People in ghetto areas pay higher prices for individual items because costs are greater in such areas.
   d. All of the above.

10. Assume that at a given output a monopolist's marginal revenue is $10 per unit and its marginal cost is $5. If the monopolist increases output, then
    a. price, marginal cost, and total profit will fall.
    b. price will fall, marginal cost will rise, and total profit will rise.
    c. price will rise, marginal cost will fall, and total profit will rise.
    d. price, marginal cost, and total profit will rise.

■ Matching

Choose the item in Column (2) that best matches an item in Column (1).

(1)		(2)	
(a)	perfect competitor	(g)	nonlinear total revenue curve
(b)	monopolist	(h)	firm with a downward-sloping demand curve
(c)	price differentiation	(i)	great economies of scale
(d)	price discrimination	(j)	price taker
(e)	barrier to entry	(k)	students pay higher rents for apartments than do nonstudents who damage them less
(f)	price searcher	(l)	students pay different tuition costs depending on need

■ Working with Graphs

1. Suppose you are given the demand schedule for a monopolist and the total cost figures below. Plot the monopolist's demand curve, marginal revenue curve, and marginal cost curve on the graph provided. Determine the optimal level of output for the monopolist. What do total profits equal? (Plot *MC* and *MR* on the midpoints.)

Output per Unit of Time	Price	Total Cost
0	$32	$12
1	28	20
2	24	25
3	20	31
4	16	41
5	12	56
6	8	79
7	4	117

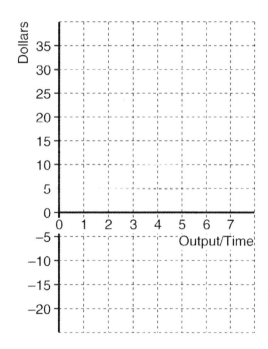

2.   Suppose you are given the graphical summary of a monopolist below. Answer the following questions using this information.

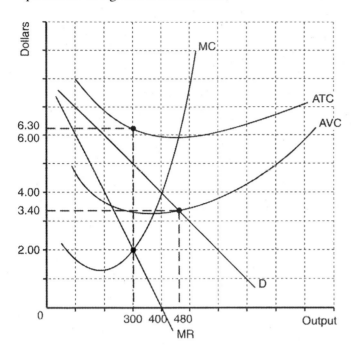

a.   The optimal short-term output level for the monopolist is _____.

b.   At the optimal level of output, marginal cost is _____.

c.   At the optimal level of output, total cost is _____.

d.   At the optimal level of output, price is _____ and total revenue is _____.

e.   The monopolist is earning a (<u>profit, loss</u>) of _____ in the given situation.

f.   Suppose that the above graph represented a perfectly competitive industry and the demand curve given was the market demand curve for the entire industry. The competitive level of output would be _____, sold at a price of _____.

g.   The average total cost per unit of output in the competitive case would fall by _____, as compared with the average total cost under a monopoly.

■ Problems

1. Indicate whether the following may characterize the perfect competitor (PC), the monopolist (M), or both (B).

        _____   (a) perfectly elastic demand curve
        _____   (b) increasing marginal cost curve
        _____   (c) downward-sloping demand curve
        _____   (d) linear total revenue curve
        _____   (e) total profit maximizer
        _____   (f) possibility of earning long-run economic profits
        _____   (g) $P > MR$
        _____   (h) homogeneous output
        _____   (i) price discriminator
        _____   (j) barriers to entry
        _____   (k) free exit and entry
        _____   (l) price searcher
        _____   (m) price taker
        _____   (n) produces where $MR = MC$
        _____   (o) $P = MC$ in equilibrium
        _____   (p) long-run equilibrium at minimum AC
        _____   (q) $P = MR$
        _____   (r) $P = AR$

■ Answers

Completion Questions

1. single; negatively
2. barriers
3. ownership of resources without close substitutes; legally required licenses, franchises, or certificates of convenience; patents; economies of scale; safety and quality regulations; high tariffs
4. remains constant; remains constant
5. falls; falls
6. less than
7. maximized; 1; elastic; inelastic
8. price; average total cost
9. *MR*; *MC*; must
10. price discriminate; resale
11. high; low; less

True-False Questions

1. T
2. F   An inefficient monopolist need not earn economic profits.
3. T
4. F   A monopolist can price discriminate under certain conditions.
5. F   It is not linear because price falls as the monopolist produces more.
6. T
7. T
8. F   Profit maximization occurs where $MR = MC$. If $TR = TC$, then economic profits are zero.
9. F   If $MR > MC$, profits will rise if the firm produces more.
10. T
11. T
12. T
13. F   A monopolist is a price searcher.
14. F   A monopolist's demand curve has various ranges of elasticity.

Multiple Choice Questions

1. (d)
2. (d)
3. (a)
4. (b)
5. (a)
6. (c)
7. (a)
8. (b)
9. (d)
10. (b)

Matching

(a) and (j)
(b) and (g)
(c) and (k)
(d) and (l)
(e) and (i)
(f) and (h)

Working with Graphs

1.

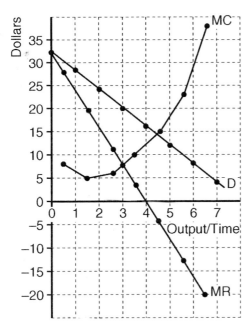

The profit-maximizing level of output is 3 units sold at a price of $20 each. This can be seen graphically. Total profits equal $29 at that output.

2. a. 300
    b. $2
    c. $1,890
    d. $5, $1,500
    e. loss, $390
    f. 400, $4
    g. $0.30

Problems

1. a. PC
    b. B
    c. M
    d. PC
    e. B
    f. M
    g. M
    h. B
    i. M

    j. M
    k. PC
    l. M
    m. PC
    n. B
    o. PC
    p. PC
    q. PC
    r. B

■ Glossary

Monopolist   The single supplier of a good or service for which there is no close substitute. The monopolist therefore constitutes its entire industry.

Natural monopoly   A monopoly that arises from the peculiar production characteristics in an industry. It usually arises when there are large economies of scale relative to the industry's demand such that one firm can produce at a lower average cost than can be achieved by multiple firms.

Price differentiation   Establishing different prices for similar products to reflect only differences in marginal cost in providing those commodities to different groups of buyers.

Price discrimination   Selling a given product at more than one price, with the price difference being unrelated to differences in marginal cost.

Price searcher   A firm that must determine the price-output combination that maximizes profit because it faces a downward-sloping demand curve.

Tariffs   Taxes on imported goods.

# 25 Monopolistic Competition

■ Learning Objectives

After you have studied this chapter, you should be able to

1. list the characteristics of the monopolistic competition market structure;

2. distinguish between the monopolistic competitor's demand curve and the perfect competitor's demand curve;

3. explain the profit-maximizing behavior of a monopolistically competitive firm;

4. discuss why brand names and trademarks are important to monopolistically competitive firms and describe different methods of and forms of advertising;

5. identify the key characteristics of information products;

6. describe the shapes of the short-run cost curves of a firm that sells information products and explain the concept of short-run economies of operation for producers of information products; and

7. explain why firms that sell information products charge prices above marginal cost.

■ Outline

1. There are four characteristics of the theory of *monopolistic competition*, which was developed simultaneously by Edward Chamberlin and Joan Robinson in 1933.
   a. A significant number of sellers in a highly competitive market
   b. Differentiated products
   c. Sales promotion and advertising
   d. Easy entry of new firms in the long run

2. Although there are many sellers in a monopolistically competitive industry, there are not as many as there are in the perfect competition model. Each monopolistic competitor has a little control over its price, but collusion is difficult and each firm acts independently of the others.

3. Perhaps the most important feature of a monopolistically competitive industry is *product differentiation.*

    a. Differentiation refers to differences in physical characteristics.

    b. Each separate differentiated product has close substitutes.

4. It is possible to predict the optimal price–output combination of the monopolistic competitor.

    a. The monopolistic competitor's demand curve is downward sloping. Thus, its marginal revenue curve lies below its demand curve.

    b. Short-run equilibrium exists where $MR = MC$. Economic profits or losses are possible in the short run.

    c. In the long run, because of free entry, the monopolistic competitor must earn exactly zero economic profits. Nevertheless, social inefficiency exists in the long run because the price of its product exceeds marginal cost, and its rate of output lies to the left of the minimum point on the *ATC* curve.

5. Because product differentiation is such an important aspect of monopolistically competitive industries, firms in these industries promote brand names via advertising.

    a. Firms can register trademarks—words, symbols, and logos—with the U.S. Patent and Trademark Office, and they can seek legal damages if anyone makes false use of trademarks and thereby damages the image of the firm's brand names.

    b. To promote their product brands, firms use three basic advertising methods: direct marketing, mass marketing, and interactive marketing.

    c. Search goods, which are items with qualities that can be assessed in advance of their purchase, are best marketed via informational advertising that acquaints consumers with their features. Experience goods, which are items with qualities that can only be assessed following their purchase, are best marketed via persuasive advertising that induces consumers to discover previously unknown tastes for those items. Credence goods are items with qualities that consumers lack the expertise to assess without assistance.

6. Information products are goods produced using information-intensive inputs at a relatively high fixed cost but distributed for sale at a relatively low marginal cost.

    a. Because fixed costs are relatively high, the average fixed cost of producing the first copy of an information product is significant. Average fixed cost declines as the firm increases its sale of additional units.

    b. The per-unit cost of distributing additional copies of an information product is the same, relatively low amount no matter how many units are sold. Thus, marginal cost and average variable cost are equal to the same constant per-unit cost.

    c. The average total cost curve for a firm that makes and sells an information product is the sum of the downward-sloping average fixed cost curve and the constant per-unit average variable cost, so the average total cost curve for the firm that produces an information product slopes downward. Hence, the firm experiences short-run economies of operation.

    d. If the price of an information product were equal to marginal cost, and hence average variable cost, the firm would only earn sufficient revenues to cover its variable costs but not its fixed costs.

e. In a long-run monopolistically competitive equilibrium, a firm that produces an information product just earns sufficient revenues to cover its total costs, thereby earning zero economic profits, when its price equals average total costs.

■ Key Terms

Credence good	Monopolistic competition
Experience good	Search good
Information product	Short-run economies of operation

■ Key Concepts

Direct marketing	Interactive marketing	Persuasive advertising
Informational advertising	Mass marketing	Product differentiation

■ Completion Questions

Fill in the blank or circle the correct term.

1. The four characteristics of monopolistic competition are _____,
   _____, _____,
   and _____.

2. Under monopolistic competition, collusion is (easy, difficult). Each firm (must, need not) take into account the reactions of rivals, and each firm has (a little, much, no) control over its selling price.

3. The demand curve for the monopolistic competitor is _____ sloped. Consequently, the monopolistic competitor's marginal revenue curve is (below, above) its demand, or *AR* curve.

4. In the short run, a profit-maximizing monopolistically competitive firm produces to the point at which (price, marginal revenue) equals (marginal cost, average total cost).

5. In a long-run monopolistically competitive equilibrium, the price of a firm's product must be (less than, greater than, equal to) marginal cost. Thus, social (inefficiency, efficiency) exists in the monopolistic competition market structure.

6. In a long-run monopolistically competitive equilibrium, the price of a firm's product is (less than, equal to, greater than) the average total cost of producing its actual output level, but the price is (less then, equal to, greater than) the minimum feasible average total cost of producing the product.

7. Brand names and trademarks have value for firms in monopolistically competitive industries because these are important factors affecting the (<u>demand for, supply of</u>) products that are (<u>homogeneous, differentiated</u>) among the firms in this industry.

8. The main methods of advertising are _____ marketing, _____ marketing, and _____ marketing.

9. An item possessing qualities that are relatively easy for consumers to evaluate in advance of purchasing the item is _____ good. An item with qualities that are relatively difficult for consumers to evaluate in advance of purchasing the item is _____ good. An item with qualities that consumers lack the expertise to assess without assistance is _____ good.

10. Advertising that focuses on explaining the features of a product is _____ _____ advertising that is more likely to be used by a firm seeking to market (<u>a search, an experience</u>) good.

11. Advertising that is intended to induce a consumer to discover previously unknown tastes for an item is _____ advertising that is more likely to be used by a firm seeking to market (<u>a search, an experience</u>) good.

12. For the producer of an information product, in the short run a relatively low average _____ cost of producing the item is equal to marginal cost at any given amount of output, and the average _____ cost curve slopes downward over its entire range.

13. If the producer of an information product were required to set the price of the item equal to marginal cost, then price would equal average (<u>fixed, variable</u>) cost at any given amount of output, so that total revenues would exactly equal (<u>total fixed, total variable</u>) costs; this means that the firm would not earn sufficient total revenues to cover any of its (<u>total fixed, total variable</u>) costs, so it would earn (<u>zero, negative</u>) economic profits.

14. If the producer of an information product sets the price of the item equal to average total cost, then total revenues would exactly equal _____ costs, and the firm would earn _____ economic profits.

■ True-False Questions

Circle the **T** if the statement is true, the **F** if it is false. Explain to yourself why a statement is false.

T F   1. The monopolistic competitor has a negatively sloped demand curve.

T F   2. The monopolistic competitor must take into account the reactions of its competitors.

T F   3. The most important feature of the monopolistically competitive market is product differentiation.

T F   4. Product differentiation exists in the wheat industry.

T F   5. One important goal of advertising is to convey quality information.

T F   6. The monopolistic competition model leads to social efficiency because in the long run $P = MC$.

T F   7. A firm that produces a search good is likely to market the item using exclusively persuasive advertising.

T F   8. Based on the advertising expenses of U.S. firms, the most used advertising method is direct marketing.

T F   9. Informational advertising focuses on enlightening consumers about the features of a product.

T F 10. A problem with heavy spending on advertising is that it can signal that a firm is mismanaged and consequently may be exiting the market in the near future.

T F 11. The production of information products entails incurring relatively low fixed costs and relatively high marginal costs.

T F 12. The reason why a firm that sells an information product experiences short-run economies of operation is that the average total cost curves slopes downward over its entire range.

T F 13. If the price of an information product is equal to marginal cost, then the firm producing this item fails to earn sufficient revenues to cover fixed costs.

T F 14. The price of an information product exceeds average total cost in a long-run monopolistically competitive equilibrium.

■ Multiple Choice Questions

Circle the letter that corresponds to the best answer.

1. Which one is **not** a characteristic of monopolistic competition?
    a. Each firm must take into account its rivals' reactions to price changes.
    b. There are a significant number of sellers.
    c. There are differentiated products.
    d. Advertising is prevalent.

2. Which one of the following is an important characteristic of monopolistic competition?
    a. It is difficult to enter the industry.
    b. It is easy for firms to establish collusive agreements.
    c. Each firm has very small shares of total market production and sales.
    d. Firms are all interdependent, so decisions made by each firm affect choices of others.

3. Because each separate differentiated product sold by a monopolistically competitive firm has numerous similar substitutes, we can say for certain that the demand for each individual firm's product is relatively

   a. low, so that no one firm can sell more than a few units of its output.
   b. high, so that in principle any given firm can sell the most output in the market.
   c. elastic, as compared with the demand for the product of a monopoly producer.
   d. inelastic, as compared with the demand for the product of a monopoly producer.

4. As is also true in a perfectly competitive industry, in a monopolistically competitive industry,

   a. in the long run firms can easily enter the market in response to positive economic profits.
   b. in the short run the demand curve for each firm's product slopes downward.
   c. in the long run the price of each firm's output equals marginal cost.
   d. in the short run firms always earn positive economic profits.

5. As is also true of a monopoly, in a monopolistically competitive industry,

   a. in the long run more firms cannot enter the market in response to positive economic profits.
   b. in the short run each firm's marginal revenue declines as it increases its production and sales.
   c. in the short run the price of each firm's product is always less than marginal cost.
   d. in the long run the price of each firm's product equals average total cost.

6. For the monopolistic competitor, in the long run

   a. economic profits can be positive.
   b. output is too high, from society's point of view.
   c. the demand curve must be tangent to the *ATC* curve.
   d. output is produced to the right of the minimum *ATC* point.

7. The U.S. Patent and Trademark Office

   a. registers trademarks, which gives an owner the right to seek legal relief in the event it can prove misuse of the brand name by another party.
   b. acts as both judge and jury for determining whether a company has misused another firm's brand name and assessing fines on offending firms.
   c. creates all company trademarks, thereby determining the names of the brands that companies market to consumers via advertising.
   d. has its own police force, which seeks evidence of unauthorized uses of firms' brand names or false information about brands.

8. Advertising

   a. attempts to increase the demand for a firm's product.
   b. can provide more information to buyers.
   c. helps to differentiate a firm's product.
   d. All of the above.

9. Persuasive advertising is
    a. most appropriate for search goods.
    b. aimed toward reducing the degree of product differentiation.
    c. designed to provide information about the main features of a good or service.
    d. intended to acquaint consumers with a taste or preference previously unknown to them.

10. Experience goods
    a. have qualities consumers can assess before purchase.
    b. must be consumed for buyers to evaluate their qualities.
    c. are most successfully marketed by way of informational advertising.
    d. are homogeneous items sold only in perfectly competitive industries.

11. In the United States, firms spend the majority of their advertising dollars on
    a. interactive marketing.
    b. direct marketing.
    c. mass marketing.
    d. None of the above.

12. For a firm that sells an information product, which one of the following pairs of cost curves *both* slope downward in the short run?
    a. *AFC* and *ATC*
    b. *AVC* and *ATC*
    c. *MC* and *AVC*
    d. *MC* and *ATC*

13. For a firm that sells an information product, which of the following costs are identical, constant, and relatively small over all ranges of output in the short run?
    a. *AFC* and *ATC*
    b. *AVC* and *ATC*
    c. *MC* and *AVC*
    d. *MC* and *ATC*

14. The term short-run economies of operation refers to decreasing
    a. marginal cost as more units of an information product are sold.
    b. average total cost as more units of an information product are sold.
    c. average fixed cost as more units of an information product are sold.
    d. marginal cost above the minimum point of the *AVC* curve for an information product.

15. If the producer of an information product faces a strictly enforced legal requirement that any units of output it produces and sells must be offered at a price equal to marginal cost, then
    a. the firm's desired output will be at the minimum point of the average total cost curve.
    b. the firm will earn positive economic profits.
    c. the firm's desired output will be zero units.
    d. the firm will earn zero economic profits.

16. In a long-run equilibrium for a profit-maximizing, monopolistically competitive producer of an information product,
    a. the firm's desired output will be at the minimum point of the average total cost curve.
    b. the firm will earn positive economic profits.
    c. the firm's desired output will be zero units.
    d. the firm will earn zero economic profits.

17. If a firm that manufactures and sells an information product sets the price of the product equal to marginal cost, it will earn
    a. total revenues equal to its total costs.
    b. an economic loss equal to its fixed costs.
    c. an economic loss equal to its variable costs.
    d. total revenues equal to its total fixed costs

18. In the short run, a monopolistically competitive firm that manufactures and sells an information product maximizes its economic profits by producing to the point at which
    a. price equals marginal cost.
    b. price equals average total cost.
    c. price equals average variable cost.
    d. marginal revenue equals marginal cost.

■ Matching

Choose the item in Column (2) that best matches an item in Column (1).

(1)	(2)
(a) monopolistic competition	(g) direct marketing
(b) search good	(h) informational advertising
(c) information product	(i) persuasive advertising
(d) TV and radio advertisements	(j) product differentiation
(e) mail advertisements	(k) short-run economies of operation
(f) experience good	(l) mass marketing

■ Working with Graphs

1.   Use the graph of a monopolistic competitor below to answer each of the following questions.

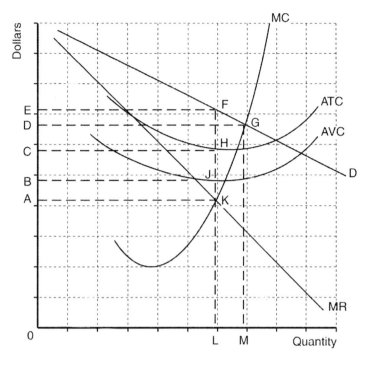

a.   At what level of output will this firm operate? _____

b.   What is marginal revenue at this level of output? _____

c.   What price will this firm charge for its product? _____

d.   The area of what rectangle is equal to total revenue? _____

e.   What is the firm's average cost in equilibrium? _____

f.   The area of what rectangle is equal to the firm's total cost? _____

g.   Is the firm making profits or incurring losses? _____

h.   The area of what rectangle is equal to profits or losses? _____

2.   Use the graphs below to answer the questions that follow.

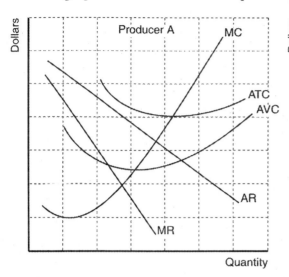

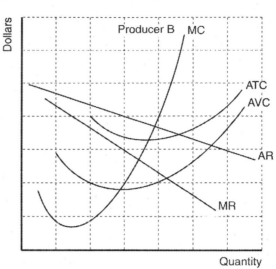

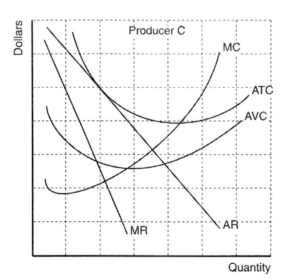

a.   Which of the producers is a monopolistic competitor making positive economic profits?

_____

b.   Which of the producers appears to be in an industry that may have reached a long-run equilibrium? _____

c.   Which of the producers is most likely to leave the industry in which it is currently operating? _____

d.   Which of the producers is in an industry that is most likely to attract additional firms?

_____

e.   If all the firms in Producer C's industry are currently in a similar situation, what will most likely happen if there is a decrease in demand for the products of that industry?

_____

f.   Which producer(s) is/are incurring short-run losses? _____

■ Problems

1. Let PC = perfect competition, M = monopoly, and MC = monopolistic competition. Indicate by writing down the appropriate initials which of the following may be consistent with one, several, or all of those markets.

   _____   (a) profit maximizer

   _____   (b) advertising

   _____   (c) long-run economic profits

   _____   (d) social inefficiency

   _____   (e) $P > MC$ in equilibrium

   _____   (f) product differentiation

   _____   (g) large economies of scale relative to market demand

   _____   (h) long-run equilibrium at minimum ATC

   _____   (i) short-run economic profits

   _____   (j) easy entry

   _____   (k) ability to set price

■ Answers

Completion Questions

1. significant number of sellers; differentiated product; advertising; easy entry
2. difficult; need not; a little
3. negatively; below
4. marginal revenue; marginal cost
5. greater than; inefficiency
6. equal to; greater than
7. demand for; differentiated
8. direct; mass; interactive
9. a search; an experience; a credence
10. informational; a search
11. persuasive; an experience
12. variable; total
13. variable; total variable; total fixed; negative
14. total; zero

True-False Questions

1. T
2. F   There are so many rivals that they can be ignored.
3. T
4. F   Wheat is largely homogeneous.
5. T
6. F   Social inefficiency exists because the monopolistic competitor's demand curve is negatively sloped. Hence, $P > MC$ in equilibrium.
7. F   Exclusively persuasive advertising is more likely to be used by the producer of an experience good.
8. T
9. T
10. F   Heavy advertising expenses signals that a company intends to stay in business a long time and desires to develop a loyal customer base.
11. F   In fact, producing an information product typically requires incurring relatively high fixed costs and relatively low marginal costs.
12. T
13. T
14. F   In long-run equilibrium for an information-product firm in monopolistically competitive industry, price is equal to average total cost.

Multiple Choice Questions

1. (a)	7. (a)	13. (c)
2. (c)	8. (d)	14. (b)
3. (c)	9. (d)	15. (c)
4. (a)	10. (b)	16. (d)
5. (b)	11. (b)	17. (b)
6. (c)	12. (a)	18. (d)

Matching

(a) and (j)   (d) and (l)

(b) and (h)   (e) and (g)

(c) and (k)   (f) and (i)

Working with Graphs

1. a.   0L

    b.   0A

    c.   0E

    d.   0EFL

    e.   0C

    f.   0CHL

    g.   Profits

    h.   CEFH

2. a.   B

    b.   C

    c.   A

    d.   B

    e.   Some firms will exit the industry.

    f.   A

Problems

1. a.   *PC, M, MC*

    b.   *M, MC*

    c.   *M*

    d.   *M, MC*

    e.   *M, MC*

    f.   *MC*

    g.   *M*

    h.   *PC*

    i.   *PC, M, MC*

    j.   *PC, MC*

    k.   *M, MC*

■ Glossary

Credence good   A product with qualities that consumers lack the expertise to assess without assistance.

Direct marketing   Advertising targeted at specific consumers, typically in the form of postal mailings, telephone calls, or e-mail messages.

Experience good   A product that an individual must consume before the product's quality can be established.

Information product   An item that is produced using information-intensive inputs at a relatively high fixed cost but distributed for sale at a relatively low marginal cost.

Informational advertising   Advertising that emphasizes the transmission of knowledge about the features of a product.

Interactive marketing   Advertising that permits a consumer to follow up directly by searching for more information and placing direct product orders.

Mass marketing   Advertising intended to reach as many consumers as possible, typically through television, newspaper, radio, or magazine ads.

Monopolistic competition   A market situation in which a large number of firms produce similar but not identical products. Entry into the industry is relatively easy.

Persuasive advertising   Advertising that is intended to induce a consumer to try a product and discover a previously unknown taste for the item.

Product differentiation   The distinguishing of products by brand name, color, and other minor attributes. Product differentiation occurs in other than perfectly competitive markets in which products are, in theory, homogeneous, such as wheat or corn.

Search good   A product with characteristics that enable an individual to evaluate the product's quality in advance of a purchase.

Short-run economies of operation   A distinguishing characteristic of an information product arising from declining short-run average total cost as more units of the product are sold.

26 Oligopoly and Strategic Behavior

■ Learning Objectives

After you have studied this chapter, you should be able to

1. outline the fundamental characteristics of oligopoly;

2. understand how to apply game theory to evaluate the pricing strategies of oligopolistic firms;

3. identify features of an industry that help or hinder efforts to form a cartel that seeks to restrain output and earn economic profits;

4. illustrate how network effects and market feedback can explain why some industries are oligopolies;

5. explain why multiproduct firms selling complementary sets of products may or may not want their products to be compatible with those of their competitors.

■ Outline

1. *Oligopoly* is a market structure in which there are very few sellers, each of which expects a reaction from its rivals to changes in its price and quantity. There are two major characteristics of oligopolies: a small number of firms and interdependence.

2. There are at least three reasons for the emergence of oligopolistic industries: economies of scale, barriers to entry, and merger (horizontal or vertical).
    a. Four- or eight-firm *concentration ratios* are often calculated to determine the extent to which an industry is "monopolized."
    b. Over time some industries experience drastic changes (up or down) in their concentration ratios. Other industries show little change.

3. Before an oligopoly situation can be analyzed with respect to price and output, specific assumptions about rival *reactions* must be made. A different model arises with each assumption regarding the oligopolist's reaction function.

4. Because there is interdependence among oligopolistic firms, economists have developed an approach, called game theory, to describe how such firms interact rationally.
   a. If firms collude and form a cartel, the game is referred to as a cooperative game.
   b. If cartels are too expensive to form or enforce, then a noncooperative game is played among oligopolists.
   c. Games are classified as being zero sum, positive sum, or negative sum.

5. Oligopolistic decision makers derive a strategy, or rule, used to make a choice. A dominant strategy is one that always yields the highest benefit, regardless of what the other oligopolists do.

6. The most famous example of game theory is called the prisoners' dilemma, in which it can be shown that (under specified conditions) in situations in which there is more than one party to a crime, the dominant strategy for each prisoner is to confess.

7. A payoff matrix indicates the consequences of the strategies chosen by the players in the game.

8. A cartel is an association of producers in an industry that agree to set common prices and output quotas to prevent competition.

9. A cartel faces two fundamental problems.
   a. To maximize joint profits, firms in a cartel must restrain industry-wide production, so the cartel must determine how much each member should restrain its output.
   b. When all members of a cartel reduce their production and charge a higher price, there is a profit incentive for each member to increase its own output to sell that that price. Thus, a cartel must establish a mechanism for enforcing the cartel agreement.

10. Four conditions that make it more likely that a cartel agreement will prove enforceable are (i) a small number of firms in the industry, (ii) relatively undifferentiated products, (iii) easily observable prices, and (iv) little variation in prices.

11. Network effects occur when the willingness of consumers to buy a product depends on how many other consumers purchase it.
    a. When network effects are an important feature of a product, an industry can experience positive market feedback, or a tendency for its product to come into favor with additional consumers because other consumers have chosen to purchase it. If a few firms can reap most of the benefits of positive market feedback, then the result can be greater concentration in the industry.
    b. Network effects can also result in negative market feedback, which occurs if some consumers cut back on purchases of a product, causing it to fall out of favor with other consumers.

12. Network effects are especially important to firms operating in two-sided markets.
    a. In a two-sided market, an intermediary firm, or platform, provides services that link groups of producers and consumers, or end users.
    b. There are four types of two-sided markets: (i) audience-seeking markets, in which media platforms link advertisers to consumers; (ii) matchmaking markets, in which intermediary firms bring together consumers or firms from groups seeking partners for exchanges;

(iii) transaction-based markets, in which companies finalize transactions between members of different groups; and (iv) shared-input markets, in which groups of end users use a key input obtained from a platform in order to be able to interact.

c. In a number of two-sided markets, platform firms charge an explicit price of zero to one group of consumers or firms to induce them to interact with another group of end users, with positive prices charged to the latter group generating the platform's revenues. In some two-sided markets, platforms charge negative prices (that is, offer subsidies) to one end-user group to give members of that group and incentive to participate in the market.

■ Key Terms

Cartel	Horizontal merger	Reaction function
Concentration ratio	Network effect	Strategic dependence
Cooperative game	Noncooperative game	Strategy
Dominant strategies	Oligopoly	Two-sided market
Game theory	Payoff matrix	Vertical merger
Herfindahl-Hirschman Index	Prisoner's dilemma	

■ Key Concepts

Audience-seeking market	Negative-sum game	Shared-input market
Matchmaking market	Opportunistic behavior	Tit-for-tat strategic behavior
Multiproduct firm	Positive market feedback	Transaction-based market
Negative market feedback	Positive-sum game	Zero sum game

■ Completion Questions

Fill in the blank or circle the correct term.

1. Two key characteristics of oligopoly are _____ and _____.

2. Oligopolies may emerge because of _____, _____, _____, and _____.

3. Concentration ratios (fall, rise) as the definition of "industry" is narrowed, and they _____ as the definition is broadened.

4. Economists have developed an approach to analyze the interdependence among oligopolists called _____ theory.

5. If oligopolists collude and form a cartel, this is a(n) _____ game. If cartels are too expensive to form or enforce, then oligopolists will play a(n) _____ game.

6. Games are referred to as _____ sum if one player's benefit is exactly equal to the expense of the other, _____ sum if the sum of the players' benefit is positive, and _____ sum if the sum of the players' benefit is negative.

7. The most famous example of game theory is _____ in which the dominant strategy of prisoners is (usually) to (<u>confess, not confess</u>).

8. The two fundamental problems that a cartel must solve are (i) determining the _____ of each cartel member and (ii) setting up an enforcement mechanism to prevent _____ on the agreement by individual members.

9. A cartel agreement is easier to establish and enforce under the following conditions: (i) a(n) _____ number of firms in the industry; (ii) firms' products are _____; (iii) prices are not _____; and (iv) prices are _____ to observe.

10. When a consumer's willingness to purchase a good or service is influenced by how many other consumers also purchase the item, there is a(n) _____.

11. (<u>Positive; Negative</u>) market feedback arises when there is a tendency for a good or service to come into favor with additional consumers because other consumers have chosen to buy the item. (<u>Positive, Negative</u>) market feedback arises when there is tendency for a good or service to fall out of favor with more consumers because other consumers have stopped purchasing the item.

12. In a two-sided market, an intermediary firm known as a(n) _____ provides services that link together groups of consumers or firms known as _____.

■ True-False Questions

Circle the **T** if the statement is true, the **F** if it is false. Explain to yourself why a statement is false.

T F   1. The main characteristic of the oligopoly market structure is that an oligopolist must consider the reaction of its rivals.

T F   2. Perhaps the strongest reason for the existence of oligopolies is economies of scale relative to market demand.

T F   3. Concentration ratios provide an accurate measure of the degree of monopoly power in an industry.

T F   4. The fundamental problem faced by a cartel is what price to charge, and once this problem is solved, each member can produce a quantity that maximizes its own economic profits.

T F   5. Cartel agreements are easier to establish and enforce if firms' products are homogeneous.

T F   6. A dominant strategy is one that is always preferred by a player, regardless of what other players do.

T F   7. By definition, in a zero-sum game no player can experience a positive payoff.

T F   8. A four-firm concentration ratio is the share of total industry sales by all firms in the industry except the four firms with the lowest sales.

T F   9. A key condition for a cartel agreement to be easier to implement and enforce is stability of firms' prices.

T F 10. Opportunistic behavior helps keep collusive agreements together.

T F 11. If a firm's strategy is to continue to cooperate with other firms in a collusive manner as long as other firms also do so, then it engages in tit-for-tat strategic behavior.

T F 12. A network effect arises any time that one consumer's demand for an item is influenced by how many other consumers purchase the item.

T F 13. Positive market feedback can help explain why one firm can develop a position of dominance within an industry, but it cannot help explain why an entire industry might rapidly expand when the industry product is subject to network effects.

T F 14. An example of a matchmaking two-sided market is the market for online dating.

T F 15. In a number of two-sided markets, groups of end users on one side of the market pay explicit prices that are equal to zero or, in some cases, pay negative prices—that is, receive subsidies.

■ Multiple Choice Questions

Circle the letter that corresponds to the best answer.

1. In which of the following will the players' sum of benefits be positive?
   a. negative sum game
   b. zero-sum game
   c. positive-sum game
   d. prisoners' dilemma

2. In any situation of oligopolistic dependence,
   a. a firm's choice of how much to produce depends on the production choices of other firms.
   b. a firm's choice of how much to produce does not depend on other firms' production choices.
   c. all firms collusively determine how much to produce in order to maximize their joint profits.
   d. all firms collusively determine what price to charge in order to maximize their joint profits.

3. In long-run equilibrium for a profit-maximizing oligopolist,
   a. $MR = MC$.
   b. $P > MR$.
   c. economic profits can be greater than zero.
   d. All of the above.

4. Which firms must have zero economic profits in the long run?
   a. monopolist, perfect competitor
   b. oligopolist, monopolistic competitor
   c. perfect competitor, monopolistic competitor
   d. perfect competitor, oligopolist

5. Of the following, the *best* explanation for the existence of oligopolies is
   a. no economies of scale exist.
   b. large economies of scale relative to market demand.
   c. advertising.
   d. one firm has exclusive ownership of an important raw material.

6. In an oligopolistic industry, entry will result if
   a. normal profits exist.
   b. the industry *LAC* curve is below the market demand curve.
   c. the industry *LAC* curve is above the market demand curve.
   d. advertising is permitted.

7. Which one of the following is a key problem in any cartel agreement?
   I. Determining how much output each cartel member should produce
   II. Deciding whether restraining output would enable charging a higher price
   III. Establishing an agreement that successfully dissuades individual cartel members from cheating
   a. I only
   b. II only
   c. both I and III only
   d. both II and III only

8. Which one of the following is **not** a condition that contributes to successful establishment and enforcement of a cartel agreement?
   a. highly variable demand for the product the cartel members
   b. highly differentiated products of cartel members
   c. a large number of firms in the industry
   d. easily observable prices

9. The four-firm concentration ratio is
   a. the sum of the dollar sales of the four top-selling firms in an industry.
   b. the sum of the physical outputs of the top four producing firms in an industry.
   c. the percentage of total industry output produced by the leading four firms in an industry.
   d. the percentage of total industry dollar sales received by the leading four firms in an industry.

10. In the context of game theory, collusion is always a
    a. noncooperative game.
    b. negative-sum game.
    c. cooperative game.
    d. zero-sum game.

11. The strategy that always yields the highest benefit to a player in a game regardless of what other players may do is that player's
    a. dominant strategy.
    b. tit-for-tat strategy.
    c. positive-sum strategy.
    d. opportunistic strategy.

12. Which one of the following is **not** a condition that contributes to successful establishment and enforcement of a cartel agreement?
    a. easily observable prices
    b. little variation in prices
    c a small number of firms in the industry
    d. considerable heterogeneity in the products of firms in the industry

13. A network effect exists for a product when
    a. the willingness of consumers to buy that product is influenced by how many other consumers purchase it.
    b. the willingness of consumers to buy that product is influenced by how many firms offer the item for sale.
    c. the willingness of firms to sell that product is influenced by how many consumers purchase the product.
    d. the willingness of firms to sell that product is influenced by how many other firms sell the product.

14. A situation in which a significant number of consumers have chosen to purchase more units of a good or service in response to purchases by other consumers, thereby causing an industry to experience surging sales, is an example of
    a. negative market feedback.
    b. positive market feedback.
    c. collusive positive profits.
    d. a cartel agreement.

15. An audience-making market is a two-sided market in which
    a. the intermediating platform assists end users seeking to find counterparts with common interests.
    b. end users on one side require a key input from a platform in order to obtain access to participants on the other side of the market.
    c. a platform provides services clearing exchanges between end users on the two sides of the market.
    d. a platform offers some forms of entertainment or sources of information that brings together advertisers and people that advertisers desire to reach with their messages.

16. Which firm has the **least** control over its price?
    a. monopolistic competitor
    b. perfect competitor
    c. monopolist
    d. oligopolist

17. In the United States, a good example of an oligopolistic industry is
    a. a single local power company.
    b. the college textbook industry.
    c. the roofing nail industry.
    d. the retail trade industry.

■ Matching

Choose the item in Column (2) that best matches an item in Column (1).

(1)	**(2)**
(a) positive-sum game	(g) a rule for making a choice
(b) oligopoly	(h) strategic dependence among a few firms
(c) Herfindahl-Hirschman Index	(i) following the crowd to buy a hot product
(d) cooperative game	(j) all players benefit
(e) strategy	(k) sum of squared sales shares for an industry
(f) positive market feedback	(l) collusive behavior

■ Working with Graphs

1. Consider the payoff matrix for two oligopolists below, and answer the questions that follow.

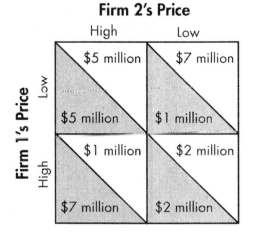

   a. If Firm 1 sets a high price, will Firm 2 set a high price or a low price?
   b. If Firm 2 sets a high price, will Firm 1 set a high price or a low price?
   c. If Firm 1 sets a low price, will Firm 2 set a high price or a low price?

d. If Firm 2 sets a low price, will Firm 1 set a high price or a low price?

e. If the two firms are unable to collude, what pricing strategies will they select?

■ Problems

1. Consider the table below, and then answer the questions that follow.

Firms in Industry A	Annual Sales (Millions of dollars)
1	20
2	15
3	10
4	10
5	10
6	10
7	10
8	5
9	5
10	5

a. What is the four-firm concentration ratio?

b. What is the eight-firm concentration ratio?

c. What is the value of the Herfindahl-Hirshman Index (HHI) for this industry?

■ Answers

Completion Questions

1. small number of firms; interdependence
2. economies of scale; barriers to entry; product differentiation and advertising; merger
3. rise; fall
4. game
5. cooperative; noncooperative
6. zero; positive; negative
7. the prisoners' dilemma; confess
8. output; cheating
9. small; homogeneous; variable; easy
10. network effect
11. Positive; Negative
12. platforms; end users

True-False Questions

1. T
2. T
3. F They are very inaccurate, if only because interindustry competition exists. Foreign competition exists too.
4. F The cartel's fundamental problem is deciding how much each member should produce so as to restrain total industry output to the level that maximizes industry profit.
5. F In a zero-sum game, some players experience positive payoffs while others experience negative payoffs, and the aggregate sum of all players' payoffs is zero.
6. F A four-firm concentration ratio is the share of industry sales by the four firms with the largest sales in the industry.
7. F They result when price leadership strategies break down.
8. F They set price at the highest level that *will still discourage entry*.
9. T
10. F By definition, opportunistic behavior involves actions that ignore possible long-run benefits of cooperation.
11. T
12. T
13. F Positive market feedback can occur either for an individual firm or for an entire industry.
14. T
15. T

Multiple Choice Questions

1. (c)	10. (c)
2. (a)	11. (a)
3. (d)	12. (d)
4. (c)	13. (a)
5. (b)	14. (b)
6. (b)	15. (d)
7. (c)	16. (b)
8. (d)	17. (b)
9. (d)	

Matching

(a) and (j)   (d) and (l)

(b) and (h)   (e) and (g)

(c) and (k)   (f) and (i)

Working with Graphs

1.   a.   low

b.   low

c.   low

d.   low

e.   The dominant strategy for each firm is to select the low price.

Problems

1.   a.   0.55 (or 55 percent)

b.   0.90 (or 90 percent)

c. $20^2 + 15^2 + (5 \times 10^2) + (3 \times 5^2) = 400 + 225 + 500 + 75 = 1,200$

■ Glossary

Cartel   An association of producers in an industry that agree to set common prices and output quotas to prevent competition.

Concentration ratio   The percentage of all sales contributed by the leading four or leading eight firms in an industry; sometimes called the *industry concentration ratio*.

Cooperative game   A game in which the players explicitly cooperate to make themselves jointly better off. As applied to firms, it involves companies colluding in order to make higher than perfectly competitive rates of return.

Dominant strategies   Strategies that always yield the highest benefit. Regardless of what other players do, a dominant strategy will yield the most benefit for the player using it.

Game theory   A way of describing the various possible outcomes in any situation involving two or more interacting individuals when those individuals are aware of the interactive nature of their situation and plan accordingly. The plans made by these individuals are known as *game strategies.*

Herfindahl-Hirschman Index (HHI)   The sum of the squared percentage sales shares of all firms in an industry.

Horizontal merger   The joining of firms that are producing or selling a similar product.

Multiproduct firm   A firm that produces and sells two or more different items.

Negative market feedback   A tendency for a good or service to fall out of favor with more consumers because other consumers have stopped purchasing the item.

Negative-sum game   A game in which players as a group lose during the process of the game.

Network effect   A situation in which a consumer's willingness to purchase a good or service is influenced by how many others also buy or have bought the item.

Noncooperative game   A game in which the players neither negotiate nor cooperate in any way. As applied to firms in an industry, this is the common situation in which there are relatively few firms and each has some ability to change price.

Oligopoly   A market structure in which there are very few sellers. Each seller knows that the other sellers will react to its changes in prices, quantities, and qualities.

Opportunistic behavior   Actions that focus solely on short-run gains because long-run benefits of cooperation are perceived to be smaller.

Payoff matrix   A matrix of outcomes, or consequences, of the strategies chosen by players in a game.

Positive market feedback   A tendency for a good or service to come into favor with additional consumers because other consumers have chosen to buy the item.

Positive-sum game   A game in which players as a group are better off at the end of the game.

Prisoners' dilemma   A famous strategic game in which two prisoners have a choice between confessing and not confessing to a crime. If neither confesses, they serve a minimum sentence. If both confess, they serve a longer sentence. If one confesses and the other does not, the one who confesses goes free. The dominant strategy is always to confess.

Reaction function   The manner in which one oligopolist reacts to a change in price, output, or quality made by another oligopolist in the industry.

Strategic dependence   A situation in which one firm's actions with respect to price, quality, advertising, and related changes may be strategically countered by one or more other firms in the industry. Such dependence can only exist when there are a limited number of major firms in an industry.

Strategy   Any rule that is used to make a choice, such as "Always pick heads."

Tit-for-tat strategic behavior   In game theory, cooperation that continues so long as the other players continue to cooperate.

Two-sided market   A market in which an intermediary firm provides services that link groups of producers and consumers.

Vertical merger   The joining of a firm with another to which it sells an output or from which it buys an input.

Zero-sum game   A game in which any gains within the group are exactly offset by equal losses by the end of the game.

27 Regulation and Antitrust Policy in a Globalized Economy

■ Learning Objectives

After you have studied this chapter, you should be able to

1. distinguish between economic regulation and social regulation;

2. recognize the practical difficulties in regulating the prices charged by natural monopolies;

3. explain the main rationales for regulation of industries that are not inherently monopolistic;

4. identify alternative theories aimed at explaining the behavior of regulators;

5. understand the foundation of antitrust laws and regulations;

6. discuss basic issues in enforcing antitrust laws.

■ Outline

1. There are two forms of industry regulation.
   a. Economic regulation is aimed at controlling prices in industries considered to be natural monopolies or influencing the characteristics of products or processes of firms in a variety of industries without inherently monopolistic features.
   b. Social regulation applies to all firms in the economy and is often intended to promote improved products, a less polluted environment, and better working conditions.

2. A natural monopoly arises when there are large economies of scale relative to industry demand and one firm can produce at a lower cost than can be achieved by multiple firms.
   a. When long-run average costs are falling, the long-run marginal cost curve is below the long-run average cost curve. The first firm to take advantage of decreasing costs can drive out all competitors by underpricing them.
   b. If regulators force the natural monopolist to engage in marginal cost pricing, the firm will suffer economic losses and will shut down.

c. There are two basic ways governments typically go about regulating natural monopolies.

    i. Cost-of-service regulation allows regulated companies to charge in accordance with actual average costs.

    ii. Rate-of-return regulation allows regulated firms to earn a normal rate of return on their investment in the business.

3. There are two key rationales for consumer protection regulations applied to nonmonopolistic industries: The existence of market failures, including negative externalities such as pollution, and asymmetric information, which can create a lemons problem and thereby bring about a general decline in product quality in an industry.

    a. Market solutions to the lemons problem include product guarantees and warranties and product certification programs.

    b. Licensing programs, legal liability legislation and enforcement, and direct oversight programs are all ways in which the government implements consumer protection regulations.

4. Because satisfying regulations is costly, businesses engage in a number of activities intended to avoid the intent of regulations or to bring about changes in established regulations.

    a. Regulated firms engage in creative response, which is a response to a regulation that conforms to the letter of the law while undermining its spirit.

    b. The regulator behavior model suggests that regulation benefits firms already in a regulated industry—not potential entrants or consumers.

        i. The capture hypothesis predicts that regulators will eventually be controlled by the special interests of the industry that is being regulated.

        ii. The share-the-gains, share-the-pains theory maintains that regulators must take into account the demands of three groups: legislators, firms in the industry, and consumers of the regulated industry.

5. By some estimates, regulation costs our nation between $800 billion and $1 trillion per year, or roughly between 6 and 9 percent of the aggregate income of all U.S. residents.

6. Antitrust policy attempts to prevent the emergence of monopoly and monopolistic behavior.

    a. The Sherman Act, which was passed in 1890, made illegal every contract and combination, in the form of a trust, that restrained trade.

    b. The Clayton Act, which was passed in 1914, made price discrimination and interlocking directorates illegal.

    c. The Federal Trade Commission Act of 1914 established the commission to prevent "unfair competition," and later legislation amended the 1914 act to allow the FTC to battle against false or misleading advertising.

    d. The Robinson-Patman Act of 1936 was aimed at preventing large producers from driving out small competitors by means of selective discriminatory price cuts.

    e. Numerous antitrust acts serve to exempt certain business (and union) practices from antitrust action.

7. The Sherman Act does not define monopoly, but the Supreme Court has defined the term monopolization as involving:

    a. the possession of monopoly power in the relevant market, and

    b. the willful acquisition or maintenance of the power as distinguished from growth or development as a consequence of a superior product, business acumen, or historical accident.

8. In practice it is difficult to measure (and define) market power. Doing so requires identifying the relevant market.

    a. The relevant market consists of two elements: a relevant product market and a relevant geographic market.

    b. Defining the relevant market is increasingly difficult because firms face increasing competition from abroad as well as within U.S. borders.

    c. For assessment of whether proposed mergers might violate antitrust laws, guidelines utilized by the U.S. Department of Justice and the Federal Trade Commission take into account both the change that the merger would induce in the relevant market's Herfindahl-Hirschman Index (HHI) and the resulting level of the post-merger HHI.

9. In recent years, the manner in which firms offer products for sale has raised antitrust issues.

    a. Product versioning, which entails selling a product in slightly altered forms to different groups of consumers, might be regarded as a means of engaging in price discrimination. Because versioning also can be viewed as selling distinctive products in different markets, it has not raised significant antitrust concerns.

    b. Product bundling, which entails offering two or more products for sale as a set, sometimes raises antitrust issues. When a consumer can only buy one of the products if it is within a bundled set, then this can be interpreted as a tie-in sale, in which a firm permits purchase of one product only if a consumer buys another product as well.

■ Key Terms

Bundling	Rate-of-return regulation
Cost-of-service regulation	Tie-in sales
Lemons problem	Versioning

■ Key Concepts

Capture hypothesis	Monopolization
Creative response	Share-the-gains, share-the-pains theory

■ Completion Questions

Fill in the blank, or circle the correct term.

1. The two primary types of government regulation are _____ regulation and _____ regulation.

2. A natural monopoly arises when there are large _____ of scale relative to _____. In such a case, the firm's average total costs persistently _____, and its marginal cost curve lies (<u>below, above</u>) its average cost curve. The first firm to expand will be able to offer a price that is _____ than those of its rivals and drive them out of business.

3. If a natural monopolist were forced to engage in marginal cost pricing for social efficiency, that firm would experience _____ economic profits. In order to counter such an outcome, regulators might _____ the natural monopolist.

4. Cost-of-service regulation requires firms to charge customers based on actual (<u>marginal, average</u>) costs. Rate-of-return regulation permits regulated firms to earn _____ profits. Because price is easier to measure and regulate than quality, regulated firms can (<u>lower, raise</u>) the price per constant-quality unit, even if price is constant.

5. Two key rationales for consumer protection regulations are market failures and _____, which in some industries can create _____ problems.

6. Regulated firms often try to avoid the effects of regulation, so they react to regulation by making a(n) _____ response. That is, the regulated firms follow the letter, but not the spirit, of a regulation.

7. The regulator behavior model suggests that much regulation is for the benefit of (<u>consumers, firms already in the industry</u>). Two such theories are _____ and _____.

8. Monopolization is the possession of monopoly power in the _____ market, and the _____ acquisition or maintenance of the power, as distinguished from growth as a consequence of _____, _____, or _____.

9. The Sherman Act makes illegal those contracts or trusts that act to _____ trade. The provisions of this act are (<u>vague, clear</u>). The Clayton Act makes price _____ illegal if it substantially lessens competition.

10. The Federal Trade Commission (FTC) Act attempts to prevent _____ competition. In addition, Congress has authorized the FTC to battle against false or misleading _____.

11. The _____ Act is aimed at preventing producers from driving out competitors by means of selected discriminatory price cuts. This legislation is commonly referred to as the _____ act.

12. Four exemptions to antitrust laws are _____, _____, _____, and _____.

13. Current enforcement guidelines for U.S. antitrust policy emphasize both the _____ in the value of the Herfindahl-Hirschman Index (HHI) that a merger would generate and the resulting _____ of the HHI after the merger would be completed.

14. (Versioning, Bundling) is the act of selling a product in slightly altered forms to different groups, while (versioning, bundling) is the act of selling two or more products together as a single set.

15. If a firm sells (versioned, bundled) products as a set, so that a consumer can purchase one of the products in the set only if the others are also purchased, such an arrangement is sometimes regarded by antitrust enforcement authorities as an example of _____ sales.

■ True-False Questions

Circle the **T** if the statement is true, the **F** if it is false. Explain to yourself why a statement is false.

T F 1. Natural monopolies arise mainly due to large economies of scale.

T F 2. If a natural monopolist is required to engage in marginal cost pricing, it will earn abnormal profits.

T F 3. The lemons problem arises as a result of asymmetric information.

T F 4. Traditionally in the United States, inherently competitive industries have not been regulated.

T F 5. Regulated firms often follow the letter of a rule but violate its spirit.

T F 6. Regulators can easily regulate the price per constant-quality unit of regulated firms.

T F 7. According to the regulator behavior theory, regulators are mostly concerned with the well-being of consumers.

T F 8. Monopolization, according to the Supreme Court, requires a willful act.

T F 9. The Robinson-Patman Act was aimed at preventing producers from driving out smaller competitors by means of selected discriminatory price cuts.

T F 10. Labor unions are exempted from antitrust laws, even if their actions restrain trade.

T F 11. Monopolization requires a willful acquisition of monopoly power in the relevant market.

T F 12. When a firm engages in product versioning, it seeks to envision all the possible ways in which producing and marketing a new product may face government regulation and antitrust enforcement.

T F 13. If a firm offers a product available for sale either individually or as part of a bundled set, then it has engaged in a tie-in sale.

■ Multiple Choice Questions

Circle the letter that corresponds to the best answer.

1. Which of the following is the best example of a government regulator that engages in economic, not social, regulation?
   a. Environmental Protection Agency
   b. Federal Aviation Administration
   c. Food and Drug Administration
   d. Federal Trade Commission

2. A natural monopoly results because
   a. of large economies of scale.
   b. of persisting declining average and marginal costs.
   c. the largest firm can underprice its competitors.
   d. All of the above.

3. If the natural monopolist were forced to price at marginal cost, it would earn
   a. abnormal profits.
   b. economic profits.
   c. economic losses.
   d. zero economic profit.

4. Which one of the following is **not** a recognized type of government regulation?
   a. regulation of natural monopolies
   b. regulation for the benefit of congress
   c. regulation of inherently competitive industries
   d. regulation for public welfare across all industries

5. Which one of the following is probably the most difficult to regulate?
   a. price
   b. output
   c. quality
   d. profit

6. Which one of the following is **not** consistent with the regulator behavior model?
   a. Regulators are concerned with benefiting themselves.
   b. Regulators are concerned with benefiting vocal customers.
   c. Regulators are concerned with benefiting firms already in the industry.
   d. Regulators are concerned with benefiting potential entrants into an industry.

7. Which one of the following best describes the nature of the lemons problem?

   a. Asymmetric information causes buyers to be uncertain about product quality, which reduces the price they are willing to pay for a product and thereby can ultimately generate a general decline in quality.

   b. Asymmetric information causes sellers to be uncertain about whether buyers will really pay for the item, which causes sellers to cut back on production of the product.

   c. Market failures generate negative externalities for products with broad costs imposed on all members of society, resulting in overproduction of these items by firms.

   d. Market failures generate positive externalities for products with broad benefits for all members of society, resulting in underproduction of these items by firms.

8. Which action is considered monopolization?

   a. willful acquisition of monopoly power

   b. producing a superior product

   c. business acumen

   d. historical accident

9. Which one of the following are **not** exempt from antitrust laws?

   a. labor unions

   b. professional baseball

   c. suppliers of military equipment

   d. all unincorporated businesses

10. Under current U.S. antitrust enforcement guidelines, in which one of the following circumstances would either the Department of Justice or the Federal Trade Commission become most concerned about the potential for a proposed merger to violate antitrust law?

    a. The merger causes the relevant market's HHI to increase by 10 and results in a post-merger HHI level exceeding 250.

    b. The merger causes the relevant market's HHI to increase by 25 and results in a post-merger HHI level exceeding 400.

    c. The merger causes the relevant market's HHI to increase by 50 and results in a post-merger HHI level exceeding 500.

    d. The merger causes the relevant market's HHI to increase by 150 and results in a post-merger HHI level exceeding 1,000.

11. When a firm sells slightly altered versions of the same product to different groups of consumers, it engages in

    a. tie-in sales.

    b. mixed sales.

    c. product bundling.

    d. product versioning.

■ Matching

Choose the item in Column (2) that best matches an item in Column (1).

	(1)		**(2)**
(a)	lemons problem	(g)	willful acquisition of monopoly power
(b)	monopolization	(h)	persistent fall in long-run *AC*
(c)	natural monopoly	(i)	behavior of regulated firms
(d)	creative response	(j)	behavior of regulators
(e)	capture hypothesis	(k)	product bundling
(f)	tie-in sales	(l)	asymmetric information

■ Working with Graphs

1. Suppose you are an analyst for a regulatory board that is in charge of the regulation of local monopolies. Given the information in the graph that follows, answer the list of questions submitted by your supervisor.

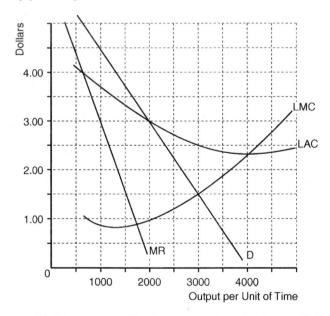

a. If this monopolist is not regulated, what will be the level of output? Price? Total revenue? Total costs? Profit or loss?

b. If this monopolist is regulated by marginal cost pricing, what will be the level of output? Price? Total revenue? Total costs? Profits or loss? Will the monopoly need a subsidy? If so, how much?

c. If cost-of-service regulation is imposed on this monopolist, what will be the level of output? Price? Total revenue? Total costs? Profit or loss?

■ Answers

Completion Questions

1. economic; social
2. economies; industry demand; fall; below; lower
3. negative; subsidize
4. average; normal; raise
5. asymmetric information; lemons
6. creative
7. firms already in the industry; capture theory; share-the-gains; share-the-pains theory
8. relevant; willful; a superior product; business acumen; historical accident
9. restrain; vague; discrimination
10. unfair; advertising
11. Robinson-Patman; chain store
12. any of the following: labor unions; public utilities; professional baseball; cooperative acts among U.S. exporters; hospitals; public transit and water systems; suppliers of military equipment; joint publishing arrangements by two or more newspapers in a single city
13. change; level
14. Versioning; bundling
15. bundled; tie-in

True-False Questions

1. T
2. F It will realize losses.
3. T
4. F Inherently competitive industries such as trucking and airlines have been regulated.
5. T
6. F It is difficult to regulate quality.
7. F They, like the rest of us, are assumed to be concerned with their own well-being.
8. T
9. T
10. T
11. T
12. F Versioning is the act of selling slightly altered forms of a product to different groups.
13. F A tie-in sale occurs when a consumer can purchase a product only if it is bought along with another product offered by the firm, such as only within a bundled set.

Multiple Choice Questions

1. (b)
2. (a)
3. (c)
4. (b)
5. (c)
6. (d)
7. (a)
8. (a)
9. (d)
10. (d)
11. (d)

Matching

(a) and (l)	(d) and (i)
(b) and (g)	(e) and (j)
(c) and (h)	(f) and (k)

Working with Graphs

1. a. 1,700 units, $3.50, $5,950, $5,440 (or 1,700 × $3.20), profit of $510 (*Note:* Dollar figures are approximations.)

   b. 3,000 units, $1.50, $4,500, $7,500, loss of $3,000, yes, $3,000

   c. 2,000, $3, $6,000, $6,000, $0

■ Glossary

Bundling   Offering two or more products for sale as a set.

Capture hypothesis   A theory of regulatory behavior that predicts that the regulators will eventually be captured by special interests of the industry being regulated.

Cost-of-service regulation   Regulation that allows prices to reflect only the actual average cost of production and no monopoly profits.

Creative response   Behavior on the part of a firm that allows it to comply with the letter of the law but violate the spirit, significantly lessening the law's effects.

Lemons problem   The potential for asymmetric information to bring about a general decline in product quality in an industry.

Monopolization   The possession of monopoly power in the relevant market and the willful acquisition or maintenance of that power, as distinguished from growth or development as a consequence of a superior product, business acumen, or historical accident.

Rate-of-return regulation   Regulation that seeks to keep the rate of return in an industry at a competitive level by not allowing prices that would produce economic profits.

Relevant market   A group of firms' products that are closely substitutable and available to consumers within a geographic area.

Share-the-gains, share-the-pains theory   A theory of regulatory behavior that holds that regulators must take account of the demands of three groups: legislators, who established and who oversee the regulatory agency; firms in the regulated industry; and consumers of the regulated industry's products.

Tie-in sales   Purchases of one product that are permitted by the seller only if the consumer buys another good or service from the same firm.

Versioning   Selling a product in slightly altered forms to different groups of consumers.

28 The Labor Market: Demand, Supply, and Outsourcing

■ Learning Objectives

After you have studied this chapter, you should be able to

1. understand why a firm's marginal revenue product curve is its labor demand curve;

2. explain in what sense the demand for labor is a "derived" demand;

3. identify the key factors influencing the elasticity of demand for inputs;

4. describe how equilibrium wage rates are determined for perfectly competitive firms;

5. explain what labor outsourcing is and how it is ultimately likely to affect U.S. workers' earnings and employment prospects;

6. contrast the demand for labor and wage determination by a product market monopolist with outcomes that would arise under perfect competition.

■ Outline

1. What is the profit-maximizing quantity of labor to hire for a firm that is a perfect competitor in both the labor market and the product market?

    a. The marginal physical product of labor is the change in total output accounted for by hiring one more worker, holding all other factors of production constant.

    b. Because of the law of diminishing marginal product, the marginal physical product of labor eventually declines.

    c. Because this firm is in a competitive labor market, it is a price taker. The firm can hire as much labor as it wants to hire at the going wage rate.

    d. The marginal benefit from hiring one more unit of labor is that laborer's marginal physical product multiplied by the firm's constant product selling price, or the marginal revenue product (MRP).

    e. The profit-maximizing rule for hiring is to hire laborers up to the point where the wage rate equals the MRP of labor.

2. The demand for labor is a derived demand. Laborers (or other inputs) are desired only because they can be used to produce products that are expected to be sold at a profit.

3. The market demand for labor curve is negatively sloped.

4. There are four principal determinants of the price elasticity of demand for an input. The price elasticity of demand for a variable input will be greater under the following conditions:

    a. the greater the price elasticity of demand for the final product;

    b. the easier it is to substitute for that variable input;

    c. the larger the proportion of total costs accounted for by a particular variable input;

    d. the longer the time period being considered.

5. In a perfectly competitive labor market, the equilibrium market wage rate is determined at the point at which the industry demand for labor curve intersects the industry supply of labor curve.

    a. The industry supply of labor curve is upward sloping from left to right.

        i. As wage rates rise in an industry, more laborers are willing to accept jobs there.

        ii. Nevertheless, the individual firm faces a horizontal supply curve at the going wage rate.

    b. When nonwage determinants of the supply of and the demand for labor change, those curves shift.

        i. The labor demand curve shifts if there is a change in (1) the demand for the final product, (2) labor productivity, or (3) the price of related factors of production.

        ii. The labor supply curve shifts if there is a change in the (1) alternative wage rate offered in other industries or (2) nonmonetary aspects of the occupation under study.

6. When a firm employs labor outside the country in which the firm is located, it engages in international outsourcing.

    a. In the short run, outsourcing by U.S. firms causes the demand for U.S. labor to decline, which results in decreases in the market wage rate and equilibrium employment in the affected U.S. labor market.

    b. In the short run, outsourcing by foreign firms in the United States causes the demand for U.S. labor to rise, which results in increases in the market wage rate and equilibrium employment in the affected U.S. labor market.

    c. Specialization and trade of labor services through outsourcing generate overall gains from trade for participating nations.

7. What is the profit-maximizing quantity of labor to hire for a firm that is a perfect competitor in the labor market but a monopolist in the product market?

    a. Such a firm's demand for labor (or any other input) is negatively sloped because (1) the marginal physical product falls and (2) the price (and therefore *MR*) falls as output increases.

    b. Such a firm's labor demand curve is its MRP curve, which equals labor's marginal physical product multiplied by the firm's *MR*. Thus, MRP = $MR \times$ MPP.

    c. Given the going market wage rate, this firm hires up to the point where MRP equals the wage rate.

d. The monopolist hires fewer workers than a perfectly competitive producer would, other things being constant.

8. How much of *each* variable factor should the firm use when combining those factors to produce a given output?

   a. The firm will hire all variable inputs up to the point where each input's MRP equals its price.

   b. In order to minimize the total cost of producing a given output, the firm should equate the ratios of each factor's marginal physical product to its respective price. This condition is referred to as the *least-cost combination of resources.*

■ Key Terms

Marginal factor cost (MFC)   Marginal revenue product (MRP)

Marginal physical product (MPP) of labor

■ Key Concepts

Derived demand

Outsourcing

■ Completion Questions

Fill in the blank or circle the correct term.

1. To a firm that is a perfect competitor in both the labor and the product market, the marginal benefit from hiring labor equals labor's _____ times _____, or MRP.

2. A perfectly competitive firm's MRP curve is negatively sloped because labor's _____ falls, due to the law of _____.

3. To such a perfectly competitive firm, the marginal cost of hiring labor is the _____, which (<u>falls, rises, remains constant</u>) as the firm hires more laborers. In the labor market, such a firm is a price (<u>taker, searcher</u>).

4. The perfectly competitive firm hires labor up to the point where _____ equals _____. At that point, the firm is maximizing _____.

5. The demand for labor is a(n) _____ demand. Consequently, if the product's selling price increases, the perfectly competitive firm's demand for labor curve will shift to the _____. The market demand curve for labor will be _____ sloped.

6. Determinants of the price elasticity of demand for an input include _____, _____, _____, and _____.

7. The supply of labor to a perfectly competitive firm is _____ elastic, therefore its labor supply curve is (<u>vertical, horizontal</u>). The supply of labor curve for the industry, however, is _____ sloped.

8. The industry demand for labor curve shifts if there is a change in the _____, _____, or _____. The industry supply curve shifts if there is a change in the _____ or _____.

9. In the short run, outsourcing by U.S. firms causes the market wage rate to (<u>rise, fall</u>) and equilibrium employment to (<u>rise, fall</u>) in U.S. labor markets. At the same time, outsourcing by foreign firms in the United States cause the market wage rate to (<u>rise, fall</u>) and equilibrium employment to (<u>rise, fall</u>) in U.S. labor markets.

10. Labor outsourcing allows nations' residents to specialize according to their (<u>absolute, comparative</u>) advantages and thereby obtain (<u>gains, losses</u>) from trade.

11. Assume a firm is a perfect competitor in the labor market but a monopolist in the product market. Its marginal benefit from hiring labor equals _____ times _____, or MRP of labor. This firm's MRP curve is negatively sloped because _____ falls due to the law of _____ and because _____ falls due to the fact that this firm must reduce its _____ as it produces more. This firm will hire labor up to the point where _____ equals _____.

12. If a perfectly competitive firm hires more than one variable input, its equilibrium condition is that _____. Stated alternatively, the firm can minimize the total cost of producing a given output by equating _____.

■ True-False Questions

Circle the **T** if the statement is true, the **F** if it is false. Explain to yourself why a statement is false.

T F 1. A firm that is perfectly competitive both in the market for its final output and in the market for labor will discover that its demand for labor curve is horizontal at the going wage rate.

T F 2. A perfectly competitive firm will hire labor up to the point where MRP equals the going wage rate.

T F 3. The marginal physical product of labor declines due to diseconomies of scale.

T F 4. Because the demand for labor is a derived demand, it shifts when wage rates change.

T F 5. The price elasticity of demand for labor will be higher the lower the price elasticity of demand is for the final good.

T F 6. A perfectly competitive firm's supply of labor curve is perfectly elastic, but the labor supply curve for the entire industry is upward sloping.

T F 7. If labor productivity rises, the demand for labor increases.

T F 8. In the short run, the net effects of outsourcing are general declines in wages and employment in U.S. labor markets.

T F 9. If labor is outsourced in both directions between two nations, the result is reduced employment in both nations and hence overall losses for both.

T F 10. A firm that operates in a perfectly competitive labor market but acts as a monopolist in the product market hires labor up to the point where the MRP of labor equals the going wage rate.

T F 11. If a firm suddenly monopolizes a perfectly competitive industry, more workers will be hired.

T F 12. If a perfectly competitive firm hires two factors of production it will hire up to the point where the MRP of one factor divided by that factor's price equals the MRP of the other factor divided by that factor's price.

■ Multiple Choice Questions

Circle the letter that corresponds to the best answer.

1. Which one of the following is **not** true about a firm that is a perfect competitor in all markets?
   a. Its supply of labor curve is perfectly elastic.
   b. Its demand for labor curve is downward sloping.
   c. Its price falls as it produces more output.
   d. Its marginal physical product of labor falls as it hires more labor.

2. For a firm that is a perfect competitor in all markets, the profit-maximizing quantity of labor to hire occurs where
   a. a falling MRP equals a rising wage rate.
   b. a rising MRP equals a rising wage rate.
   c. a falling MRP equals a falling wage rate.
   d. a falling MRP equals a constant wage rate.

3. A firm that is a perfect competitor in all markets finds that its MRP for labor falls because as it hires more labor
   a. the marginal physical product of labor falls.
   b. the price of output falls as output increases.
   c. Both of the above.
   d. None of the above.

4. The marginal factor cost of labor
    a. equals the going wage rate to a competitive firm.
    b. equals the change in wage rates divided by the change in labor.
    c. rises for the competitive firm.
    d. equals the change in total cost divided by the change in wage rates.

5. The demand for labor
    a. is a derived demand.
    b. shifts as selling price of the good produced changes.
    c. shifts to the right if labor productivity increases.
    d. All of the above.

6. Which one of the following will **not** lead to a relatively high price elasticity of demand for labor?
    a. high price elasticity of demand for the final product
    b. no good substitutes for the labor skill in question
    c. high ratio of labor to total costs
    d. a very long period of time after the wage change

7. The supply of labor
    a. to a perfect competitor is positively sloped.
    b. for the entire industry is perfectly elastic.
    c. is positively sloped for the industry.
    d. depends on labor's marginal physical product.

8. Which one of the following will **not** lead to an increase in the demand for labor?
    a. Price of labor falls.
    b. The productivity of labor increases.
    c. The price of a labor substitute input increases.
    d. The demand for the final product increases.

9. In the short run, which of the following will occur in U.S. labor markets as a result of outsourcing by U.S. firms?
    a. a fall in labor supply
    b. a rise in labor demand
    c. an increase in market wages
    d. a decrease in equilibrium employment

10. Which one of the following will occur as a result of outsourcing by both U.S. and foreign firms?
    a. higher employment levels in labor markets in which each nation has a comparative advantage
    b. specialization in tasks by workers in both nations
    c. gains from trade in both nations
    d. All of the above

11. If Firm B is a perfectly competitive firm in the labor market and a monopolist in the product market, then
    a. its demand for labor is negatively sloped.
    b. its supply of labor is positively sloped.
    c. its selling price is a constant.
    d. its wage rates rise as it hires more labor.

12. If Firm B is a perfect competitor in the labor market and a monopolist in the product market, then
    a. its supply of labor curve is perfectly elastic at the going wage rate.
    b. it hires labor up to the point where MRP of labor equals the going wage rate.
    c. its MRP curve falls because the marginal product of labor falls and its selling price falls.
    d. All of the above.

13. The monopolist in the product market finds that its MRP for labor falls as it hires labor because the MPP of labor
    a. falls and output price is constant.
    b. falls and output price falls.
    c. is constant and output price falls.
    d. rises but output price falls faster.

14. If a perfectly competitive market is suddenly monopolized, the amount of labor hired will
    a. remain constant.
    b. fall.
    c. rise.
    d. fall in the short run, rise in the long run.

15. If a firm hires two variable inputs, A and B, it is minimizing costs when
    a. MPP of A/price of A = MPP of B/price of B.
    b. MPP of A/price of B = MPP of B/price of A.
    c. MRP of A/MPP of B = MRP of B/MPP of A.
    d. MRP of A/price of B = MRP of B/price of A.

■ Matching

Choose the item in Column (2) that best matches an item in Column (1).

(1)

(a) MPP

(b) MPP × *MR*

(c) MPP × price

(d) least-cost combination

(e) derived demand

(f) uncertain short-run effects

(2)

(g) outsourcing

(h) MRP of perfectly competitive firm

(i) MRP of monopolistic firm

(j) labor demand curve

(k) change in output for a unit input change

(l) equate MPP/price of all factor inputs

■ Working with Graphs

1.   Analyze the diagram below, and then answer the questions that follow. Assume that a union bargains for a wage rate equal to $22.50 per hour.

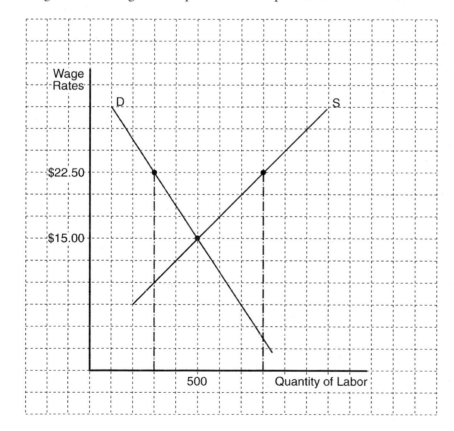

a.   What is the equilibrium wage rate in this market?

b.   What is the quantity of labor supplied at the wage rate negotiated by the union?

c.   What is the quantity of labor demanded at the union-negotiated wage rate?

d. What market situation exists at the union-negotiated wage rate?

e. How many workers were laid off, due to the union-negotiated wage rate?

f. How many workers entered the labor force, seeking a job, due to the union-negotiated wage rate?

g. Are workers in this industry better off or worse off as a result of this union-negotiated wage?

h. Which workers are more likely to be laid off?

■ Problems

1. In the following table you are given information about a firm operating in a perfectly competitive market. Consider all factors of production fixed at the moment, with the exception of labor services. The other factors of production cost the firm $50 per day, which may be thought of as a fixed cost. Assume that the firm maximizes economic profits.

Labor Input (workers per day)	Total Physical Product (units per day)	Marginal Physical Product (units per day)	Marginal Revenue Product ($ per worker)
0	0	_____	_____
1	22	_____	_____
2	40	_____	_____
3	56	_____	_____
4	70	_____	_____
5	82	_____	_____
6	92	_____	_____
7	100	_____	_____
8	106	_____	_____

a. Assume that the firm sells its output at $3 per unit. Complete the last two columns in the table above.

b. If the going market wage is $36 per day, the firm will hire _____ workers per day and produce _____ units of output.

c. Given your answer to part (b), the firm will have total revenues of _____ per day and total costs of _____ per day.

d. The above will result in a (<u>profit, loss</u>) of _____ per day.

2.   Suppose you work for a firm that sells its output in a monopoly market. Answer the following questions.

   a.   If you hire an additional worker, output goes up by 50 units to 125 units per day. If you wish to sell the additional 50 units, you must lower your price from $3 per unit to $2 per unit. What is the maximum wage you would be willing to pay the additional worker?

   b.   Assume you hired the worker from Part a and output now stands at 125 units per day. If another worker is hired, output rises to 165 units per day. Given the demand curve for your product, you know that in order to sell the additional output, price will have to be dropped from $2 per unit to $1 per unit. What is the maximum wage you would be willing to pay this additional worker?

■ Answers

Completion Questions

1. marginal physical product; price
2. marginal physical product; diminishing marginal product
3. wage rate; remains constant; taker
4. MRP of labor; wage rate; total profits
5. derived; right; negatively
6. price elasticity of demand for final good; ease with which other inputs can substitute for this input; proportion of total costs accounted for by the input in question; length of time period being considered
7. perfectly; horizontal; positively
8. demand for the final good; labor productivity; price of related factors; wage rate in other industries; nonmoney job aspects
9. fall; fall; rise; rise
10. comparative; gains
11. marginal physical product of labor; *MR*; marginal physical product; diminishing marginal product; *MR*; price; MRP; the wage rate
12. the ratio of MRP to price of factor is equated for all factors; the ratio of marginal physical product to factor price for all factors

True-False Questions

1. F   Its demand for labor curve is negatively sloped.
2. T
3. F   It declines due to the law of diminishing marginal product.
4. F   If wage rates change, we move along a given labor demand curve.
5. F   It will be lower.
6. T
7. T
8. F   In the short run, outsourcing by U.S. firms does tend to push down U.S. wages and employment, but outsourcing by foreign firms in the United States tends to push up market wages and employment levels in U.S. labor markets, so the net short-run wage and employment effects are uncertain.
9. F   Labor outsourcing between two nations permits their residents to specialize according to their comparative advantages, so that on net both countries experience gains from trade.
10. T
11. F   Fewer workers will be hired, because output falls.
12. T

Multiple Choice Questions

1. (c)	9. (d)
2. (d)	10. (d)
3. (a)	11. (a)
4. (a)	12. (d)
5. (d)	13. (b)
6. (b)	14. (b)
7. (c)	15. (a)
8. (a)	

Matching

(a) and (k)	(d) and (l)
(b) and (i)	(e) and (j)
(c) and (h)	(f) and (g)

Working with Graphs

1. a. $15.00
   b. 800
   c. 300
   d. Surplus, or excess quantity supplied of labor
   e. 200
   f. 300
   g. Those who kept their jobs are better off; those who became unemployed are worse off. Group income fell from $7,500 to $6,750.
   h. Younger, lower income-lower productivity workers

Problems

1. a. MPP: 22, 18, 16, 14, 12, 10, 8, 6
      MRP: 66, 54, 48, 42, 36, 30, 24, 18
   b. 5, 82
   c. $246, (5 × $36) + $50 = $230
   d. Profit, $16

2. a. $25 per day since MRP = $25
   b. A negative wage, because the price decrease necessary to sell the additional output causes total revenues to decline ($MR < 0$), MRP for this worker is negative, and the firm must be paid to hire another unit of labor.

■ Glossary

Derived demand   Input factor demand derived from demand for the final product being produced.

Marginal factor cost (MFC)   The cost of using an additional unit of an input. For example, if a firm can hire all the workers it wants at the going wage rate, the marginal factor cost of labor is the wage rate.

Marginal physical product (MPP) of labor   The change in output resulting from the addition of one more worker. The MPP of the worker equals the change in total output accounted for by hiring the worker, holding all other factors of production constant.

Marginal revenue product (MRP)   The marginal physical product (MPP) times marginal revenue (*MR*). The MRP gives the additional revenue obtained from a one-unit change in labor input.

Outsourcing   A firm's employment of labor outside the country in which the firm is located.

29 Unions and Labor Market Monopoly Power

■ Learning Objectives

After you have studied this chapter, you should be able to

1. outline the essential history of the labor union movement;

2. discuss the current status of labor unions;

3. describe the basic economic goals and strategies of labor unions;

4. evaluate the potential effects of labor unions on wages and productivity;

5. explain how a monopsonist determines how much labor to employ and what wage rate to pay;

6. compare wage and employment decisions by a monopsonistic firm with the choices made by firms in industries with alternative market structures.

■ Outline

1. Unions are workers' organizations that usually seek to secure economic improvements for their members.
    a. The U.S. labor movement started with craft unions, which are composed of workers who engage in a particular skill or trade.
    b. The American Federation of Labor (AFL), a craft union, was formed by Samuel Gompers in 1886. AFL membership growth flourished until World War I, when the government withdrew its support.
    c. The Great Depression brought the National Recovery Act in 1933, which attempted to raise wages to pre-Depression levels. This law's key provision was to guarantee the right of labor to bargain collectively.
    d. The Wagner Act also guaranteed collective bargaining and granted workers the right to form unions.
    e. In 1938, John L. Lewis formed the Congress of Industrial Organizations (CIO), which was composed of industrial unions; that is, unions with membership from an entire industry.

f.   The Taft-Hartley Act was enacted to stem union power. The law allows individual states to pass right-to-work laws, which make the requirement of union membership for continued employment illegal. It also bans the closed shop everywhere and the union shop in states with right-to-work laws and outlaws jurisdictional disputes, sympathy strikes, and secondary boycotts.

2.   There is a worldwide trend toward declining unionization, and there has been a change in the types of occupations attracting union members.

a.   The percentage of the U.S. labor force that is unionized has fallen because of a decrease in the relative importance of manufacturing, industry deregulation, increased immigration, and greater global competition.

b.   A shift toward more workers employed in service occupations has produced a corresponding shift toward greater unionization of these workers, particularly among workers employed by federal, state, and municipal governments.

3.   Unions can be analyzed as setters of minimum wages. The strike is the ultimate bargaining tool for unions.

4.   It is not clear what unions wish to maximize. Unions can either set wage rates or select the quantity of its membership that will be employed. Unions cannot do both.

a.   To the extent that unions set wage rates above equilibrium, they create a surplus of labor, or a shortage of jobs that they ration.

b.   If unions wish to employ all members, they must accept a relatively low wage rate.

c.   If unions wish to maximize total labor income, they set wage rates at the point at which the price elasticity of demand equals 1. Some members will be unemployed.

d.   If unions maximize wage rates for a given number of workers—presumably high-seniority workers—low-seniority workers will become unemployed because wage rates probably will be set above equilibrium.

e.   One union strategy is to limit total union membership to the original quantity. Over time, if demand increases, wage rates will rise.

f.   Unions can raise wage rates for members by (a) limiting membership, and (b) increasing union labor productivity, thereby increasing the demand for union labor relative to nonunion labor.

5.   Unionization has conflicting effects on wages, productivity, and employment.

a.   There is evidence that unions do succeed in achieving higher hourly wage rates for their members but not significantly higher annual earnings than nonunion workers.

b.   While certain union practices such as featherbedding and strikes reduce labor productivity, other practices such as airing grievances and concerns about inefficient production methods may increase productivity.

c.   Employment growth has slowed significantly in the most heavily unionized industries, but the overall effects of unionization on U.S. employment are probably relatively small.

6. Consider a firm that is a perfect competitor in the product market and a monopsonist in the labor market.

   a. That firm faces an upward-sloping supply of labor curve. Before it can hire more labor, the firm must raise wage rates for *all* of its employees.

   b. As a consequence, the marginal factor cost of hiring labor to that firm exceeds the wage rate. The MFC curve is that firm's additional cost of hiring labor, and it rises as the firm hires more labor.

   c. The marginal benefit of hiring labor to such a firm is its MRP curve, which falls (due to declining marginal product of labor) as it hires more labor.

   d. The profit-maximizing employment level occurs at the point at which the decreasing MRP curve intersects the rising MFC curve. The wage rate is set on the supply curve, consistent with that quantity of labor.

   e. In such a situation, monopsonistic exploitation of labor results because the wage rate is below the MRP of labor.

7. A summary of monopoly, monopsony, and perfectly competitive situations is presented in Figure 29-8.

■ Key Terms

Collective bargaining	Jurisdictional dispute	Right-to-work laws
Craft unions	Labor unions	Strikebreakers
Industrial unions	Monopsonist	

■ Key Concepts

Bilateral monopoly	Marginal factor cost (MFC)	Sympathy strike
Closed shop	Monopsonistic exploitation	Union shop
Featherbedding	Secondary boycott	

■ Completion Questions

Fill in the blank, or circle the correct term.

1. The U.S. labor movement started with local _____ unions, which are comprised of workers in a particular _____. The other major type of union is the _____ union, which consists of workers from a particular _____.

2. The Great Depression generated legislation that (<u>helped, hurt</u>) the union movement.

3. The Taft-Hartley Act of 1947 (<u>is, is not</u>) considered pro-labor union. The law allows states to pass _____ laws. The act makes illegal the following union practices: _____, _____, _____ strikes, and _____ boycotts.

4. The original craft unions were the _____.

5. The ultimate bargaining tool for the union is the _____.

6. If a union sets wage rates above market clearing levels, it creates a(n) _____ of labor. Viewed alternatively, the union creates a(n) _____ of jobs, which it must then ration to workers.

7. If a union chooses to employ all of its members, it (<u>must, need not</u>) accept a lower wage rate. If the union wants to maximize the value of total wages, it sets the wage rate at the point at which the price elasticity of demand for labor equals the number _____. If the union wants to set relatively high wages for its high-seniority members, its _____ members will be laid off.

8. Assume that a firm is a perfect competitor in the product market and a monopsonist in the labor market. The marginal benefit of hiring labor for such a firm is its _____ curve, which is (<u>horizontal, negatively sloped, positively sloped</u>), due to the law of _____. The marginal cost of hiring labor for such a firm is its _____ curve, which is (<u>horizontal, positively sloped, negatively sloped</u>). The firm's MFC curve rises because as it hires more labor, wage rates (<u>fall, rise, remain constant</u>) since the industry supply of labor curve is _____ sloping. The firm's MFC is (<u>equal to, greater than, less than</u>) the wage rate.

9. Assume a firm is a monopolist in the product market and a monopsonist in the labor market. The marginal benefit of hiring labor for that firm is its _____ curve, which falls due to _____ and _____ as output increases. The marginal cost of hiring labor is that firm's _____ curve, which rises because in order to hire more labor, that firm must _____ wage rates of _____ employees. This is because the firm's supply of labor curve is _____ sloping.

10. A firm maximizes total profits by hiring labor up to the point at which the marginal benefit (<u>exceeds, equals, is less than</u>) the marginal cost from doing so. Suppose Firm A is a perfect competitor in the product market and a monopsonist in the labor market. Firm A will hire labor up to the point at which a downward-sloping _____ curve intersects an upward-sloping _____ curve. Given that quantity of labor, the wage rate will be set at that level consistent with the (<u>supply, demand</u>) curve of labor.

11. Firm B is a monopolist in the product market and a monopsonist in the labor market. If it wants to maximize total profits, it will hire labor up to the point at which a downward-sloping _____ curve intersects an upward-sloping _____ curve.

12. When a resource is paid less than its _____, monopsonistic exploitation exists.

■ True-False Questions

Circle the **T** if the statement is true, the **F** if it is false. Explain to yourself why a statement is false.

T F   1. The growth rate of unions and the extent to which unions are effective has depended on government support.

T F   2. The Wagner Act increases union power, but the Taft-Hartley Act reduces it.

T F   3. Union power was decreased during the Great Depression.

T F   4. In recent years, public employee union membership has increased significantly.

T F   5. Unions tend to create a shortage of labor and a surplus of jobs.

T F   6. In the United States, unions can set wage rates or determine the quantity of labor hired, but they cannot do both.

T F   7. If a union wants to maximize the value of total wages, it sets wage rates as high as it possibly can.

T F   8. If a union can restrict the total quantity of laborers to a fixed number, its members will earn higher wages in the future.

T F   9. Recent studies indicate that unions do not increase labor's productivity.

T F   10. A profit-maximizing firm that is a perfect competitor in the product market but a monopsonist in the labor market will hire labor up to the point at which MRP of labor equals the going wage rate.

T F   11. A firm that is a monopolist in the product market and a monopsonist in the labor market maximizes total profit by hiring labor up to the point at which the MRP of labor equals the MFC of labor.

T F   12. Monopsonistic exploitation exists when workers receive a wage below their MRP.

T F   13. Government action to impose a minimum wage that is higher than the wage rate currently paid by a monopsonist causes employment at the monopsonist to decline.

■ Multiple Choice Questions

Circle the letter that corresponds to the best answer.

1. Which one of the following is **not** associated with a craft union?
   a. United Auto Workers
   b. AFL
   c. Knights of Labor
   d. Pipefitters Union

2. Which one of the following acts is **not** pro-labor union?
   a. National Industrial Recovery Act
   b. Wagner Act
   c. Taft-Hartley Act
   d. National Labor Relations Act

3. Which one of the following is legal in **non**–right-to-work states?
   a. closed shop
   b. union shop
   c. sympathy strike
   d. secondary boycott

4. Which one of the following is true about the union movement?
   a. The growth and effectiveness of unions depends in part on the extent of government help.
   b. Since 1968, private-employee union membership has risen.
   c. Since 1968, public-employee union membership has fallen dramatically.
   d. All of the above.

5. Unions tend to
   a. set minimum wages for members above the market clearing level.
   b. create unemployment for low-seniority members.
   c. create surpluses of labor and shortages of union jobs.
   d. All of the above.

6. If a union sets wage rates above market clearing levels, then
   a. jobs must be rationed among union members.
   b. a surplus of jobs is created.
   c. a shortage of labor is created.
   d. high-seniority members will complain.

7. Which one of the following is inconsistent with the others?
    a. surplus of labor
    b. shortage of jobs
    c. wage rate above the market clearing level
    d. wage rate below the market clearing level

8. If unions want to maximize the value of total wages, they set wage rates
    a. as high as they can.
    b. as low as they can.
    c. at the point at which the price elasticity of demand for labor equals 1.
    d. in the inelastic range of the product demand curve.

9. If unions maximize the wage rate of high-seniority workers, then
    a. low-seniority workers will become laid off.
    b. all union members will remain employed.
    c. they violate the Wagner Act.
    d. they violate the Taft-Hartley Act.

10. Which one of the following statements probably best describes the impact of unions on wage rates?
    a. Unions have increased all wage rates in the economy.
    b. Unions have increased all union worker wage rates.
    c. Unions increase the wage rates of some workers at the expense of other workers.
    d. Unions cannot raise wage rates for their members.

11. Unions can set
    a. wage rates but not employment levels.
    b. wage rates and employment levels.
    c. neither wage rates nor employment levels.
    d. either wage rates or employment levels, but not both.

12. If Firm B is a monopsonist in the labor market and a perfect competitor in the product market, then
    a. it faces a horizontal supply of labor curve.
    b. it faces a horizontal demand for labor curve.
    c. its wage rate equals its MFC.
    d. its marginal benefit from hiring labor equals the MRP of labor.

13. Firm B from Question 12 can maximize total profits by hiring labor up to the point at which
    a. a decreasing MRP of labor curve intersects a decreasing MFC of labor curve.
    b. a decreasing MRP of labor curve intersects a rising MFC of labor curve.
    c. a decreasing MRP of labor curve intersects a horizontal supply of labor curve, at the going wage rate.
    d. a horizontal MRP of labor curve is intersected by a rising MFC of labor curve.

14. Firm B from Questions 12 and 13 faces
    a. a rising MFC of labor.
    b. a declining labor MRP.
    c. an upward-sloping supply of labor curve.
    d. All of the above.

15. If Firm A is a monopolist in the product market and a monopsonist in the labor market, then
    a. it faces a horizontal labor supply and a horizontal labor demand curve.
    b. it faces a downward-sloping supply of labor curve.
    c. the marginal revenue product of labor falls and the marginal factor cost of labor rises.
    d. the marginal revenue product of labor is constant and the marginal factor cost of labor rises.

16. Firm A from Question 15 can maximize total profits by hiring labor up to the point at which
    a. a downward-sloping MRP of labor curve intersects an upward-sloping MFC of labor curve.
    b. an upward-sloping MRP of labor equals a constant wage rate.
    c. a constant MRP of labor curve equals a falling MFC of labor.
    d. a horizontal MRP of labor curve is intersected by a rising supply of labor curve.

17. Firm A from Question 15
    a. observes an MFC that exceeds the wage rate.
    b. observes a selling price that exceeds the marginal revenue of an extra unit of output.
    c. maximizes profits by hiring to the point at which MRP of labor = MFC of labor.
    d. All of the above.

18. Which one of the following is probably an example of monopsony exploitation, as defined in this text?
    a. A low-skilled laborer is paid $1 per hour in a perfectly competitive labor market
    b. A professional athlete gets paid $1 million per year, but his MRP is $1.5 million per year.
    c. Mr. Smith can earn $35,000 per year as a plumber but chooses to work as a high school teacher for $20,000 per year.
    d. Mrs. Calvo has a Ph.D. in English but only earns $10,000 per semester teaching university English because there are so many qualified teachers in that area.

19. Monopsonistic exploitation equals
    a. marginal physical product of labor minus the wage rate.
    b. marginal revenue product of labor minus the wage rate.

c.   marginal physical product of labor minus marginal revenue product of labor.

d.   marginal factor cost of labor minus marginal physical product.

■ Working with Graphs

1.   Suppose you are given the following graphical representation for a monopsonist selling its output in a perfectly competitive market. Answer the following questions.

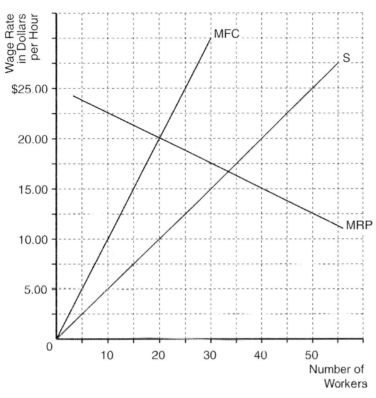

a.   Given the market conditions that exist in the above graph, the monopsonist will hire _____ workers per day at a wage of _____ per hour.

b.   Suppose that the government (or a labor union) initiates a minimum wage of $12.50 per hour in this particular market. As a result, the monopsonist will (<u>increase, decrease</u>) its employment rate to _____ workers per day at a wage of _____ per hour.

2. Use the graph below to answer the following questions. *Note:* Define monopolistic exploitation as being equal to the difference between *VMP* (or price times the marginal product of labor) and MRP—as defined in the text. (*Note: VMP* is not defined in your text. Consequently, this is a difficult question. It is purely optional.)

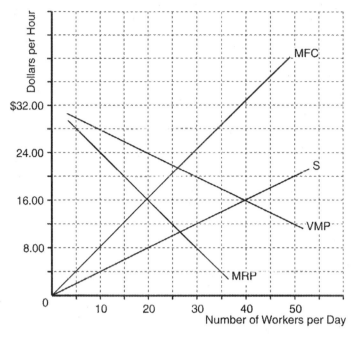

a. This monopolist-monopsonist will hire _____ workers per day and pay a wage of _____ per hour.

b. At this rate of employment, the value of marginal product of labor (*VMP*) is _____ per hour.

c. With no outside intervention in this market, we will observe (<u>monopsonistic, monopolistic, both monopsonistic and monopolistic</u>) exploitation.

d. The level of monopsonistic exploitation is _____ per hour, and the level of monopolistic exploitation is _____ per hour.

e. The total level of exploitation is _____ per hour, represented by the difference between the _____ and the _____.

■ Answers

Completion Questions

1. craft; skill or trade; industrial; industry

2. helped

3. is not; right-to-work; closed shop (union shop in right-to-work states); jurisdictional disputes; sympathy; secondary

4. European merchant guilds

5. strike

6. surplus; shortage

7. must; l; low-seniority

8. MRP of labor; negatively sloped; diminishing returns; MFC of labor; positively sloped; rise; upward; greater than

9. MRP of labor; diminishing marginal physical product of labor; decreasing product price; MFC of labor; raise; all; upward

10. equals; MRP of labor; MFC of labor; supply

11. MRP of labor; MFC of labor

12. marginal revenue product

True-False Questions

1. T

2. T

3. F It was increased by President Roosevelt.

4. T

5. F They create a surplus of labor and a shortage of jobs.

6. T

7. F It sets the wage rate at the point at which the price elasticity of demand equals l.

8. F Not necessarily. Demand may fall dramatically.

9. F They may increase productivity by creating a safer and more secure environment.

10. F It hires up to the point at which MRP = MFC of labor.

11. T

12. T

13. F The monopsonist hires labor to the point where MRP = MFC, at which the profit-maximizing quantity of labor hired is less than would be true in a perfectly competitive market. A minimum wage above the profit-maximizing wage reduces MFC to the fixed minimum wage rate, so the monopsony hires more workers.

Multiple Choice Questions

1. (a)	11. (d)
2. (c)	12. (d)
3. (b)	13. (b)
4. (a)	14. (d)
5. (d)	15. (c)
6. (a)	16. (a)
7. (d)	17. (d)
8. (c)	18. (b)
9. (a)	19. (b)
10. (c)	

Working with Graphs

1. a. 20, $10
    b. increase, 25, $12.50

2. a. 20, $8
    b. $24
    c. both monopsonistic and monopolistic
    d. $8, $8
    e. $16, *VMP* of $24 per hour, wage of $8 per hour

■ Glossary

Bilateral monopoly   A market structure consisting of a monopolist and a monopsonist.

Closed shop   A business enterprise in which employees must belong to the union before they can be employed and must remain in the union after they are hired.

Collective bargaining   Negotiation between the management of a company and the management of a union for the purpose of setting a mutually agreeable contract that sets wages, fringe benefits, and working conditions for all employees in the unions involved.

Craft unions   Labor unions composed of workers who engage in a particular trade or skill, such as baking, carpentry, or plumbing.

Featherbedding   Any practice that forces employers to use more labor than they would otherwise or to use existing labor in an inefficient manner.

Industrial unions   Labor unions that consist of workers from a particular industry, such as automobile manufacturing or steel manufacturing.

Jurisdictional dispute   A disagreement involving two or more unions over which should have control of a particular jurisdiction, such as a particular craft or skill or a particular firm or industry.

Labor unions   Worker organizations that seek to secure economic improvements for their members. They also seek to improve the safety, health, and other benefits (such as job security) of their members.

Monopsonist   The only buyer in a market.

Monopsonistic exploitation   Paying a price for the variable input that is less than its marginal revenue product; the difference between marginal revenue product and the wage rate.

Right-to-work laws   Laws that make it illegal to require union membership as a condition of continuing employment in a particular firm.

Secondary boycott   A refusal to deal with companies or purchase products sold by companies that are dealing with a company being struck.

Strikebreakers   Temporary or permanent workers hired by a company to replace union members who are striking.

Sympathy strike   A work stoppage by a union in sympathy with another union's strike or cause.

Union shop   A business enterprise that may hire nonunion members, conditional on their joining the union by some specified date after employment begins.

30 Income, Poverty, and Health Care

■ Learning Objectives

After you have studied this chapter, you should be able to

1. describe how to use a Lorenz curve to represent a nation's income distribution;

2. identify the key determinants of income differences across individuals;

3. discuss theories of desired income distribution;

4. distinguish among alternative approaches to measuring and addressing poverty;

5. recognize the role played by third-party payments in rising health care costs;

6. explain the key elements of the new U.S. national health insurance program and evaluate its potential economic effects.

■ Outline

1. This chapter attempts to define distribution of income and present theories of why income is unevenly distributed across the population.

2. The Lorenz curve is a geometric representation of the distribution of income.
   a. There are some criticisms of using the Lorenz curve to measure the degree of income inequality in a nation.
      i. The curve does not take into account income in kind.
      ii. It does not account for differences in family size and effort.
      iii. It does not account for age differences.
      iv. It measures pretax money income.
      v. It does not measure underground economy earnings.
   b. Since World War II the distribution of money income in the United States has not changed very much.
   c. The distribution of total income, which includes in-kind transfers, has become more equal in the United States since 1962.

3. Wealth and income are not synonymous.
   a. Wealth is a stock concept, and income is a flow concept.
   b. A stock is evaluated at a given moment in time. A flow is evaluated during a period of time.
   c. Each of us inherits a different endowment, including human attributes and nonhuman wealth, which strongly affects our ability to earn income in the marketplace.

4. There are numerous determinants of income differences.
   a. The wage–earnings cycle typically shows that at a young age income is low. Income builds gradually to a peak at around age 50, and then gradually curves down until it approaches zero at retirement age.
   b. In competitive markets, workers can expect to earn approximately their marginal revenue product (MRP).
   c. Determinants of an individual's marginal productivity include innate abilities and attributes, experience, and training.

5. Inheritance is also a determinant of income differences.

6. Discrimination undoubtedly contributes somewhat to income differences.
   a. White families earn higher median incomes than black families.
   b. Males earn higher median incomes than females.

7. There are normative standards of income distribution: equality and productivity.

8. Western nations have sustained enough economic growth over the last several hundred years so that mass poverty has disappeared.

9. If poverty is measured in absolute terms, it will be eliminated by economic growth. If poverty is defined in relative terms, it will be mathematically impossible to eliminate it, unless everyone has the same income—an improbable event. If we correct poverty rates for in-kind transfers, they fall dramatically in the United States.

10. There is a variety of income-maintenance programs designed to help the poor: They include social insurance, Supplemental Security Income, Temporary Assistance to Needy Families, food stamps, and the Earned Income Tax Credit program.

11. In spite of the numerous programs designed to reduce poverty, officially defined poverty rates have shown no long-run tendency to drop since their relatively dramatic decline through 1973.

12. In recent years the prices of health care services and health care insurance have increased considerably in the United States. U.S. citizens have been spending higher and higher percentages of their income on health care.

13. There are several explanations as to why health care costs have risen rapidly in the United States.
    a. Our population is, on average, getting older and the elderly are the main users of health care.
    b. Technological advances in medicine have spawned expensive machinery that everyone wants to use (both suppliers and demanders).

   c. The third-party payment system has created a situation in which physicians and hospitals have no incentive to keep health care costs down.

      i. Because health care is subsidized by government, people want more than they would otherwise. Thus, a moral hazard exists.

      ii. Both government and private-provided health care insurance create a situation in which third parties (insurers) pay most of the costs of medical services. Hence, people want more health care than if they were paying for it themselves.

14. Legislation passed in 2010 has given the federal government a fundamental role in the U.S. health care industry.

   a. The legislation has several components:

      i. The law requires nearly all U.S. residents either to purchase health insurance coverage or pay fines, and requires firms with more that 50 employees to offer health insurance coverage or pay fines.

      ii. The law also requires the federal government to either to pay subsidies or to extend Medicaid coverage to families with incomes up to 400 percent of the federal poverty level.

      iii. In addition, the legislation created government-directed exchanges that provide services matching individuals and firms to health insurance plans that satisfy a number of detailed regulations.

      iv. Finally, the law establishes a special tax rate of 3.8 percent to be applied to nearly all incomes earned by individuals earning more than $200,000 per year and married couples earning more than $250,000 per year.

   b. There are three key ways in which the health care legislation will affect the U.S. economy:

      i. The requirement for many firms to provide health insurance will raise the effective wage rate that they must pay per unit of labor hired, which will induce movements upward along their downward-sloping marginal-revenue-product-of-labor curves and hire less labor. Thus, the quantity of labor demanded by firms will decrease. Other things being equal, U.S. employment will decline.

      ii. In markets for goods and services, the fact that firms' costs of hiring each additional unit of labor will rise will result in higher marginal costs. Firms will respond by reducing output of goods and services at all prices, which will place upward pressure on equilibrium prices.

      iii. Most estimates indicate that the federal government's spending on health care will rise faster than receipts of new tax revenues to finance these expenditures, so the government budget deficit likely will increase, other things being equal.

■ Key Terms

Lorenz curve

■ Key Concepts

Age-earnings cycle	Income in kind
Distribution of income	Third parties

■ Completion Questions

Fill in the blank, or circle the correct term.

1. A Lorenz curve shows what portion of total money income is accounted for by different _____ of a nation's households. If it is a 45-degree line, then _____ income inequality exists.

2. The Lorenz curve as a representation of income inequality has been criticized because it does not _____, or account for _____, _____, _____, and _____.

3. Since World War II, the lowest 20 percent of the income distribution in the United States had a combined money income of _____ percent of the total money income of the entire population. If income in kind is taken into account, however, income inequality has (decreased, increased) relative to the period immediately following World War II.

4. (Wealth, Income) is a stock concept, while _____ is a flow concept.

5. One determinant of income inequality is age. The age-earnings cycle indicates that teenagers' incomes are relatively (low, high). Incomes rise gradually to a peak at around age _____, and then gradually fall toward zero as people approach _____. People earn different amounts over their lifetime because age is related to a worker's _____.

6. If a worker's MRP exceeds her wage rate, chances are that she will (change jobs, be laid off). If a worker's wage rate is greater than her MRP, then chances are she will be _____. As long as it is costly to obtain information about a specific worker's MRP, there (will, will not) be some difference between a worker's wage and her MRP.

7. Three determinants of an individual's marginal productivity are _____, _____, and _____. Other than differences in marginal productivity, income differences are also due to _____, _____, and _____.

8. Two theories of normative standards of income distribution are _____ and _____.

9. (Absolute, Relative) poverty will automatically be eliminated by economic growth, but _____ poverty can never be eliminated, in practice.

10. In the United States, several income-maintenance programs are aimed at eliminating poverty. The best known is _____ Security, which in effect is an intergenerational income transfer. Another is *SSI*, which establishes a nationwide _____ income for the aged, the blind, and the disabled. The TANF program is for families who are _____ in need.

11. In the United States since 1973 there (has, has not) been a long-run trend toward reduced officially defined poverty.

12. Many economists believe that the major cost to increased income equality is _____. Hence, a trade-off exists.

13. In recent years the percent of total income spent on medical care has (<u>decreased, increased</u>) dramatically because (1) our population, on average, is getting (<u>younger, older</u>); (2) technological advances in medical equipment have caused (<u>a decrease, an increase</u>) in the demand for medical services; (3) third-party billing has (<u>decreased, increased</u>) due to health insurance; and (4) physicians and hospitals have (<u>few, strong</u>) incentives to keep costs down.

14. Most national health care plans incorporate a system to put a (<u>floor, ceiling</u>) on medical fees and services. This will create (<u>surpluses, shortages</u>) eventually.

■ True-False Questions

Circle the **T** if the statement is true, the **F** if it false. Explain to yourself why a statement is false.

T   F   1. In the real world, no country has a linear (straight-line) Lorenz curve.

T   F   2. Third-party paying avoids the moral hazard problem that exists in the health care system.

T   F   3. When in-kind transfers are considered, measured income inequality in the United States rises, and poverty levels fall.

T   F   4. Not considering income in kind, the bottom 20 percent of U.S. income earners earn about 5 percent of total U.S. income.

T   F   5. Income and wealth are unrelated.

T   F   6. Income is stock concept, and wealth is a flow concept.

T   F   7. In the United States, over time, income inequality has increased dramatically.

T   F   8. An age-earnings cycle exists because age and marginal productivity are related.

T   F   9. In a competitive economy, workers tend to get paid their marginal revenue product.

T   F   10. In the United States, inheritance and discrimination are more important determinants of income differences than are marginal productivity differences.

T   F   11. In the United States, the return to investment in human capital is significantly higher than it is for other investments.

T   F   12. Mass poverty is still a problem for even the advanced Western economies.

T   F   13. Economic growth will eventually eliminate relative poverty.

T   F   14. Despite massive sums of money devoted to income redistribution programs in the United States, officially measured poverty has remained roughly unchanged since 1973.

T F 15. All economists agree that more income equality in the United States is desirable.

T F 16. Because health care is usually paid for by third parties, buyers are largely insensitive to price increases.

T F 17. Physicians and hospitals, like other service providers, have an incentive to keep costs down.

T F 18. To help fund the national health care program, the federal government has imposed a special 3.8 percent tax rate on all of the incomes of all households.

■ Multiple Choice Questions

Circle the letter that corresponds to the best answer.

1. The Lorenz curve
   a. gives a numerical measure of a nation's degree of income inequality.
   b. is a straight line in modern, industrial societies.
   c. is a straight line in socialist countries.
   d. overstates the true degree of income inequality, as it is currently measured.

2. Which one of the following statements about the Lorenz curve is correct?
   a. It accounts for age differences.
   b. It considers income-in-kind transfers.
   c. It considers pretax income.
   d. It considers income earned in the underground economy.

3. In 2011, in the United States, the lowest 20 percent of income earning families had a combined income of about _____ percent of the total money income of the entire population.
   a. 5
   b. 10
   c. 15
   d. 20

4. Which one of the following statements is **false**?
   a. The U.S. population, on average, is getting older.
   b. Technological advances in medicine have reduced health care costs.
   c. Much of health care is subsidized by governments.
   d. Most health care is paid for by third parties.

5. *Analogy:* Income is to flow as _____ is to stock.
   a. wealth
   b. poverty
   c. consumption
   d. investment

6. Total economic wealth
    a. is a flow concept.
    b. includes human attributes.
    c. excludes nonhuman wealth.
    d. is zero for most people in the United States.

7. In the United States, the long-run trend shows
    a. increased poverty.
    b. increased income inequality.
    c. little change in officially measured poverty.
    d. increased poverty once income-in-kind adjustments are made.

8. In the United States, over the age-earnings cycle,
    a. productivity changes.
    b. income peaks at about age 65.
    c. income rises with age, throughout.
    d. income first falls with age, then rises with age.

9. In the United States, an age-earnings cycle exists because
    a. age is unrelated to income.
    b. age and income are related by law.
    c. productivity and age are related.
    d. of minimum-wage laws.

10. Which one of the following is probably the **most** important determinant of income differences in the United States?
    a. differences in marginal productivity
    b. inheritance of nonhuman wealth
    c. discrimination
    d. income assistance programs

11. Which one of the following is the **least** like the others, with respect to productivity?
    a. innate abilities and attributes
    b. experience
    c. education and training
    d. inheritance of nonhuman wealth

12. Which one of the following is **not** a key component of the federal government's national health care program?
    a. fines on individuals who do not buy health insurance
    b. fines on businesses that do not provide health insurance
    c. nearly complete deregulation of private health insurance plans to enable providers to reduce their costs
    d. government-directed health insurance exchanges to match individuals and firms to available insurance plans

13. Which one of the following does **not** occur with economic growth?
    a. elimination of absolute poverty
    b. elimination of relative poverty
    c. increasing living standards
    d. increasing life expectancy

14. In recent years in the United States,
    a. health care costs have increased as a percentage of national income.
    b. the population, on average, has been getting younger.
    c. technological discoveries have reduced the cost of medical care.
    d. health care costs have risen, but national income has risen more rapidly.

15. The Earned Income Tax Credit (EITC) program creates
    a. incentives for those taxed to work.
    b. disincentives for its recipients to work.
    c. incentives for its recipients to increase MRP.
    d. neither incentives nor disincentives for anyone to work.

16. We have to worry about greatly increasing Medicare expenditures because
    a. the U.S. population is getting older.
    b. there is a moral hazard issue with respect to Medicare.
    c. Congress keeps adding to eligible expenses for Medicare repayment.
    d. All of the above.

17. The optimal amount of income inequality is
    a. zero.
    b. a positive economics concept.
    c. a normative economics concept.
    d. agreed on by all economists.

18. In a nation in which complete income equality has been achieved,
    a. economic incentives would be reduced dramatically.
    b. economic freedom would be curtailed dramatically.
    c. national output and national income would fall dramatically.
    d. All of the above.

■ Matching

Choose the item in Column (2) that best matches an item in Column (1).

(1)		(2)	
(a)	Lorenz curve	(f)	inherited traits or MRP
(b)	moral hazard	(g)	stock
(c)	determinant of income inequality	(h)	third-party payments
(d)	wealth	(i)	flow
(e)	income	(j)	geometric measure of income distribution

■ Working with Graphs

1. Use the table below and the grid provided to construct a Lorenz curve.

Cumulative Percent of Population	Cumulative Percent of Income
20	5
40	10
60	30
80	70
100	100

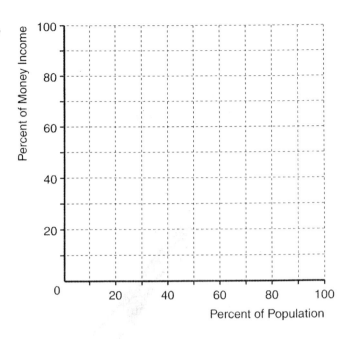

2. Below are income figures for two countries. Plot the Lorenz curve for both countries on the grid provided.

Cumulative Percent of Population	Cumulative Percent of Income	
	Country A	Country B
20	5	10
40	20	20
60	40	30
80	60	50
100	100	100

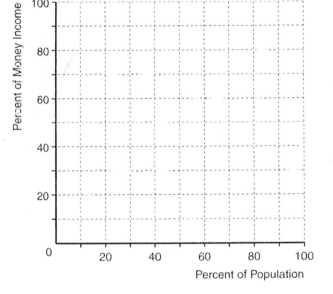

Which of the two countries has the more equal distribution?

■ Problems

1. In your text you learned that income and wealth are different concepts. However, they can be related via the discounting technique that you learned in Chapter 21. How?

■ Answers

Completion Questions

1. proportions; zero
2. include income in kind; differences in family size and effort; age; taxes; underground economy earnings
3. about 5; decreased
4. Wealth; income
5. low; 50; retirement; productivity
6. change jobs; laid off; will
7. talent; experience; training; age, inheritance, discrimination
8. equality; productivity
9. Absolute; relative
10. Social; minimum; temporarily
11. has not
12. less economic efficiency
13. increased; older; an increase; increased; few
14. ceiling; shortages

True-False Questions

1. T
2. F Third-party paying causes a moral hazard problem.
3. F Income inequality and poverty both fall.
4. T
5. F The present value of income equals "human" wealth. See the problem section.
6. F Income is a flow during an interval, and wealth is a stock at a point in time.
7. F It has remained constant or fallen somewhat.
8. T
9. T
10. F Marginal productivity differences are the most important.
11. F The rate of return is about the same.
12. F Economic growth has eliminated it.
13. F Relative poverty can never be eliminated.
14. T
15. F Many believe it undesirable. Almost all recognize its costs.
16. T
17. F No, such a lack of incentive is one reason costs have risen.
18. F The 3.8 percent tax rate applies to nearly all incomes above $200,000 per year earned by individuals and above $250,000 per year earned by married couples.

Multiple Choice Questions

1. (d)
2. (c)
3. (a)
4. (b)
5. (a)
6. (b)
7. (c)
8. (a)
9. (c)
10. (a)
11. (d)
12. (c)
13. (b)
14. (a)
15. (b)
16. (d)
17. (c)
18. (d)

Matching

(a) and (j)	(d) and (g)
(b) and (h)	(e) and (i)
(c) and (f)	

Working with Graphs

1.   See the graph to the right.

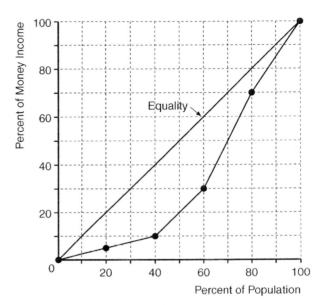

2.   See the graph to the right. Country A has a more equal distribution of income.

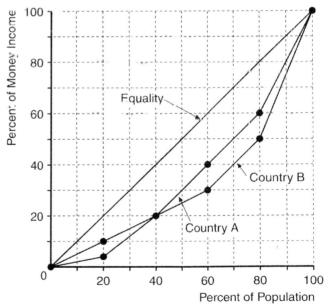

Problems

1.   The value of "human" wealth can be considered as being the present value of the (net) income stream that a person earns over his or her work life.

■ Glossary

Age-earnings cycle   The regular earnings profile of an individual throughout his or her lifetime. The age-earnings cycle usually starts with a low income, builds gradually to a peak at around age 50, and then gradually curves down until it approaches zero at retirement.

Distribution of income   The way income is allocated among the population based on groupings of residents.

Health insurance exchanges   Government agencies to which the national health care program assigns the task of assisting individuals, families, and small businesses in identifying health insurance policies to purchase.

Income in kind   Income received in the form of goods and services, such as housing or medical care. Income in kind differs from money income, which is simply income in dollars or general purchasing power, that can be used to buy *any* goods and services.

Lorenz curve   A geometric representation of the distribution of income. A Lorenz curve that is perfectly straight represents perfect income equality. The more bowed a Lorenz curve, the more unequally income is distributed.

Third parties   Parties who are not directly involved in a given activity or transaction. For example, in the relationship between caregivers and patients, fees may be paid by third parties (insurance companies, government).

31 Environmental Economics

■ Learning Objectives

After you have studied this chapter, you should be able to

1. distinguish between private costs and social costs;

2. understand market externalities and possible ways to correct externalities;

3. explain how economists can conceptually determine the optimal quantity of pollution;

4. contrast the roles of private and common property rights in alternative approaches to addressing the problem of pollution;

5. describe how many of the world's governments are seeking to reduce pollution by capping and controlling the use of pollution-generating resources;

6. discuss how the assignment of property rights may influence the fates of endangered species.

■ Outline

1. It is important to distinguish between private costs and social costs.
   a. Private costs are those incurred by individuals when they use scarce resources.
   b. Social costs include private costs plus the cost of actions borne by people other than those who commit those actions. Social costs embody the full opportunity cost of a resource-using action.
   c. When people use resources in production or consumption, pollution may be an unwanted by-product. If so, the social costs of consuming and producing will exceed the private costs of doing so.

2. An externality exists when a private cost or benefit diverges from a social cost or benefit. If an externality exists, the costs or benefits of an action are not fully borne by the two parties engaged in an exchange or by an individual using resources.

3. In theory, it is possible to change the signals in an economy so that individuals can be forced to take into account all the costs of their actions.
    a. If polluters are charged to pollute, they will (i) install pollution-abatement equipment, (ii) reduce pollution-causing activities, or (iii) pay the price to pollute.
    b. In general, charging a uniform price to pollute is inefficient because a given physical quantity of pollution has different social costs in different places.

4. Ultimately, the optimal quantity of pollution is a normative, not a positive, economics concept.
    a. The waste-disposing capacity of our ecosystem is a scarce resource that can be analyzed like any other resource. The marginal benefit curve for a cleaner environment declines, and the marginal cost curve for a cleaner environment rises.
    b. The optimal quantity of pollution occurs where the declining marginal benefit curve intersects the rising marginal cost curve. In general, the optimal quantity of pollution will exceed zero.

5. Common property is owned by everyone. Hence, private property rights, which allow the use, transfer, and exchange of property, do not exist for common property.
    a. If a resource is scarce and it is common property, it will be wasted. Certain species will become extinct if people value them but property rights do not exist.
    b. A resource that is scarce, but is not common property, can be used efficiently under certain conditions.
    c. Externalities can be internalized via voluntary contracting, even when property rights do not exist,
        i. if the transaction costs associated with making, reaching, and enforcing agreements are low relative to the expected benefits of reaching an agreement, and
        ii. if the number of individuals involved is small.
    d. Private property rights can be assigned (through governments) so that an externality can be internalized.

6. The European Union (EU) is mixing government controls and market processes in an effort to reduce emissions of greenhouse gases that might be contributing to global warming.
    a. After setting an overall national cap on greenhouse-gas emissions, the EU established allowances of such emissions for individual firms and distributed permits to firms allowing greenhouse-gas emissions.
    b. Firms wishing to emit more greenhouse gases than their allowances can purchase additional permits from firms that opt to emit fewer greenhouse gases than their permits allow, and a market clearing price of emission-allowance permits adjusts to equate the quantity of permits demanded with the quantity supplied.

■ Key Terms

Private costs	Transaction costs
Social costs	

■ Key Concepts

Common property   Optimal quantity of pollution
Externality   Private property rights

■ Completion Questions

Fill in the blank, or circle the correct term.

1. Costs incurred by individuals when they use scarce resources are called _____ costs. _____ costs include private costs and external costs and represent the full cost that society bears when a resource-using action occurs.

2. When we add external costs to internal costs, we get _____ costs. An externality exists if there is a divergence between _____ and _____.

3. In theory, decision makers can be made to take into account all of the costs of their actions if people who impose costs on others are (taxed, subsidized).

4. If polluters are charged to pollute, they have the following three options: _____ _____, _____, and _____ _____.

5. A uniform tax on polluters will not be economically efficient if a given physical quantity of pollution imposes different _____ ____ costs in different places.

6. As more and more pollution is reduced, the marginal benefit (falls, rises) and the marginal cost _____ _____. The optimal quantity of pollution occurs at the point at which _____ ___ ___ _____ .

7. If at a zero price the quantity demanded of a resource _____ its quantity supplied, that resource is scarce. If a scarce resource is common property, it probably (will, will not) be wasted.

8. Sheep, cows, and other species are not in danger of extinction because they are valued and _____ rights exist. Other species are becoming extinct because they are _____ property.

9. All costs associated with making, reaching, and enforcing contracts are known as _____ costs.

10. Externalities can be internalized if _____ costs are low and if the number of parties involved is (small, large).

11. In the late 2000s, the European Union sought to bring about a reduction in greenhouse-gas emissions by imposing an overall emissions _____ and distributing emission allowance _____ that firms could trade.

12. In the late 2000s, the decline in the market clearing price of permits allowing firms in the European Union (EU) to emit greenhouse gases was an indication that too (<u>many, few</u>) permits had been distributed in relation to the amount of emissions reduction desired by EU policymakers.

■ True-False Questions

Circle the **T** if the statement is true, the **F** if it is false. Explain to yourself why a statement is false.

T F   1. Social costs do not include private costs.

T F   2. Private costs do not include external costs.

T F   3. If social costs exceed private costs, too much of the good normally will be produced.

T F   4. Pollution is an example of a social cost.

T F   5. The optimal quantity of pollution is zero.

T F   6. Air pollution is a problem because air is common property.

T F   7. A given quantity of physical pollution causes the same amount of economic damage everywhere.

T F   8. If polluters are charged to pollute, we may end up with less pollution.

T F   9. If a use is found for a resource at a zero price, then unless a decision is made about property rights, the resource will be wasted and possibly even destroyed.

T F 10. If private property rights don't exist, the private sector cannot internalize externalities.

T F 11. Externalities may be internalized if the government assigns private property rights.

T F 12. Private property rights to sheep exist. Consequently, they are not in danger of extinction.

T F 13. Attempts to protect one species may well impose costs on humans.

T F 14. If a policy of emissions caps and permits trading is implemented at the market clearing price of emissions-allowance permits declines, then this outcome indicates that the government set the emissions cap well below the amount of emissions desired by firms.

T F 15. Shortly after the European Union introduced a system of capped emissions and permits trading in the late 2000s, the market clearing price of permits declined.

■ Multiple Choice Questions

Circle the letter that corresponds to the best answer.

1. Social costs
   a. exclude internal costs.
   b. exclude external costs.
   c. exclude both internal and external costs.
   d. include both internal and external costs.

2. Air pollution
   a. is an internal cost to firms.
   b. is an external cost to firms.
   c. exists because air is a privately owned resource.
   d. has the same costs to society everywhere.

3. A misallocation of resources may result if
   a. social costs exceed private costs.
   b. social benefits exceed private benefits.
   c. a scarce resource is communally owned.
   d. All of the above.

4. If polluters are charged to pollute, then
   a. pollution will disappear.
   b. the environment will be damaged severely.
   c. less pollution is a probable result.
   d. less voluntary pollution abatement will result.

5. Which one of the following will **not** help to reduce the problem that exists when social costs exceed social benefits?
   a. subsidize polluters
   b. subsidize parties damaged by pollution
   c. charge polluters to pollute
   d. internalize external costs

6. If polluters are charged to pollute, efficiency requires that
   a. they be charged according to the economic damages they create.
   b. they be charged the same amount.
   c. they be charged according to the physical quantity of pollution they generate.
   d. nonpolluters be charged also.

7. The optimal quantity of pollution exists when the
   a. rising marginal benefit of pollution abatement equals the falling marginal cost.
   b. rising marginal cost of pollution abatement equals the falling marginal benefit.
   c. constant marginal cost of pollution abatement equals the falling marginal benefit.
   d. constant marginal benefit of pollution abatement equals the rising marginal cost.

8. Externalities can be internalized by the private sector if
   a. transaction costs of doing so are low.
   b. benefits of doing so are high.
   c. the number of people involved is small.
   d. All of the above.

9. Which statement is **not** true?
   a. An externality is a situation in which a private cost (or benefit) diverges from a social cost (or benefit).
   b. The optimal quantity of pollution is typically greater than zero.
   c. Private costs of any activity always exceed social costs.
   d. Transaction costs include contract-enforcement costs.

10. Under a policy strategy in which a government imposes an emissions cap and issues tradable emissions-allowance permits to firms, the government
    a. places a limit on how many emissions-allowance permits each firm can buy or sell.
    b. issues an unlimited number of emissions-allowance permits but limits the total number of permits that firms may trade.
    c. anticipates that if the strategy is successful in reducing emissions, the market clearing price of permits should fall.
    d. seeks to cap nationwide emissions and then distributes emission-allowance permits across firms.

11. Which one of the following gives people an economic incentive to actively assist in repopulating an endangered species?
    a. making hunting of the endangered species illegal
    b. legalizing trading in the hides, bones, or other body parts of members of the endangered species
    c. allowing people to own the endangered species and to charge the public to view them in nature displays, safaris, and the like
    d. completely separating the endangered species from people, perhaps by placing members of the species in compounds that few humans can visit

■ Matching

Choose the item in Column (2) that best matches an item in Column (1).

(1)	**(2)**

(a)   optimal quantity of pollution

(b)   social costs

(c)   common property

(d)   transaction costs

(e)   private costs

(f)   costs of making, reaching, and enforcing agreements

(g)   internal costs

(h)   owned by all and hence by none

(i)   sum of internal and external costs

(j)   equalization of marginal cost and marginal benefit of pollution abatement

■ Working with Graphs

1.   Use the graph below to answer the questions that follow. Note that *S* represents the industry supply curve and *SS* represents the marginal costs to society—which include marginal private costs and external costs. Assume that no positive externalities exist.

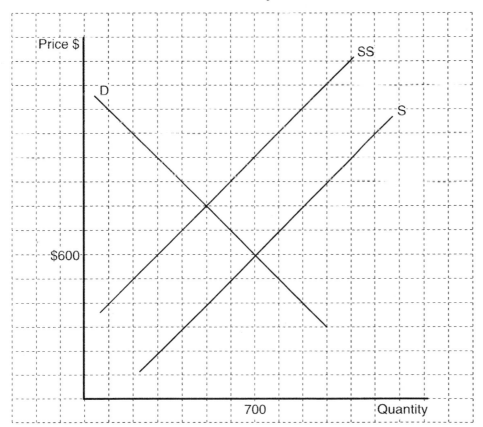

a.   Which curve represents the marginal private costs of producing the good in question?

b.   Which curve reflects the marginal social costs of producing this good?

c. Which curve represents both the marginal private benefits and the marginal social benefits of this good?

d. How many units of this good will be produced by the private sector? What is the value of the marginal social cost of that quantity? The value of the marginal social benefits?

e. What is the optimal quantity of this good, from society's point of view? Why?

2. Suppose you are given the following graph for the demand and supply of fertilizer per week. As a by-product of fertilizer production, the fertilizer plant dumps harmful chemicals into local streams. A local agency has determined that if fertilizer production were limited to two tons per week, the local streams would be able to handle the by-products without harm. The agency has decided to impose a tax on the fertilizer plant. What tax per unit of output is necessary to achieve the agency's goal of no harm to the local streams? Can we conclude that if the agency charges this tax that society is better off? Why or why not?

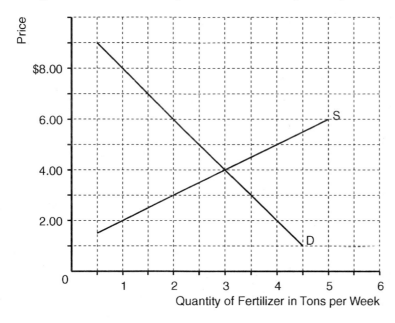

■ Problems

1. Suppose you live in a small town with a privately owned solid-waste disposal facility (garbage dump) just west of town that services a larger city about 30 miles away. Because of the prevailing westerly wind, your town suffers from an unpleasant odor generated at the dump. The more garbage that arrives at the dump in a given week, the more unpleasant the odor is. A study is undertaken, and the results are partially summarized in the table that follows.

(1) Garbage Processed in Tons per Week	(2) Dump's Marginal Cost	(3) Consumers' Valuation of Disposal Services	(4) External Costs Due to Odor	(5) Marginal Social Cost
5	$4.00	$8.00	$0.00	$4.00
10	4.25	7.60	0.20	4.45
15	4.50	6.60	0.50	5.00
20	4.80	5.80	1.00	_____
25	5.20	5.20	1.75	_____
30	5.80	4.80	2.75	_____

Column (1) represents the quantity of garbage disposed of at the dump in tons per week.

Column (2) is the private marginal cost of disposing of various quantities of garbage—the supply of disposal services.

Column (3) represents the demand (willingness to pay) for various quantities of garbage disposal by the consumers of the service in the city to the west.

Column (4) is the external costs that are imposed on residents in your town by the dumping of various quantities of garbage.

Column (5) is the marginal social cost of the dumping services, which includes both private and external costs.

a. Under present conditions, with the disposal plant ignoring external cost, what is the equilibrium price and quantity of disposal services in the market?

b. Complete Column (5).

c. Using your answers from (a) and (b), can you tell what is happening in this market at the present?

d. If the disposal plant were forced to internalize all the relevant costs of operation, what would be the equilibrium price and quantity in this market?

■ Answers

Completion Questions

1. private; Social
2. social; social costs and private costs or social benefits and private benefits
3. taxed
4. install pollution-abatement equipment; reduce pollution-causing activity; pay the price to pollute
5. social
6. falls; rises; $MB = MC$ of pollution reduction
7. exceeds; will
8. private property; common
9. transaction
10. transaction; small
11. cap; permits
12. many

True-False Questions

1. F   They are the sum of private costs and negative externalities (if any).
2. T
3. T
4. T
5. F   It is a positive amount because it costs society resources to have a cleaner environment.
6. T
7. F   The next unit of air pollution causes more economic damage in New York City than it does in a small town in Arizona.
8. T
9. T
10. F   The private sector, throughout history, has sometimes been able to do so, when transaction costs are low.
11. T
12. T
13. T
14. F   If the emissions cap had been set well-below desired emissions, then the market clearing price of permits should have increased.
15. T

Multiple Choice Questions

1. (d)   7. (b)
2. (b)   8. (d)
3. (d)   9. (c)
4. (c)   10. (d)
5. (a)   11. (c)
6. (a)

Matching

(a) and (j)   (d) and (f)
(b) and (i)   (e) and (g)
(c) and (h)

Working with Graphs

1. a. curve *S*
    b. curve *SS*
    c. curve *D*
    d. 700; $1,000; $600
    e. 500; that is where the *MB* to society equals the *MC* to society

2. $3 per ton of fertilizer. No. We are given no information about how much society values unharmed streams in the area, so we are not justified in concluding that the tax has made society better off.

Problems

1. a. $5.20, 25 tons per week
    b. Marginal social cost: $5.80, $6.95, $8.55
    c. With the external costs being ignored, the disposal plant's marginal cost at the equilibrium level is below the true marginal social cost.
    d. $5.80, 20 tons per week

■ Glossary

Common property Property that is owned by everyone and therefore by no one. Air and water are examples of common property resources.

Externality A consequence of a diversion of private cost (or benefit) from a social cost (or benefit). A situation in which the costs (or benefits) of an action are not fully borne (or gained) by the decision makers engaged in an activity that uses scarce resources.

Optimal quantity of pollution The level of pollution for which the marginal benefit of one additional unit of pollution abatement just equals the marginal cost of that additional unit of pollution abatement.

Private costs Costs borne solely by the individuals who incur them. Also called *internal costs*.

Private property rights Exclusive rights of ownership that allow the use, transfer, and exchange of property.

Social costs The full costs borne by society whenever a resource use occurs. Social costs can be measured by adding external costs to private, or internal, costs.

Transaction costs All costs associated with making, reaching, and enforcing agreements.

32 Comparative Advantage and the Open Economy

■ Learning Objectives

After you have studied this chapter, you should be able to

1. discuss the worldwide importance of international trade;

2. explain why nations can gain from specializing in production and engaging in international trade;

3. understand common arguments against free trade;

4. describe ways that nations restrict foreign trade;

5. identify key international agreements and organizations that adjudicate trade.

■ Outline

1. The proportion of GDP accounted for by trade varies greatly among individual nations, but if trade were curtailed, even such nations as the United States would be affected significantly.
    a. A nation ultimately pays for its imports by exports. Thus, restrictions on imports ultimately reduce exports.
    b. If trade is voluntary, then both nations participating in an exchange benefit.

2. A nation has a comparative advantage in producing good A if out of all the goods it can produce, good A has the lowest opportunity cost.

3. Opportunity costs, and hence comparative advantages, differ among nations.

4. There are numerous arguments that have been presented as being anti-free trade. Such arguments include the infant industry argument, protecting domestic jobs, countering foreign subsidies and dumping, protecting the environment, and national defense concerns. Some of these arguments are simply wrong, and others emphasize costs to the neglect of benefits.

5. There are numerous methods that nations have used to restrict foreign trade.

   a. Some nations place import quotas on foreign goods.

   b. Some nations place taxes or tariffs on foreign goods.

   c. Both quotas and tariffs raise prices to domestic consumers and reduce the quantity of goods traded.

6. There are two key types of international trade organizations.

   a. The World Trade Organization, which has more than 140 member nations, establishes and enforces rules governing trade among these nations.

   b. Regional trade blocs are separate groups of countries that grant special trade privileges only to bloc members.

      i. Trade diversion occurs when a nation's trade shifts from countries outside a regional trade bloc to a country within the bloc, whereas trade deflection takes place when final assembly of products is conducted in a nation within a regional trade bloc so that the products can be exported under beneficial terms to other nations within the bloc.

      ii. Rules of origin define categories of products eligible for trading preferences within a regional trade bloc.

■ Key Terms

Comparative advantage	Infant industry argument
Dumping	Quota system
General Agreement on Tariffs and Trade (GATT)	World Trade Organization (WTO)

■ Key Concepts

Regional trade bloc	Trade diversion
Rules of origin	Voluntary import expansion (VIE)
Trade deflection	Voluntary restraint agreement (VRA)

■ Completion Questions

Fill in the blank, or circle the correct term.

1. A nation ultimately pays for imports by _____.

2. If world trade ceased to exist, all trade-related jobs (would, would not) be lost in the long run. Instead, nations would simply _____. Nevertheless, worldwide living standards would (fall, rise) significantly.

3. International trade permits each nation to specialize in the production of those goods for which it has a(n) _____ advantage. Each nation specializes in the production of goods for which its opportunity costs are the (<u>lowest, highest</u>).

4. Nations have an incentive to specialize and trade because they have different collective tastes and because different nations will always have different _____ costs to producing goods.

5. There are numerous arguments against free trade. These arguments include the _____ industry argument, the argument that trade may impede _____ _ protection, and the contention that trade may interfere with national _____ efforts.

6. Two ways to restrict foreign trade analyzed in the text are _____ on imports and _____ on imported goods.

7. Most restrictions on international trade have one major element in common: They interfere with nations' specializing in the production of goods for which they have a(n) _____ advantage. Therefore they are economically (<u>inefficient, efficient</u>).

8. Because a nation ultimately pays for imports with its _____, restricting imports to save jobs destroys jobs in the _____ sector of the economy. Hence, on net, import restrictions (<u>do, do not</u>) save jobs.

9. The _____ _____ is a global organization of more than 140 nations that establishes general rules governing trade among those nations, whereas a(n) _____ _ is a smaller group of countries that agree to grant special trade privileges to all countries within this smaller group.

10. Trade _____ is the shifting of existing international trade from countries outside a regional trade bloc to nations within the bloc, whereas trade _____ __ _____ is the completion of assembly of products in a country within a bloc with the intent of gaining from trade preferences granted when the products are exported to other nations within the bloc.

■ True-False Questions

Circle the **T** if the statement is true, the **F** if it is false. Explain to yourself why a statement is false.

T F   1. If all world trade ceased, import sector jobs and export sector jobs would be permanently destroyed.

T F   2. Because international trade is voluntary in the private sector, both nations benefit from trade that is continued.

T F   3. In the long run, imports are paid for by exports.

T F   4. In effect, a tariff makes the supply of the good in question a vertical line at a level below the original equilibrium quantity.

T F   5. A U.S. tariff on Japanese-made goods will lead to an increase in the demand for U.S. goods that are substitutes for those Japanese-made goods.

T F   6. Import quotas harm domestic consumers but help domestic producers of those goods on which quotas are placed.

T F   7. Tariffs harm domestic consumers and harm domestic producers of goods that compete with the goods on which tariffs are placed.

T F   8. A tariff on good X will cause a leftward shift of the supply curve for good X in the foreign country, and a rightward shift of the demand curve for good X in the country that imposed the tariff.

T F   9. In a two-country world, it is possible for both countries to have a comparative advantage in the production of a specific good.

T F   10. If the United States has a comparative advantage in producing wheat, it must be true that the opportunity cost for producing wheat in the United States is below that opportunity cost in other nations.

T F   11. Because in the real world nations have different resource endowments and different collective tastes, trade will always be advantageous.

T F   12. It is easy to determine the industries to which the infant industry argument applies.

T F   13. If a nation imposes anti-dumping laws, its consumers will pay lower prices for goods.

T F   14. Free trade may increase a nation's instability in the short run because over time a nation's comparative advantage can change.

T F   15. When a nation restricts imports to protect jobs, it in effect preserves less productive employment at the expense of more productive employment.

T F   16. One difference between the economic effects of quotas versus tariffs is that tariffs lead to a higher price to consumers but quotas do not.

T F   17. The World Trade Organization enforces agreements forged among countries in various regional trade blocs.

T F   18. Rules of origin specify categories of products eligible for trading preferences within a regional trade bloc.

■ Multiple Choice Questions

Circle the letter that corresponds to the best answer.

1. In the long run, a nation pays for its imports by
   a. exporting.
   b. creating money.
   c. extending credit to the exporting nation.
   d. All of the above.

2. The U.S. ratio of imports to GDP is about _____ percent.
   a. 5
   b. 10
   c. 17
   d. 25

3. If trade between two nations is voluntary and continued, then
   a. both nations benefit.
   b. one nation could benefit more than the other.
   c. living standards are higher in both nations than if trade were not permitted.
   d. All of the above.

4. Country A's opportunity cost of producing a mobile phone is 5 microchips, and Country B's opportunity cost of producing a microchip is 0.25 mobile phone. Which one of the following statements is true?
   a. Country A has a comparative advantage in producing mobile phones.
   b. Country B has a comparative advantage in producing mobile phones.
   c. Country A has a comparative advantage in producing both goods.
   d. Country B has a comparative advantage in producing both goods.

5. If Country C has a comparative advantage in producing wheat, then its opportunity cost of producing wheat
   a. is maximized.
   b. equals the opportunity cost of producing other goods.
   c. cannot be determined.
   d. is lowest among its trading partners.

6. Nations find it advantageous to trade because they
   a. have different resource endowments.
   b. have different collective tastes.
   c. have different comparative advantages.
   d. All of the above.

7. Which one of the following is **not** an argument used against free trade?
   a. Free trade makes nations more interdependent.
   b. Free trade leads nations to specialize in production.
   c. Free trade increases average and total worldwide incomes.
   d. Imports may destroy some domestic jobs.

8. Which one of the following is most **unlike** the others?
   a. import quota
   b. tariff
   c. free trade
   d. anti-dumping laws

9. Concerning import quotas and tariffs, which of the following statements is true?
   a. Both lead to lower prices for consumers.
   b. Both lead to more imports.
   c. Tariffs lead to higher prices, but quotas do not.
   d. Quotas directly restrain imports, while tariffs induce people to choose fewer imports.

10. Which statement is **not** true, concerning the use of import restrictions to save jobs?
    a. The cost to consumers often exceeds the value of the jobs saved.
    b. Some jobs are destroyed in the export sector.
    c. In the long run, they do not save jobs in those industries in which a nation has lost its comparative advantage.
    d. They are the most efficient way to help domestic workers threatened by foreign competition.

11. Which statement is true of a typical regional trade bloc?
    a. It has more than 140 member nations.
    b. It was originally established by the General Agreement on Tariffs and Trade.
    c. Each nation can appeal perceived violations of regional agreements to the WTO.
    d. Each member nation within a bloc grants others within the bloc special trade privileges.

12. Which one of the following terms best describes trade diversion involving a regional trade bloc?
    a. shifting products from nations that are members of trade bloc to countries outside the bloc for the purpose of avoiding rules of origin
    b. shifting existing international trade from countries outside of a regional trade bloc to nations within the bloc
    c. assembling products outside a regional trade bloc to avoid restrictions specified by the bloc's rules of origin
    d. assembling products in a country within a regional trade bloc to gain from trading the products within the bloc

■ Matching

Choose the item in Column (2) that best matches an item in Column (1).

(1)

(a)   anti-dumping law

(b)   tariff

(c)   trade deflection

(d)   comparative advantage

(e)   trade diversion

(f)   quota system

(2)

(g)   minimum opportunity cost of production

(h)   trade restriction

(i)   tax on foreign-produced goods

(j)   set of restrictions on quantities of imports

(k)   completion of product assembly and sale in a trade bloc

(l)   shifting existing trade from outside a trade bloc to countries within the bloc

■ Working with Graphs

1.   Analyze the graph below, and then answer the questions that follow. The graph deals with an import quota set on foreign-made sugar. Start at Point A.

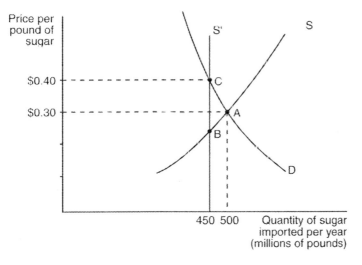

a.   What is the price of sugar in this country, without the import quota?

b.   What is the maximum amount of imported sugar given the quota?

c.   What is the price of sugar, given the import quota?

d.   What is the effective import supply curve, given the quota?

2. Analyze the graphs below, which deal with a U.S. tariff placed on Japanese-made autos, and then answer the questions that follow. Start at Point A.

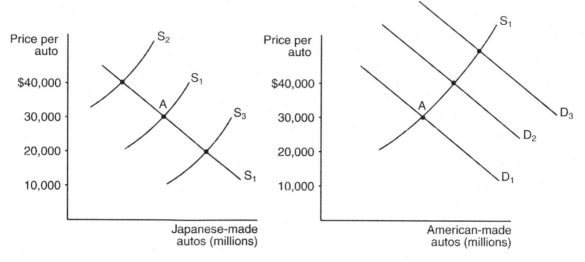

a. What is the price of U.S.- and Japanese-made autos in the United States without the tariff?
b. Which curve represents the supply of Japanese-made autos in the United States after the tariff?
c. Which curve shows the demand for U.S.-made autos in the United States after the tariff?
d. What is the price of autos in the United States after the tariff is imposed?

■ Problems

1. Suppose that Germany and the United States are both experiencing full employment and can produce the following amounts of wine and beer per week. Use this information to answer the following questions.

	Wine (gallons)	Beer (gallons)
Germany	600	1,200
United States	400	1,600

a. Germany has a comparative advantage in the production of _____, whereas the United States has a comparative advantage in the production of _____.
b. What is the cost of wine in terms of beer in Germany? What is the cost of wine in terms of beer in the United States?

2. Let us assume we are again in a two-country world, with the countries being Germany and the United States. Again, to simplify, let us assume that there are only two goods produced, coal and steel. In the table that follows, you will find the production possibilities of both countries. Assume that each country is currently operating at combination B on its production possibilities schedule. Use this information to answer the following questions. (*Hint:* Remember that movements along production possibilities curves involve opportunity costs and that comparative advantage and trade depend on opportunity costs.) Entries are in thousands of tons per week.

		A	B	C	D
Germany:	Coal	0	24	48	72
	Steel	18	12	6	0
United States:	Coal	0	36	72	108
	Steel	36	24	12	0

a. Which country has a comparative advantage in the production of steel?

b. Which country has a comparative advantage in the production of coal?

c. What is the cost of coal in terms of steel in Germany? What is the cost of coal in terms of steel in the United States?

(Remember that these are opportunity costs as determined by production possibilities.)

d. What is the current world production of coal and steel?

e. If both countries specialize in the production of goods in which they have a comparative advantage, Germany will produce _____ thousand tons of _____, the United States will produce _____ thousand tons of _____, and the world output of coal will increase by _____ thousand tons.

■ Answers

Completion Questions

1. exporting

2. would not; produce the goods themselves; fall

3. comparative; lowest

4. opportunity

5. infant; environmental; defense

6. quotas; tariffs

7. comparative; inefficient

8. exports; export; do not

9. World Trade Organization; regional trade bloc

10. diversion; deflection

True-False Questions

1. F   Eventually each nation will produce its own goods—but at a higher cost and (perhaps) lower quality.

2. T

3. T

4. F   That describes the effect of an import quota.

5. T

6. T

7. F   They help domestic producers of such goods.

8. T

9. F   Not for a *specific* good.

10. T

11. T

12. F   In practice, it is difficult to predict which industries will eventually be successful without aid.

13. F   Consumers will pay higher prices.

14. T

15. T

16. F   Both lead to higher prices for consumers.

17. F   The World Trade Organization only enforces WTO rules. Regional trade blocs have their own, separate trade agreements.

18. T

Multiple Choice Questions

1. (a)

2. (c)

3. (d)

4. (b)

5. (d)

6. (d)

7. (c)

8. (c)

9. (d)

10. (d)

11. (d)

12. (b)

Matching

(a) and (h)	(d) and (g)
(b) and (i)	(e) and (k)
(c) and (l)	(f) and (j)

Working with Graphs

1. a. 30 cents per pound
    b. 450 million pounds
    c. 40 cents per pound
    d. The same as the regular supply curve up to 450 million pounds and vertical from that point on

2. a. $30,000 per auto
    b. S_2
    c. D_2
    d. $40,000 per auto

Problems

1. a. wine; beer
    b. 1 gallon wine = 2 gallons beer; 1 gallon wine = 4 gallons beer

2. a. United States
    b. Germany
    c. 4,000 tons coal = 1,000 tons steel; 3,000 tons coal = 1,000 tons steel
    d. 60,000 tons coal; 36,000 tons steel
    e. 72; coal, 36; steel; 12

■ Glossary

Comparative advantage The ability to produce a good or service at a lower opportunity cost than other producers.

Dumping Selling a good or service abroad at a price below the price charged in the home market or at a price below its cost of production.

General Agreement on Tariffs and Trade (GATT) An international agreement established in 1947 to further world trade by reducing barriers and tariffs. GATT was replaced by the World Trade Organization in 1995.

Infant industry argument The contention that tariffs should be imposed to protect from import competition an industry that is trying to get started. Presumably, after the industry becomes technologically efficient, the tariff can be lifted.

Quota system A government-imposed restriction on the quantity of a specific good that another country is allowed to sell in the United States. In other words, quotas are restrictions on imports. These restrictions are usually applied to one or several specific countries.

Regional trade bloc A group of nations that grants members special trade privileges.

Rules of origin Regulations that nations in regional trade blocs establish to delineate product categories eligible for trading preferences.

Trade deflection Moving partially assembled products into a member nation of a regional trade bloc, completing assembly, and then exporting them to other nations within the bloc, so as to benefit from preferences granted by the trade bloc.

Trade diversion Shifting existing international trade from countries outside a regional trade bloc to nations within the bloc.

Voluntary Import Expansion (VIE) An official agreement with another country in which it agrees to import more from the United States.

Voluntary Restraint Agreement (VRA) An official agreement with another country that "voluntarily" restricts the quantity of its exports to the United States.

World Trade Organization (WTO) The successor organization to the GATT that handles trade disputes among its member nations.

33 Exchange Rates and the Balance of Payments

■ Learning Objectives

After you have studied this chapter, you should be able to

1. distinguish between the balance of trade and the balance of payments;

2. identify the key accounts within the balance of payments;

3. outline how exchange rates are determined in the markets for foreign exchange;

4. discuss factors that can induce changes in equilibrium exchange rates;

5. understand how policymakers can go about attempting to fix exchange rates.

■ Outline

1. A balance of trade reflects the difference between the value of a nation's merchandise exports and its merchandise imports. The balance of payments reflects all economic transactions between a nation and the rest of the world.

   a. The current account balance equals the sum of (1) the balance of trade, (2) the balance of services, and (3) net unilateral transfers (private gifts and government grants). If the current account balance is negative, a current account deficit exists. If the current account balance is positive, a current account surplus exists.

   b. Capital account transactions consist of direct investment purchases in financial assets among countries and loans to and from foreigners. If the capital account balance is a negative number, a capital account deficit exists. If the capital account balance is positive, a capital account surplus exists.

   c. If the sum of a nation's current account and its capital account is negative, that nation has an international payments disequilibrium (deficit) that must be financed by official (government) reserve account transactions. Of course, another nation must have an international payments surplus.

      i. Official reserve account transactions include sales or purchases of foreign currencies, gold, special drawing rights, the reserve position in the International Monetary Fund, and financial assets held by official government agencies.

    ii.   Official transactions must exactly equal (but be of opposite sign to) the balance of payments.

2.   Under a flexible exchange rate system of international payments, exchange rates between nations are determined by the forces of supply and demand.

    a.   When U.S. residents import a foreign good or service, this leads to a supply of dollars and a demand for foreign currency on foreign exchange markets.

    b.   When U.S. residents export goods and services to a foreign country, this leads to a supply of foreign currency and a demand for dollars.

    c.   The equilibrium exchange rate is determined in the same way that the equilibrium price for anything is established.

        i.   The U.S. demand curve for (say) European Monetary Union euros is negatively sloped. As the dollar price of the euro falls—it takes fewer dollars to purchase a given quantity of euros—the quantity of euros demanded by U.S. residents rises.

        ii.   The U.S. demand for euros is a derived demand. We demand euros because we demand goods and services produced in nations of the European Monetary Union.

        iii.   Residents of nations in the European Monetary Union supply euros because they want (say) U.S. goods and services. As the dollar price of euros rises—it takes fewer euros to purchase one dollar—European residents will increase their quantity supplied of euros in order to purchase more U.S. goods.

        iv.   The equilibrium dollar price per euro is established at the intersection of the U.S. demand for euros curve and the European Monetary Union supply of euros curve. The equilibrium euro price per dollar is automatically determined thereby.

    d.   If U.S. residents experience a change in tastes in favor of goods and services produced in nations of the European Monetary Union, the demand for euros will increase. The dollar price of the euro rises and the euro price of dollars falls. The dollar depreciates and the euro appreciates.

    e.   Other determinants of exchange rates include (relative) changes in real interest rates, changes in productivity, changes in tastes, and perceptions of economic stability.

3.   Under a gold standard, each nation fixes its exchange rate in terms of gold. Consequently, all exchange rates are fixed. Under the pure gold standard, each nation would have to abandon an independent monetary policy. Each nation's money supply would automatically change whenever a balance of payments disequilibrium occurred.

4.   In 1944, representatives of the world's capitalist nations met in Bretton Woods to create a new international payments system to replace the gold standard that had collapsed in the 1930s.

    a.   The International Monetary Fund (IMF) was established in 1944. The IMF established a system of fixed exchange rates and a means to lend foreign exchange to deficit nations.

    b.   Member governments were obligated to intervene in foreign exchange markets, to maintain the values of their currencies within 1 percent of the declared par value.

    c.   In 1971, the United States ended the connection between the value of the dollar and gold, and in 1973, the Bretton Woods system ended.

5. To fix a nation's exchange rate, a central bank must influence the demand for its nation's currency in the foreign exchange market.

    a. To do this, the central bank must buy or sell foreign exchange reserves. If the central bank must persistently sell reserves of foreign currencies to keep the value of its currency at a pegged level, then the exchange rate can remain fixed only as long as the central bank's foreign exchange reserves last.

    b. A key rationale for fixing the exchange rate is to limit foreign exchange risks so that a nation's residents do not have to hedge against losses from fluctuations in exchange rates.

■ Key Terms

Appreciation

Balance of payments

Balance of trade

Depreciation

Exchange rate

Flexible exchange rates

Foreign exchange market

Foreign exchange risk

Gold standard

Hedge

International Monetary Fund (IMF)

Special drawing rights (SDRs)

■ Key Concepts

Accounting identities

Bretton Woods system

Capital account

Current account

Gold standard

Par value

■ Completion Questions

Fill in the blank, or circle the correct term.

1. When U.S. residents wish to import European-made goods, they supply _____ to the foreign exchange market and demand _____ on that market. When residents of nations in the European Monetary Union wish to import U.S.-made goods, they supply _____ and demand _____ on the foreign exchange market.

2. In a flexible exchange rate system, exchange rates are determined by (<u>governments,</u> <u>supply and demand</u>). If the exchange rate goes from $1.25 per euro to $1.30 per euro, the dollar has (<u>appreciated, depreciated</u>), and the euro has _____.

3. If the euro depreciates, it takes (<u>fewer, more</u>) euros to purchase a dollar. This leads to (<u>an increase, a decrease</u>) in the quantity of euros demanded by U.S. residents and (<u>an increase,</u> <u>a decrease</u>) in the quantity of euros supplied by residents of nations in the European Monetary Union.

4. If U.S. tastes move in favor of European goods, there will be a(n) _____ in the demand for euros. Other things being constant, the euro will (<u>appreciate, depreciate</u>) on the foreign exchange market. This will eventually induce U.S. residents to export (<u>less, more</u>) to Europe and import _____ from Europe.

5. Under a pure gold standard, exchange rates (<u>float, are fixed</u>).

6. If the value of U.S. imports exceeds the value of its exports, the U.S. balance of trade will be a (<u>negative, positive</u>) number, and another country's balance of trade must be a(n) _____ number. The United States then is said to have a trade (<u>deficit, surplus</u>), while the other nation has a trade _____ .

7. If governments do not intervene, by definition the sum of a nation's balance on current account plus its balance on capital account will equal _____. If governments intervene in the balance of payments process, then the sum of a nation's balance on current account plus its balance on capital account must exactly _____, but be of opposite sign to, its official transactions.

8. Official reserve account transactions involve the following assets of individual countries: _____ _____, _____, _____, _____, and _____.

9. A nation's balance of payments is affected by, among other things, relative changes in that nation's _____ and _____.

10. If the value of a nation's exports is less than the value of its imports, it is running a trade _____. The nation's currency will (<u>depreciate, appreciate</u>) under a flexible exchange rate system.

11. The possibility that people may incur losses as a result of unexpected variations in the value of a nation's currency in foreign exchange markets is called _____.

■ True-False Questions

Circle the **T** if the statement is true, the **F** if it is false. Explain to yourself why a statement is false.

T F   1. If you wish to buy German goods, you ultimately offer dollars and demand euros.

T F   2. If you wish to send money to your relatives in England, you ultimately offer dollars and demand English currency.

T F   3. In a flexible exchange rate system, gold flows lead to international payments equilibrium.

T F   4. If French tastes move in favor of U.S. goods, the supply of dollars on the foreign exchange market rises relative to the demand for dollars.

T F   5. The U.S. demand for British pounds rises if the British inflation rate exceeds the U.S. inflation rate.

T F   6. In a flexible exchange rate system, if Canadian tastes move away from U.S. goods (other things being constant), both the U.S. dollar and the Canadian dollar will depreciate.

T F   7. The gold standard is one form of a fixed exchange rate system.

T F   8. Under the gold standard, if disequilibrium exists in the world's balance of payments, gold will flow from one nation to another until payments equilibrium is restored.

T F   9. Under a flexible exchange rate system, if disequilibrium exists in the world's balance of payments, exchange rates will change until payments equilibrium is restored.

T F   10. Under a flexible exchange rate system, each nation must give up control over its own monetary policy.

T F   11. In today's world, the sum of a nation's current account balance plus its capital account balance must be zero.

T F   12. If one nation has a current account deficit, another nation must have a current account surplus.

T F   13. A nation can finance a current account deficit with a capital account surplus.

T F   14. Under a flexible exchange rate system, payments equilibrium is brought about by a change in the exchange rate. Under a gold standard, national price levels change to restore payments equilibrium.

T F   15. To fix, or peg, the exchange rate for its nation's currency, a central bank must buy or sell domestic securities such as bonds issued by the nation's government.

■ Multiple Choice Questions

Circle the letter that corresponds to the best answer.

1. If the foreign exchange rate is that $1 is equivalent to 4 Polish zlotys, then 1 zloty is worth
    a. $4.
    b. 40 cents.
    c. 25 cents.
    d. 4 cents.

2. The demand schedule for euros on the foreign exchange market
    a. is derived partially from foreign demand for European goods.
    b. reflects the fact that European residents want to import goods and services.
    c. shows the quantity of euros demanded at different income levels.
    d. is unimportant if the European Monetary Union is on a fixed exchange rate system.

3. Which one of the following does **not** lead to an increase in the demand for Mexican pesos?
   a. A worldwide change in tastes in favor of Mexican goods occurs.
   b. The Mexican inflation rate exceeds the world inflation rate.
   c. Mexico's interest rate rises relative to world rates.
   d. World real income rises.

4. Which one of the following leads to an increase in the demand for the U.S. dollar on the foreign exchange market?
   a. An increase in U.S. exports
   b. an increase in foreign investment in the United States
   c. an increase in gifts from foreigners to U.S. residents
   d. All of the above.

5. If a nation has an international payments surplus in a flexible exchange rate system, then
   a. its currency will appreciate.
   b. its price level will rise.
   c. gold will flow from it to nations with a payments deficit.
   d. All of the above.

6. Which one of the following statements is **not** true?
   a. Under flexible exchange rates, international payments equilibrium is restored through changes in exchange rates.
   b. Under a gold standard, international payments equilibrium is restored through changes in national price levels.
   c. Under a flexible exchange rate system, a nation cannot pursue a monetary policy that is independent of its trading partners.
   d. Under the gold standard, international payments disequilibrium leads to gold flows, which restore equilibrium.

7. If Thailand has a payments deficit, payments equilibrium can be restored if Thailand's
   a. price level rises relative to the world's.
   b. interest rate rises relative to the world's.
   c. real national income rises relative to the world's.
   d. money supply rises relative to the world's.

8. A nation can finance a deficit on its current account with
   a. a surplus on its capital account.
   b. a deficit on its capital account.
   c. official purchases of foreign currencies with its own currency.
   d. purchases of gold from foreign countries with its own currency.

9. If a nation has a deficit on both its current account and its capital account, then

    a. it is in a balance of payments equilibrium.

    b. the world must be on a flexible exchange rate system.

    c. it must have official transactions that are identical to (but opposite in sign to) the sum of those two deficits.

    d. it will experience gold inflows.

10. A nation's balance of payments is affected by its relative

    a. interest rate.

    b. political stability.

    c. inflation rate.

    d. All of the above.

11. When the price of the Chinese yuan, measured in dollars per yuan, rises in the foreign exchange market,

    a. the quantity of yuan demanded in the foreign exchange market increases.

    b. the quantity of yuan supplied in the foreign exchange market increases.

    c. an increase in the supply of yuan could have generated this higher exchange rate.

    d. a decrease in the demand for yuan could have generated this higher exchange rate.

12 A key requirement for a nation's central bank to be able to keep the exchange rate for its currency fixed is

    a. allowing the equilibrium exchange rate to rise when there is an increase in the demand for its currency.

    b. allowing the equilibrium exchange rate to fall when there is a decrease in the demand for its currency.

    c. possession of sufficient foreign exchange reserves to be able to sell foreign currencies whenever there is pressure for the nation's currency to depreciate.

    d. possession of sufficient foreign exchange reserves to be able to buy foreign currencies whenever there is pressure for the nation's currency to depreciate.

■ Matching

Choose the item in Column (2) that best matches an item in Column (1).

(1)	**(2)**
(a) appreciation	(f) rise in one currency's value relative to another's
(b) depreciation	(g) fall in one currency's value relative to another's
(c) fixed exchange rate system	(h) balance of payments settlements
(d) special drawing right	(i) gold standard
(e) trade deficit	(j) value of imports exceeds value of exports

■ Working with Graphs

1. Consider a situation in which exchange rates are flexible. Consumers in the United States wish to import a good from Germany, a nation that is part of the European Monetary Union.

    a. Calculate the U.S. price of this good, given the German price of the good and the different exchange rates that might prevail as listed in the table below, and place these calculations in the appropriate column. Calculate the quantity of euros demanded by U.S. consumers in order to purchase the import good at different exchange rates. Enter these numbers in the last column.

Exchange Rate ($/euro)	German Price of the Good	U.S. Price of the Good	Quantity Demanded	Total U.S. Euro Expenditures
0.80/1	1 euro	_____	90	_____
0.85/1	1 euro	_____	80	_____
0.90/1	1 euro	_____	70	_____
0.95/1	1 euro	_____	60	_____
1.00/1	1 euro	_____	50	_____

    By looking at the table above, one can conclude that as it takes more dollars to purchase 1 euro, the dollar price of the import good will _____.

    b. In the table above, you are given the quantity of the import good at different prices. Graph the demand for euros on the grid provided below.

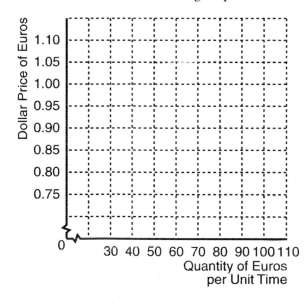

c. Let us now assume that people in Germany wish to import from the United States some good that costs $1 per unit. Calculate the German price of the good given the U.S. price and the different exchange rates that might prevail, as listed in the table below, and place these numbers in the appropriate column.

Exchange Rate ($/euro)	U.S. Price of the Good	German Price of the Good	Quantity Demanded	Total German $ Expenditures
0.80/1	$1	_____	24.0	_____
0.85/1	$1	_____	42.5	_____
0.90/1	$1	_____	63.0	_____
0.95/1	$1	_____	85.5	_____
1.00/1	$1	_____	110.0	_____

By looking at the above table, one can conclude that as it takes more dollars to purchase 1 euro, the euro price of the good will _____.

d. In the last table, you are given the quantity of the import good that German consumers wish to purchase at different German prices. Use this information to calculate the quantity of euros that German consumers will be willing to supply at different exchange rates in order to import the U.S. good. (*Note:* Round off to the nearest whole number.) Enter these numbers in the last column. Graph the supply of German euros on the same grid as your graph of part (b).

e. Assume for simplicity that the only trade between the United States and Germany involves the two goods discussed above. Under this assumption, the equilibrium exchange rate will be approximately _____ dollars per euro or _____ euros per dollar.

f. Suppose that now U.S. consumers undergo a change in tastes and preferences for the German import good. As a result, the U.S. demand for the import good increases as shown in the table below.

Exchange Rate ($/euro)	German Price of the Good	U.S. Price of the Good	Quantity Demanded	Total U.S. Euro Expenditures
0.80/1	1 euro	_____	120	_____
0.85/1	1 euro	_____	110	_____
0.90/1	1 euro	_____	100	_____
0.95/1	1 euro	_____	90	_____
1.00/1	1 euro	_____	80	_____

Enter in the last column the quantity of euros now demanded by U.S. consumers for use in purchasing the German import good. (*Note:* Round off to the nearest whole number.) Graph the new demand for euros on the same grid provided for part (b).

The new equilibrium exchange rate will be approximately _____ dollars per euro, or _____ euros per dollar. As a result of the increase in the U.S. demand for German imports, with all else constant, the dollar will _____ and the euro will _____.

g. Now consider the above problem assuming that the exchange rate was fixed at $0.90/euro. When the U.S. demand for German goods increased, the United States would have purchased _____ units and paid a total of $_____ for German imports. German residents would have bought _____ units from the United States and paid a total of $_____ for U.S. exports. As a result, the United States would have lost $_____, or approximately _____ euros, in foreign exchange.

2. The figure below shows the supply of, and the demand for, British pounds, as a function of the exchange rate—expressed in U.S. dollars per pound. Assume that Britain and the United States are the only two countries in the world.

a. How might the shift from D to D' be accounted for?

b. Given the shift from D to D', what exists at $1.60 = 1 pound?

c. Will the pound now appreciate or depreciate?

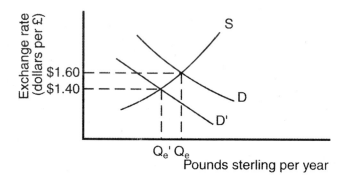

■ Problems

1. Below are balance of payments figures for North Shore during 2011. (All figures are in billions of dollars.)

Allocations of special drawing rights	$710
Balance on the capital account	−3,507
Foreign official assets	10,175
Errors and omissions	−1,879
Balance on the current account	−5,795
North Shore official assets	−4

a. The official reserve transactions balance was (+/−) _____ $_____.

b. The official reserve transactions were
   i. the sum of $_____, _____, and _____
   ii. totaled (+/−)_____ $_____

2.   Suppose both Canada and the United States had been on a pure gold standard and that the Canadian government had been willing to buy and sell gold at a price of 53.85 Canadian dollars for an ounce of gold. The U.S. government had been willing to buy and sell gold at a price of $35 an ounce. In the foreign exchange markets, the price of a Canadian dollar would have been _____ U.S. dollars and the price of a U.S. dollar would have been _____ Canadian dollars.

3.   Below are hypothetical demand and supply schedules for the European Monetary Union's euro during a week. (The quantities of euros demanded and supplied are measured in millions, and the exchange rate for the euro is measured in dollars.)

Quantity Demanded	Exchange Rate	Quantity Supplied
100	$1.28	570
200	1.27	520
300	1.26	460
400	1.25	400
500	1.24	330
600	1.23	260
700	1.22	180

a.   The equilibrium exchange rate for the euro is $_____. At this equilibrium, the rate of exchange for the dollar is _____ _____ euros.

b.   At the equilibrium exchange rate,

  i.   _____ million euros are demanded and supplied each week, and

  ii.   _____ million dollars are bought and sold each week.

c.   If the European Central Bank wished to peg the exchange rate for the euro at

  i. $1.26, it would have to (buy/sell) (how many) _____ million euros for dollars each week, and

  ii. $1.24, it would have to (buy/sell) (how many) _____ million euros for dollars each week.

4.   Which of the following will cause the Japanese yen to appreciate?

a.   U.S. real incomes increase relative to Japanese real incomes.

b.   It is expected that in the future the yen will depreciate relative to the dollar.

c.   The U.S. inflation rate rises relative to the Japanese inflation rate.

d.   The after-tax, risk-adjusted real interest rate in the United States rises relative to that in Japan.

e.   U.S. tastes change in favor of Japanese-made goods.

■ Answers

Completion Questions

1. dollars; euros; euros; dollars
2. supply and demand; depreciated; appreciated
3. more; an increase; a decrease
4. increase; appreciate; more; less
5. are fixed
6. negative; positive; deficit; surplus
7. zero; equal
8. foreign currencies; gold; SDRs; reserve position in the IMF; any financial asset held by an official government agency
9. inflation rate; political stability
10. deficit; depreciate
11. foreign exchange risk

True-False Questions

1. T
2. T
3. F Changes in exchange rates lead to payments equilibrium.
4. F The demand for dollars rises relative to the supply of dollars because the French want to buy relatively more U.S. goods.
5. F U.S. residents will demand fewer pounds because British goods are now relatively higher priced.
6. F The U.S. dollar will depreciate relative to the Canadian dollar. Thus, the Canadian dollar must appreciate relative to the U.S. dollar.
7. T
8. T
9. T
10. F Floating exchange rate systems permit an independent monetary policy.
11. F In today's world, nations intervene in exchange markets. Hence, international settlements among governments are necessary.
12. T
13. T
14. T
15. F The central bank must buy or sell foreign exchange reserves.

Multiple Choice Questions

1. (c)   7. (b)
2. (a)   8. (a)
3. (b)   9. (c)
4. (d)   10. (d)
5. (a)   11. (a)
6. (c)   12. (c)

Matching

(a) and (f)   (d) and (h)

(b) and (g)   (e) and (j)

(c) and (i)

Working with Graphs

1. a.   U.S. prices of the good: 0.80, 0.85, 0.90, 0.95, 1.00. Total U.S. euro expenditures: 90, 80, 70, 60, 50; rise

    b.   See graph below.

    c.   German prices of the good: 1.250, 1.176, 1.111, 1.053, 1.00; Total German dollar expenditures: 24.00, 42.50, 63.00, 85.50, 110.00; fall

    d.   Total German expenditures in euros: 30, 50, 70, 90, 110. See graph below.

    e.   0.90, 1.11

    f.   Total U.S. euro expenditures: 120, 110, 100, 90, 80. See graph below. 0.95; 1.053; depreciate; appreciate

    g.   100; 111.10; 63, 63.00; 48.10 (or $111.10 − $63.00), 53 (48.1 ÷ $0.90 = 53.44)

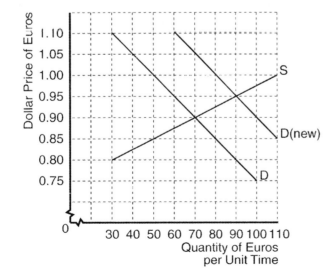

2. a. A decrease in the demand for British pounds will occur if world tastes change away from British-made goods, the British price level rises relative to the world's, world income falls relative to British income, and/or British interest rates fall relative to world interest rates, among other reasons.

    b. A surplus of British pounds, and a British balance of payments deficit.

    c. Depreciate.

Problems

1. a. +, 11181

    b. (1) 710, 10,475, –4 (any order) (2) +, 11,181

2. 0.65, 1.539

3. a. 1.25, 0.80

    b. (1) 400 (2) 500

    c. (1) buy, 160 (2) sell, 170

4. a, c, and e

■ Glossary

Accounting identities   Values that are equivalent by definition.

Appreciation   An increase in the exchange value of one nation's currency in terms of the currency of another nation.

Balance of payments   A system of accounts that measures transactions of goods, services, income, and financial assets between domestic households, businesses, and governments and residents of the rest of the world during a specific time period.

Balance of trade   The difference between exports and imports of physical goods.

Capital account   A category of balance of payments transactions that measures flows of financial assets.

Current account   A category of balance of payments transactions that measures the exchange of merchandise, the exchange of services, and unilateral transfers.

Depreciation   A decrease in the exchange value of one nation's currency in terms of the currency of another nation.

Exchange rate   The price of one nation's currency in terms of the currency of another country.

Flexible exchange rates   Exchange rates that are allowed to fluctuate in the open market in response to changes in supply and demand. Sometimes called *floating exchange rates*.

Foreign exchange market   A market in which households, firms, and governments buy and sell national currencies.

Foreign exchange risk   The possibility that changes in the value of a nation's currency will result in variations in the market value of assets.

Hedge   A financial strategy that reduces the chance of suffering losses arising from foreign exchange risk.

International Monetary Fund   An agency founded to administer an international foreign exchange system and to lend to member countries that had balance of payments problems. The IMF now functions as a lender of last resort for national governments

Par value   The officially determined value of a currency.

Special drawing rights (SDRs)   Reserve assets created by the International Monetary Fund for countries to use in settling international payment obligations.